The most obvious fact of life is that *everybody dies*. It would be irrational and foolish to live our entire lives unprepared for what we know is inevitable! That's why reading this book will be one of the wisest investments of time you'll ever make. It will end your worrying and wondering, your fretting and fearing, about life after death. Instead, you'll gain the confidence and peace of mind that come from settling your eternal destiny.

DR. RICK WARREN, *The Purpose Driven Life* and the *Daily Hope* broadcast

This is the most powerfully uplifting and extensively researched book I have ever read on the subject of heaven. If you've struggled to know what to believe and why, you will find your answers in these pages. Every human being should have the privilege of reading this book.

SHEILA WALSH, author of *Holding On When You Want to Let Go*

The Case for Heaven engages both the mind through convincing evidence and the heart through personal narratives and discoveries. I hope that you—whether a Christian or a skeptic—will read, discuss, and share this book with others.

SEAN MCDOWELL, PhD, associate professor of apologetics at Talbot School of Theology and coauthor of *Evidence That Demands a Verdict*

Lee Strobel is a national treasure. In *The Case for Heaven*, he answers tough questions, removes obstacles to belief, and gives us confidence in why we can believe that heaven is a beautiful reality we can look forward to experiencing.

Bestselling author DERWIN GRAY, lead pastor, Transformation Church

Lee Strobel tackles challenging questions about reincarnation, annihilation, and hell as he makes a convincing, compelling case for heaven. He helps the reader overcome the fear of death. I plan on getting two copies—one to keep as a reference and one to give to a skeptic.

ANNE GRAHAM LOTZ, author of *Jesus in Me*

The Case for Heaven may be Lee Strobel's best book yet. Well-researched and clearly written, it presents the evidence for heaven powerfully and faces the best arguments against it with honesty. It is so engaging and inspiring that it's difficult to put it down.

J. P. MORELAND, distinguished professor of philosophy,
Talbot School of Theology, Biola University, and author
of *A Simple Guide to Experience Miracles*

As a detective, I wish Lee Strobel had been my partner because—as always—he leaves no stone unturned. His interviews will open your eyes and encourage your soul. *The Case for Heaven* is a must-read and a powerful addition to Lee's seminal "Case For" book series.

J. WARNER WALLACE, *Dateline*-featured cold-case detective,
senior fellow at the Colson Center for Christian Worldview, and
author of *Person of Interest* and *Cold-Case Christianity*

Prepare to be taken on a journey of hearing key insights from experts in their field and heartfelt honesty from those facing death. *The Case for Heaven* may challenge the status quo, but it will not disappoint.

Neuroscientist SHARON DIRCKX (PhD, Cambridge),
author of *Am I Just My Brain?*

Lee Strobel has done it again, this time with a fascinating, challenging, thoughtful, and moving book on the realities of heaven—and hell. Through his keen research, skillful storytelling, and apt interviews with experts, Strobel makes a compelling case for the historic Christian doctrine of the afterlife.

DOUGLAS GROOTHUIS, philosophy professor, Denver Seminary

If this book were a television show, it might be called *Touched by the Truth*. Let this impressive array of experts impact your life and faith with the evidence for the world to come. You'll be encouraged as you encounter the compelling case for the life that awaits you.

Emmy-nominated actress, producer, and *New York Times* bestselling author ROMA DOWNEY

This investigator doesn't shrink from bringing up the tough topics. Lee Strobel reminds us how the gospel insightfully addresses our most challenging intellectual questions and how it powerfully meets our deepest human needs.

> PAUL COPAN, Pledger Family Chair of Philosophy and Ethics, Palm Beach Atlantic University, and author of *Is God a Moral Monster?*

No one today is more fit to make the case for heaven than Lee Strobel, the man who wrote *The Case for Easter.* If Jesus was raised from the dead to the right hand of the Father, heaven is a reality. The one implies the other, and Lee knows it.

> SCOT MCKNIGHT, professor of New Testament, Northern Seminary, and author of *The Heaven Promise* and *A Church Called Tov*

Some years ago, there was a movie titled *Heaven Can Wait.* But the truth is, heaven *can't* wait, and questions about heaven, hell, and the hereafter must be reckoned with sooner rather than later. *The Case for Heaven* is a great place to begin.

> DON SWEETING, president, Colorado Christian University

The Case for Heaven showcases why Lee Strobel is among the most unique and interesting writers of our time. In an age of pandemic, depression, and violence, I'm thrilled that Lee has focused his attention on this question of eternal significance.

> JOHN STONESTREET, president of the Colson Center and host of the *BreakPoint* podcasts

THE CASE FOR
Heaven

ALSO BY LEE STROBEL

THE CASE FOR

Heaven

—

A Journalist Investigates

Evidence for Life After Death

LEE STROBEL

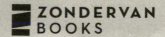

ZONDERVAN
BOOKS

Requests for information should be addressed to:
Zondervan, 3900 *Sparks Dr. SE, Grand Rapids, Michigan* 49546

Zondervan titles may be purchased in bulk for educational, business, fundraising, or sales promotional use. For information, please email SpecialMarkets@Zondervan.com.

ISBN 978-0-310-35845-9 (international trade paper edition)
ISBN 978-0-310-35844-2 (audio)

Library of Congress Cataloging-in-Publication Data

Names: Strobel, Lee, 1952- author.
Title: The case for heaven : a journalist investigates evidence for life after death / Lee Strobel.
Description: Grand Rapids : Zondervan, 2021. | Includes bibliographical references and index. |
    Summary: "In The Case for Heaven, bestselling author and investigative journalist turns a
    critical eye on the evidence for heaven, a variety of claims about the afterlife, and modern-
    day stories of near-death experiences to build a compelling case that death is not the end
    of our existence but a transition to an exciting and very real world to come"— Provided by
    publisher.
Identifiers: LCCN 2021005223 (print) | LCCN 2021005224 (ebook) | ISBN 9780310259190
    (hardcover) | ISBN 9780310358435 (ebook)
Subjects: LCSH: Heaven—Christianity. | Heaven. | Death.
Classification: LCC BT846.3 .S77 2021 (print) | LCC BT846.3 (ebook) | DDC 236/.24—dc23
LC record available at https://lccn.loc.gov/2021005223
LC ebook record available at https://lccn.loc.gov/2021005224

For Nabeel Qureshi—
I'll see you on the other side!

Contents

Introduction

Can We Know There's a Heaven?

Is this dying? Why, this is bliss . . . Earth is receding; Heaven is opening; God is calling. I must go.

DWIGHT L. MOODY, JUST BEFORE HIS DEATH

My eyes fluttered. They opened and struggled to focus. My mind fought confusion. I was on my back, stretched out on a firm surface below a bright light. A face came into view, looking at me—a doctor, his surgical mask pulled down.

"You're one step away from a coma," he said. "Two steps away from dying."

My eyelids sagged shut. I drifted back into unconsciousness—a welcomed relief from the grotesque hallucinations that had plagued me.

At times like this, hovering over the hazy border between life and death, the afterlife is no longer a mere academic topic to be researched, analyzed, and debated. Heaven and hell, our existence beyond the grave, become desperately relevant. They're all that matter.

I know what you're thinking: *Poor guy; he almost died.* But here's what *I'm* thinking: *Just wait until it happens to you!*

Because it will. One way or another, next week or in decades, you're going to creep up to the dividing line between now and

1

forever. When you slip from this world, what will you find? A void of nonexistence? A dark realm of regret and recrimination? Or a reality that's more vivid, more exhilarating, more rewarding, more *real* than anything you've ever known? At that moment, in the midst of that existential transition, nothing will be more important. And if it will matter so much then, isn't it worth investigating now?

When I was an atheist, I thought I knew what awaited me after my heart stopped pumping and my brain waves flattened. *Nothing.* My existence would cease. Activity in the world would continue unabated, but I would be absent. It was difficult—and disconcerting—to imagine.

After my wife announced that she had become a follower of Jesus, I used my journalism and legal training to investigate whether there was any credibility to Christianity or any other religion. I concluded after nearly two years that there's persuasive evidence that Jesus indeed is the unique Son of God. I ended up leaving my newspaper career to tell others what I had learned.

Of course, the Christian faith gave me a whole different picture of eternity. The Bible talks about a vivid postmortem realm. Though this is embedded in overall Christian theology, I never really studied whether there was specific evidence or compelling logic to support this heavenly vision. Essentially, I set much of the issue aside for a while. After all, I was young and healthy.

Then came that Thursday evening in the summer of 2011 when Leslie found me unconscious on our bedroom floor. The ambulance took me to a hospital in nearby Parker, Colorado, where the emergency room physician gave me the dire news that I was on the precipice of death.

It turned out I had a rare medical condition called *hyponatremia*, a frighteningly sharp drop in my blood sodium level that caused my brain to swell and threatened to snuff out my existence. Suddenly, it wasn't enough to have a few inchoate suppositions about the world to come. It was insufficient to cling to some antiseptic-sounding doctrines that had never been adequately examined. I needed to know for sure what happens when I close my eyes for the final time in this world.

The Evidence for Eternity

After recovering from my medical trauma, I decided to embark on a quest to get answers about the afterlife to satisfy my heart and soul. I traveled to South Bend, Indiana, and Portland, Oregon, to San Antonio, Denver, Chicago, and beyond as I sat down with scholars to quiz them about how they know what they know about this all-important matter.

I discussed heaven with them, but so much more. Can neuroscience tell us whether we have a soul that can survive our body's demise? Might the intriguing accounts of near-death experiences reveal something about our future? What insights can physics, history, and philosophy provide about our existence beyond this world? And what about Jesus, the one who was dead and gone but then reportedly was encountered alive a few days later? What light might he shed on the subject?

I wanted to know whether spending forever in a blissful paradise makes rational sense. And who gets to go to heaven anyway? Some Christians believe everyone wins a ticket to paradise—even our pet dogs. And how about the awful reality of that "other place"—wouldn't it be more humane for God to quickly extinguish people who are headed for hell rather than consigning them to an eternity of suffering? More and more pastors are saying so.

I also explored alternatives to the Christian worldview—for instance, reincarnation. Shouldn't we listen to people who say they've lived in the past? Maybe life *is* cyclical, as Eastern religions teach—birth and death followed by more of the same until we're ultimately absorbed into The Absolute. Millions of people believe that's true.

Let's face it, there's a lot of controversy about life after death—and sometimes religious leaders aren't much help. When Union Theological Seminary president Serene Jones was asked by a reporter what happens when we die, her first words were, "I don't know! There may be something, there may be nothing."[1]

Ask a cross section of Americans the same question, and one out of six will shrug their shoulders. They have no idea what occurs after death. Only a slim majority (54 percent) believe they'll end up in heaven.[2]

As for atheists, I suspect many of them think about death more frequently than some of them admit. At least, I did when I was a spiritual skeptic, staring at the ceiling in the middle of the night and shuddering at the prospect of my ultimate demise.

"For me, the fear of death is far and away the most immediate and challenging aspect of my atheism," one humanist told *The Atlantic*. "Death affects me in a profound way."[3] Even Bart Ehrman, the agnostic New Testament scholar, once conceded, "The fear of death gripped me for years, and there are still moments when I wake up at night in a cold sweat."[4]

Many people get to the closing moments of their life—often a time of angst and abject fear—without any certainty about what to expect next. One author tells of asking a thirty-one-year-old friend who was on his deathbed what dying was like. "I don't know," the man replied. "I don't really know. Sometimes it seems like some blackness coming toward me. And sometimes it doesn't feel like anything."[5]

That's not poetic, but it's honest. He sincerely had no idea what would transpire in those fateful moments to come. What is hidden inside that ominous approaching darkness? Will he feel anything after he breathes his last?

Truly, what's more important than answers to questions like

these? Wouldn't you rather investigate these issues now instead of being tormented by them on your deathbed? Think about how your life might change today—your priorities, decisions, and worldview—once you ascertain with confidence what awaits you at the conclusion of your time in this world. After all, if there really is an afterlife, you'll be spending a lot more time there than here.

So come with me on the path of discovery. Consider the evidence. Evaluate the logic. Pursue the truth with an open mind. Then reach your own informed verdict in the case for heaven.

CHAPTER 1

The Quest for Immortality

Our Frantic Efforts to Outlive Ourselves

How can I rest, how can I be at peace? Despair is in my heart . . . I am afraid of death.

EPIC OF GILGAMESH (CIRCA 2100 BC),

OLDEST KNOWN FICTION

No deity will save us; we must save ourselves.

HUMANIST MANIFESTO II

It was a sermon on heaven and hell by famed evangelist Billy Graham that brought a troubled twelve-year-old named Clay Jones to faith in Jesus. The son of an atheist and astrologer, he had grown up sickly and bullied, a mediocre student and a self-described "rebellious little punk." Graham's 1969 rally in Southern California became the turning point for him.

Over time, Jones was utterly transformed. He married his high school sweetheart Jean E. and ended up as a pastor and seminary professor. Then came the phone call that rocked his world—specialists had finally diagnosed his chronic back pain. The news was grim: he was suffering from a virulent form of bone cancer that kills 100 percent of its victims within two years.

Hit the pause button. Can you imagine getting a call like

that? How would you react? What emotions would surge through you? What's the first thing you would do?

As for Clay and Jean E., tears streamed down their faces. They held hands and offered a prayer of thanksgiving for what God had done in their lives and for the fact that he was in control of the situation. They asked for healing.

"This is going to sound strange," Jones said later, "but I wasn't afraid of dying. Some people scoff when I say that, but it's true. Yes, I mourned that I'd be leaving my wife. But, you see, I had a robust view of heaven—and *that's* what made all the difference. As the apostle Paul said, 'To live is Christ and to die is gain.'[1] The worst thing that could happen would be that I would graduate into God's glorious presence—forever."

How someone reacts to life-shattering news like that depends on their worldview. If there is no God, there is no hope. Said Stanford psychiatrist Irvin D. Yalom, "Despite the staunchest, most venerable defenses, we can never completely subdue death anxiety: it is always there, lurking in some hidden ravine of the mind."[2] Indeed, the desire to cheat death and live forever, to somehow achieve immortality apart from God, has been a driving force throughout history.

As for Jones, a few weeks after that initial call, a specialist realized there had been an error in the diagnosis—yes, he had bone cancer, but it was a much milder form that could be treated by surgery. Today, Jones has been healed for more than fifteen years.

Still, his own health scare, his chronic childhood illnesses, and the deaths of friends have given Jones special insights into the topic of dying.

I flew to Orange County, California, and drove to his modest Mediterranean-style house to chat with him about his latest book, a profound and provocative work whose title explains exactly what I wanted to discuss with him: *Immortal: How the Fear of Death Drives Us and What We Can Do about It.*[3]

Interview #1: Clay Butler Jones, DMin

Jones has a multifaceted background as a leader, author, and professor. After receiving an undergraduate degree in philosophy from California State University in Fullerton, he went on to earn his Master of Divinity degree from American Christian Theological Seminary and his Doctor of Ministry degree from Trinity Evangelical Divinity School.

He is widely known for his work in the apologetics program at Biola University, where he started teaching in 2004. He has taught classes on the resurrection, why God allows evil, and other topics as an associate professor at its Talbot Seminary, and he is currently a visiting scholar there.

Along the way, he hosted a national call-in talk radio program for eight years, sparring with Buddhists, Scientologists, secular humanists, Muslims, Mormons, Jehovah's Witnesses, and others from varying religious perspectives. Currently he serves as chairman of the board of Ratio Christi, a ministry that defends Christianity on more than 115 college campuses.

His 2017 book *Why Does God Allow Evil?* is a masterful treatment of a troubling topic. Philosopher J. P. Moreland said Jones "fearlessly and deftly addresses all the hard questions head-on," adding, "There is no ducking of issues."[4] Apologist Frank Turek said Jones's new book on immortality, published in 2020, "could be one of the most important books you'll ever read."[5]

We sat down in adjacent cushioned chairs in Jones's living room for our conversation. Jones is an all-too-rare combination of being an unvarnished straight shooter with a heart full of compassion and empathy. There is, to echo Moreland, no ducking of issues with him.

He was casual in his attire, unpretentious in his demeanor, and passionate in his convictions. Though over sixty years old, his hair was still pretty much black (and slightly tousled), while gray was on the verge of fully conquering his beard.

Our conversation stretched into several hours as we delved into the issue of how the fear of death drives humanity, and how the desire to achieve immortality—of *any* sort—is a relentless pursuit for so many people.

"What prompted you to research this topic?" I asked.

"I came across the book *A Brief History of Thought*, by French philosopher and secular humanist Luc Ferry," Jones explained. "Ferry wrote, 'The quest for a salvation without God is at the heart of every great philosophical system, and that is its essential and ultimate objective.'[6] That rocked me! He was saying that the heart of philosophy is trying to find a way of dealing with death without God. I needed to find out if other philosophers felt the same way."

"What did you discover?"

"That indeed much of philosophy is trying to conquer the fear of death. For example, Plato writes that in the last hours before his teacher Socrates died, Socrates said, 'Truly then . . . those who practise philosophy aright are cultivating dying.'[7] Philosopher Michel de Montaigne wrote an essay called 'To Philosophize Is to Learn How to Die,' in which he said that all the wisdom in the world eventually comes down to teaching us how not to be afraid of dying.[8] German philosopher Arthur Schopenhauer said, 'Without death men would scarcely philosophize.'[9]

"So philosophers, anthropologists, psychologists, sociologists, psychiatrists—they're fascinated with how death affects behavior," he continued. "Cultural anthropologist Ernest Becker's book *The Denial of Death* won the Pulitzer Prize in 1974.[10] Becker says that 'the idea of death, the fear of it, haunts the human animal like nothing else: it is a mainspring of human activity.'[11] His premise was that everybody is terrified by their own death and they're trying to do everything they can to compensate for it."

"How did your friends react when they found out you were writing a book on death?" I asked.

Jones chuckled. "They'd say, quite defensively, 'I'm not afraid of dying.'"

"Were they telling the truth?"

"They weren't being entirely dishonest—because they don't think about their own death. They've blocked it from their minds."

"Until they have chest pains," I offered.

He pointed at me like I'd won the jackpot. "Bingo," he declared. "Then the fear of death stands in front of them—and it won't leave the room."

Denial, Distraction, Depression

In his book, Clay Jones quotes social scientists as saying that the fear of death drives culture—in fact, some claim it fuels *all* of it. As social theorist Zygmunt Bauman wrote, "There would probably be no culture were humans unaware of their mortality."[12]

"Are these experts exaggerating?" I asked.

"Just barely," came his response. "Remember that Hebrews 2:15 says Jesus came to rescue people who are 'held in slavery by their fear of death.' So Scripture confirms that we are in bondage to a fear of dying. And I do believe that is what motivates much of human behavior. If people don't follow Jesus, who's going to free them from that slavery? They've got to somehow find a way to free themselves—and that leads to all kinds of problems."

"For example?"

"It affects people in every conceivable way. The first thing they do is deny. They shove it out of their minds and say to themselves, 'I'm the exception. If science keeps advancing and I live long enough, medicine will cure anything that threatens my life.' Then they distract. We pay entertainers and sports stars huge amounts of money because they're valuable to us—they divert our attention from the fact that we're going to die.

"Then there's depression," he added. "The prospect of our death and the deaths of those we love is *the* major reason for depression. Staks Rosch said in the *Huffington Post,* 'Depression is a serious problem in the greater atheist community and far too often, that depression has led to suicide. This is something many of my fellow atheists often don't like to admit, but it is true.'"[13]

"I can understand depression, but suicide?" I asked. "People kill themselves because they're afraid of dying? That's counterintuitive."

"Essentially, what they're doing is taking control of that which has control over them. The Spanish philosopher Miguel de Unamuno said that 'the self-slayer kills himself because he will not wait for death.'"[14]

In his book, Jones quotes research published in the *American Journal of Psychiatry:* "Religiously unaffiliated subjects had significantly more lifetime suicide attempts and more first-degree relatives who committed suicide than subjects who endorsed a religious affiliation . . . Furthermore, subjects with no religious affiliation perceived fewer reasons for living."[15]

Since my interview with Jones, Harvard researchers released a new study documenting that attendance at religious services dramatically reduces deaths from suicide, drugs, and alcohol. Attending services at least once a week cut these so-called "deaths by despair" by 33 percent among men and a whopping 68 percent among women, compared to those who never attended services.[16]

"People often talk about an epidemic of suicide," concluded Jones, "but the real epidemic is the increasing rejection of a robust belief in an afterlife. *That's* what is miring more and more people in hopelessness."

Crack-Crack-Cracking the Brain

I picked up my Bible and quoted Ecclesiastes 3:11, which says God has "set eternity in the human heart," and then I asked Jones, "What does that mean to you?"

"That there's more than just a fear of death. We want to live forever. It's implanted in us. We want to understand eternity, we want to fit into eternity, we *need* eternity," he replied.

I said, "One way that people try to achieve immortality without God is to figure out how to live longer and longer in order to cheat death. Futurologist Ian Pearson said that 'realistically by 2050 we would expect to be able to download your mind into a machine, so when you die it's not a major career problem.'[17] What do you make of that?"

Jones sighed. "There's a lot of desperation along those lines—you can see it in organic grocery stores, where shoppers scurry around to make sure everything is non-GMO, no antibiotics, and so forth, as if this can significantly prolong their life. I was at a reunion where people were passing around a book on how not to die. I said, 'By the way, if scientists were able to cure all cancers, people would only live an average of 2.265 years longer.' A Harvard demographer computed this. It doesn't matter—you'll die of something else."

"What about transhumanism?" I asked, referring to the way scientists want to alter our bodies and brains scientifically so we can live longer. Billionaire innovator Elon Musk is already experimenting with implanting computer chips into brains.[18]

"Sure, transhumanism, or human+, says that since people are no more than molecules in motion, we can replicate the synapses of the brain with circuitry not yet invented. And they can upload our mind into a computer so we can be avatars in a virtual world or transferred into a robot. Of course it's science fiction."

"Why?"

"You'd have to have circuitry that's identical to the connections in your brain. There are almost a thousand trillion connections in the brain, and we haven't figured out all its secrets yet. As one expert explained, emulating the brain on a computer isn't the same as actually making a brain. Besides, they haven't been able to reproduce the brain of a small roundworm with 302 neurons. Another expert said that even if artificial intelligence does 99 percent of the work, it would take a thousand years to map the brain.

"On top of that," he said, "even if we could produce something that's wired exactly like your brain, nobody has any idea how such a system could be conscious. Let's face it—scientists can't explain how nonconscious stuff becomes conscious. Even Michael Shermer of *Skeptic* magazine says, 'We still don't know the basis of consciousness.'[19] You're more than just your brain—your consciousness is the real *you* that provides your identity. So this is just a pipe dream."

I asked Jones about cryonics, which involves freezing a person after they die and then thawing them out once science has found a cure for what killed them. Theoretically, someone could continue this process ad infinitum. As an example, the head and body of Hall of Fame baseball player Ted Williams, who died in 2002, are frozen in separate tanks of liquid nitrogen. His daughter said cryonics is "like a religion, something we could have faith in."[20]

Numerous celebrities have said they want this ultimate ice bath for themselves when they die, including broadcaster Larry King, who didn't believe in an afterlife, and so he said, "The only hope, the only fragment of hope, is to be frozen."[21]

"This is replete with problems," Jones told me. "For one thing, you have to be frozen within a couple of minutes of dying or else your brain deteriorates. That's not very practical. Second, there's sonic fracturing."

"What's that?"

Jones reached over and poured more soda over the ice cubes in my half-empty glass, and then he paused. "Hear the cracking?"

Sure enough, the ice was making a cracking sound.

"That's what happens if you try to thaw a brain or organ—*crack, crack, crack*," he said. "Nobody knows how to fix that fracturing. One cryonics company actually suggests the possibility of sewing or gluing parts back together. Seriously? Now you've got Frankenstein!"

"Why do all these schemes for immortality fail?"

"Because God has determined that people are going to die. Hebrews 9:27 says that 'people are destined to die once, and after that to face judgment.' Adam and Eve decided to follow their hearts and violate the command of God, and we've been attending funerals ever since. You *will* die. The big question, then, becomes how to make sure you spend eternity with God."

Living On through Children

One of the most fascinating insights in Jones's book is that much of human behavior is motivated by people pursuing various forms of *symbolic immortality*—in other words, since they can't physically live forever, they doggedly pursue ways to leave a legacy or make an impact on the world so that at least their memory will be kept alive in perpetuity.

Philosopher Sam Keen said people try to "transcend death by participating in something of lasting worth. We achieve ersatz immortality by sacrificing ourselves to conquer an empire, to build a temple, to write a book, to establish a family, to accumulate a fortune, to further progress and prosperity, to create an information society and a global free market."[22]

One promoter of this strategy was Edwin S. Shneidman, the first professor of the study of death at UCLA. "A positive postself is a most worthy goal of life," he said. "To live beyond one's own breath! To be lauded in the obituary pages of the *New York Times*. To have a future in the world yet to come; to have a gossamer extension beyond the date of one's death. To escape oblivionation; to survive one's self is a lofty and reasonable aspiration." He went on to add, "To cease as though one had never been, to exit life with no hope of living on in the memory of another, to be expunged from history's record—that is a fate literally far worse than death."[23]

Really? *Literally* far worse than death? That's quite a statement. I turned to Jones. "What are some of the most common forms of symbolic immortality that people pursue?"

"Having or adopting children is a big one—trying to live on through your kids," he answered. "Nathan Heflick was explicit in *Psychology Today*: 'So why do people have children? One reason is to transcend the great specter of death.'[24] The great actor Sir Peter Ustinov said, 'Children are the only form of immortality that we can be sure of.'"[25]

"Why doesn't that work?" I asked.

"Just do the math. Our genetics quickly get watered down. In twenty generations, your future offspring will only have 0.000004 percent of your genes. You couldn't feed a mosquito with that. Actually, given the way genes are transferred in blocks, with some dominant and others recessive, it's unlikely *any* of your genes will survive that long."

"What about memories that are carried on through families?"

Jones smiled. "Do you know the first names of your great-great-grandparents?"

I felt sheepish. "Uh, no, I guess I don't."

He reassured me with a pat on my shoulder. "Don't feel bad," he said. "I'll often ask classrooms full of students if they know the first names of their great-great-grandparents—and so far only one student has said yes. Then I ask if anyone *cares* about their great-great-grandparents, and the answer is no. Not one person. *Nobody cares!* So much for trying to keep yourself alive through your family."

Jones added that he's seeing a growing trend of people engaging in genealogy research. "That's another way of trying to live forever—if you venerate your ancestors, then your kids or grandkids might feel obligated to remember you. It's fruitless, because *you're still dead!*" he said, his bushy eyebrows rising. "Even if you live on briefly in the memory of family members, it doesn't really give you authentic immortality."

Fifteen Minutes of Fame

In his book, Clay Jones quotes an exchange between atheist Richard Wade and a spiritual skeptic named Anne, who wrote to say that her fear of death was causing her such severe panic attacks that she would almost pass out.

Wade's response was that he wasn't bothered by thoughts of dying because "my legacy is already complete . . . I've made a positive difference by being here, and I'm looking forward to making even more."[26]

Jones said to me, "Essentially, Wade was telling this woman to go accomplish some things before you die so that you'll be remembered. That's another form of symbolic immortality—creating something that supposedly has lasting value."

"How common is that?"

"Very," he said. "It's what causes people to paint a masterpiece, design a building, start a website, or write a book," he said, cracking a smile as he gestured toward me.

He went on to cite some examples. "Michelangelo supposedly said, 'No thought is born in me that has not "death" engraved upon it.'[27] One of the most extravagant odes to self is the Palace of Versailles in France—the world's largest palace, with more than 720,000 square feet, over 2,000 acres—all created by King Louis XIV to secure his name in history. He told the *Academie Royale*, 'I entrust to you the most precious thing on earth, my fame.'[28] Or these days, if you're wealthy enough, you can just put your name on a building—although that doesn't always turn out well."

"What do you mean?"

"When the Lincoln Center for Performing Arts opened in New York in the 1960s, its concert auditorium was called Philharmonic Hall. A few years later, they solicited a large gift

17

to improve the acoustics and named the hall after Avery Fisher, who manufactured speakers. Then in 2015 they redid the hall again, and this time they renamed it David Geffen Hall, after a media mogul who bought the naming rights from the Avery Fisher family. Apparently, Fisher's progeny didn't care much for the idea of his symbolic immortality. As you can see, this kind of fame can be rather fleeting."[29]

"We live in such a celebrity culture," I said. "So many people are striving for fame to give them a kind of symbolic immortality."

"Absolutely—and it gets a little ridiculous, like the guy who made it into the *Guinness Book of World Records* by breaking the greatest number of toilet seats with his head in one minute."

"Seriously?"

"Yeah—forty-six in total. I don't know where he even got the idea to do that in the first place. Now he's made it into the book—until the day when he gets forced out by other bizarre accomplishments. I remember when the mayor of a city announced his long-shot bid for the presidency. One political commentator said he had zero chance, but at least it will be in his obituary. I guess it was worth it to him for that."

Then Jones added an ironic example of how this quest for fame seldom succeeds in the long term. "Remember how the artist Andy Warhol said everyone will be famous for fifteen minutes?" I nodded. "Well, in 2004, a TV commercial said, 'Somebody once said everyone will be famous for fifteen minutes.' They actually removed his name! Even *that* fame didn't last for him."

Stealing John Lennon's Fame

Then there's the dark side of symbolic immortality. Some people are driven to leave their mark on the world, even if it means achieving infamy through crime or mayhem. As one serial killer wrote to a television station before he was caught, "How many do I have to kill before I get . . . some national attention?"[30]

With that, Jones related the story of the temple of Artemis in Ephesus—considered one of the seven wonders of the ancient world. It took 120 years to build—and then one day in the year 356, someone burned it to the ground. They caught him and asked why he did it—and he said he wanted to be famous.

"Their response was to declare that his name would be forever banned—a so-called *damnatio memoriae* law that said anyone mentioning his name would be executed," Jones said. "They wanted to scrub him from history, but guess what? Today we know his name. It's Herostratus. Books and plays have been written about him. And yet we hardly know anything about the architects of the temple. Their names, for the most part, are lost.

"Why did Mark David Chapman kill John Lennon?" Jones asked. "Chapman was straightforward: he said he did it to get attention and to 'steal John Lennon's fame.'[31] He told the parole board, 'That bright light of fame, of infamy, notoriety was there. I couldn't resist it.'[32] When the Charles Lindbergh baby was kidnapped, more than two hundred people falsely confessed to the crime.[33] That illustrates the desire for attention—even bad attention.

"Tragically, we see this far too often," he said. "The Parkland school shooter, who murdered seventeen people, recorded a video prior to his crime in which he said, 'When you see me on the news you'll all know who I am.'[34] The Columbine High School killers speculated beforehand which famous director would create a movie about them. For people like them, there is no God, there is no judgment or afterlife. Why not go out in a blaze of glory and make a name for yourself?"

I shuddered at the truth of that. "In the end, all these various forms of symbolic immortality are absolutely futile, aren't they?"

"That's right. After all, they're *symbolic*—you're still dead, right? Ultimately nothing meaningful is achieved. The Roman emperor Marcus Aurelius put it well when he said, 'What is the

advantage of having one's own name on the lips of future generations when their overriding concern will be the same as ours:
to have their names on the lips of successors . . . How does that
confer any reality on us?"[35]

"Let's face it: notoriety generally fades pretty quickly. Most
perpetrators of crimes are forgotten. Our accomplishments get
eclipsed because of greater accomplishments by others. The vast
majority of people who spend their lives desperately trying to
achieve stardom fail in their quest. Those who do manage to
achieve a degree of celebrity status find that maintaining their
fame takes endless maintenance, fine-tuning, and damage
control."

He added with a smile, "Just ask Madonna!"

Of Books and Chocolate Cake

Faced with the abject failure of various attempts to achieve
immortality apart from God, many atheists have taken another
approach to dealing with the fear of death. Maybe, they say, dying
isn't so bad after all. Perhaps it's actually *better* than the idea of
immortality. Maybe the grave is a blessing in disguise.

"They try to paper over the fear of death by maintaining
that they wouldn't want to live forever anyway," Jones said to me.
"They claim that eternal life would be supremely boring. We'd
run out of pleasurable things to do. The endless repetition would
be tedious and eventually drive us crazy."

From time to time, atheists have brought up that argument in
conversations with me. It's a position reflected in a quote popu-
larly attributed to science fiction author Isaac Asimov: "Whatever
the tortures of hell, I think the boredom of heaven would be even
worse."[36]

"Of course, it's a straw man argument," said Jones. "Atheist
Stephen Fry said eating a delicious cake or reading a good book
are great pleasures because they end. But he added, 'A book that

went on forever and a cake that you never stopped eating would both soon lose their appeal.'"[37]

Jones threw up his hands. "Who in the world is talking about endless repetition?" he asked. "We could eat chocolate cake every day right now and get bored with it, but we don't. We vary our diet, and the cake becomes a periodic treat. Nobody's talking about eating the same cake, nonstop forever. And whoever heard of an endless book? All great books have a climax and conclusion—but we don't keep reading the same book over and over.

"Besides," he said, "if heaven is real, then God will make all things new,[38] and he will be continually creating a world of joy and wonder for us. If God can create all the beauty and excitement of our current universe, he's certainly capable of creating an eternally stimulating and rewarding experience for his followers in the new heaven and the new earth."

A Bible verse that says as much popped into my mind: "No eye has seen, no ear has heard, and no mind has imagined what God has prepared for those who love him."[39]

Jones added that another approach atheists take to minimize death is to say that dying is good because it clears the way for others to live. The late Apple cofounder Steve Jobs actually said in a commencement address that "death is very likely the single best invention of life" because "it clears out the old to make way for the new."[40]

Asked Jones, "Even if it were true that humanity's lifeboat is so full that someone needs to drown in the icy waters so others can survive, why should that be any comfort to us? But the truth is that this is irrelevant. That's not the situation we're in. Nobody needs to die today because we lack adequate resources."

"I Was Not; I Was; I Am Not; I Do Not Care."

Yet another popular way of mitigating the fear of death goes back to the Greek philosopher Epicurus (341–270 BC), who essentially asked why we should get worked up over dying because it's only the same kind of nonexistence we had before we were born. If your preexistence didn't bother you, why should you fear graduating into nonexistence after death? As Jones pointed out in *Immortal*, a popular Roman saying on ancient tombstones was *"Non fui, fui, non sum, non curo,"* or "I was not; I was; I am not; I do not care."[41]

"The gospel of atheism is . . . that nothing happens after death," atheist Sam Harris told a crowd of skeptics. "There's nothing to worry about, there's nothing to fear, when after you die you are returned to that nothingness that you were before you were born . . . Death, therefore, is not a problem. Life is the problem."[42]

"How do you respond to that argument?" I asked Jones.

"As the philosopher Thomas Nagel said, it's not the state of nonexistence that's objectionable, but the loss of life," he answered. "What if you were told you would soon be reduced to the mental capacity of a contented baby and you'd be happy as long as your stomach was full and your diaper was dry? After all, you were once content as an infant, so wouldn't you be content now? Frankly, I don't think that would comfort anyone. The problem is what you're deprived of. As Nagel said, if life is all we have, then losing it would be 'the greatest loss we can sustain.'"[43]

I spoke up. "Of course, the premise that there is nothingness after death presumes Christianity must be false."

"Exactly right," came Jones's reply. "If Christianity is true—and we have good reasons to believe it is—then we face judgment after death. There would be eternal consequences for those who have rejected God's offer of forgiveness for their sins. We don't face the nothingness of nonexistence; instead, we either face an eternity with God or separated from him. That's the *real* truth about immortality.

"Let's face it," he added, "skeptics like to claim that Christians invented Christianity to escape their fear of death, but look at all the nonsense skeptics need to embrace to cope with their own death fears. It's all pointless. As a physician wrote in *Psychology Today*, 'I've tried to resolve my fear of death intellectually and come to the conclusion that it can't be done, at least by me.'"[44]

In his book, Jones sums up the atheistic story of salvation without God this way: "When you die, your consciousness will cease. Your body will then decay where, as *The Hearse Song* goes, 'The worms crawl in, the worms crawl out / the worms play pinochle on your snout.' You have no hope of reuniting with loved ones. You will never again enjoy other people, or sunsets, or beaches, or breakers, or mountains, or redwoods, or roses, or anything else for that matter. Soon *everyone will forget you* except as maybe a footnote of history. But even if you are a footnote of history, does that really matter?"[45]

Christianity, in contrast, offers the best possible outcome for followers of Christ after they pass from this world. Reveling in God's presence. Reuniting with loved ones. Living without tears or struggles or fears. Experiencing a wondrous world of adventure, excitement, and exploration. Contentment, joy, love—*forever*.

It's no wonder that even the atheist philosopher Luc Ferry concedes, "I grant you that amongst the available doctrines of salvation, nothing can compete with Christianity—provided, that is, that you are a believer."[46]

And I would add, provided that our beliefs are justified by the evidence.

The *Most Important Topic*

Jones had made it clear that when it comes to dealing with our inevitable death, there is really no room for false hope, wishful thinking, desperate denials, or empty efforts to somehow achieve pseudo-immortality apart from God. On the one hand, if heaven is really just "a fairy story for people afraid of the dark," as the late theoretical physicist Stephen Hawking put it,[47] we shouldn't want anything to do with the concept.

On the other hand, if Oxford professor John Lennox is right when he says that "atheism is a fairy story for people afraid of the light"[48]—that there are legitimate reasons to believe that our death in this world can be an actual gateway to a more fabulous existence for eternity—then this is surely *the* most important topic we can ponder. This life, as precious as it is to us, is just a blink of an eye compared to staring down the infinite timeline of eternity.

Jones and I sipped the last of our soft drinks and stood just as his wife, Jean E., walked into the room. Jones introduced us and then said, "How about if we go out for lunch?"

He didn't need to twist my arm. I was looking forward to a casual meal and some light conversation before continuing to climb the mountain of research that faced me.

In the end, what Clay Jones said about our universal desire for immortality sounded accurate to me. But that doesn't make the Christian view of the afterlife true. I still needed to pursue the issue of whether surviving the death of our bodies makes any scientific sense. Logically speaking, wouldn't this require that we have a soul that can continue to endure after we take our last breath in this world? I needed to know whether there is any compelling evidence that people possess this kind of immaterial spirit.

Recently I had heard about a Cambridge-educated neuroscientist who might be able to provide solid answers. Though she lives all the way over in England, fortunately technology would enable us to connect for an in-depth interview.

I was determined to emulate the example of Jones: there would be, I resolved, no ducking of issues.

CHAPTER 2

Searching for the Soul

Are We Conscious beyond the Grave?

For me now, the only reality is the human soul.

NOBEL PRIZE–WINNING SCIENTIST

SIR CHARLES SHERRINGTON

SHORTLY BEFORE HE DIED

Ralph Lewis was raised in a Jewish family in South Africa. He always considered himself a skeptic, though he appreciated some of the rituals at his synagogue. He became a psychiatrist in Canada and joined the faculty at the University of Toronto.

During his wife Karin's battle with breast cancer—even though he sensed "some form of providence" during that period and she did regain her health through serendipitous circumstances—they both became atheists. After all, it seemed like a natural next step in their philosophy of materialism, which means that there's no spiritual dimension beyond the physical world.

To Lewis, nobody has a soul that endures after death. "There is simply no room for belief in a spiritual realm, in a scientific view of reality," he said. "Period."

Though he concedes that people have an intuitive belief in a soul, it's actually just wishful thinking. "Death has never been popular, especially when it is seen as the final and utter cessation of being. The prospect's tolerability increases only when it is framed as a mere passage to a heavenly paradise filled with all manner of delights," he said. "Humans are profoundly egocentric, and it is natural for us to frame the world in self-referential terms. We cannot easily conceive of the world existing without us, and we struggle to imagine our absolute nonexistence."

Lewis believes that matter achieved immense complexity through "spontaneous unguided processes of self-organization, further sculpted in biological organisms by powerful evolutionary forces—again, unguided." Ultimately, human consciousness, or the mind, emerged by itself during our evolutionary history in some as-yet-unexplained way. "The mind is the product of the brain and nothing but the brain," he said. "The mind is (only) what the brain does."

When our brain dies, we die and decay. What will it feel like to be dead? "Well, remember how you felt for all those eons before you were born?" he asks. "Just like that."[1]

Physicalism versus Dualism

It's easy to sympathize with Ralph and Karin Lewis. When circumstances seem dire, when health fails or death looms, it's natural to cast about for answers. Some cling to religious doctrines. Others reject their spiritual upbringing. But I was interested in a different approach—namely to analyze the evidence and see where the facts point.

Might we be more than just our brains? Should we question the Darwinian dogma that the soul is a figment of our imagination? Or is it possible that ancient teachings are true: humans are both body *and* spirit?

Many scientists today would embrace Lewis's skeptical viewpoint. To them, we are our brains and nothing more. "The prevailing wisdom . . . is there is only one sort of stuff, namely *matter*—the physical stuff of physics, chemistry, and physiology—and the mind is somehow nothing but a physical phenomenon," said atheist philosopher Daniel Dennett.

"In short, the mind is the brain," he continued. "We can (in principle!) account for every mental phenomenon using the same physical principles, laws, and raw materials that suffice to explain radioactivity, continental drift, photosynthesis, reproduction, nutrition, and growth."[2]

Said Sir Colin Blakemore, professor of neuroscience at the University of Oxford, "The human brain is a machine which alone accounts for all our actions, our most private thoughts, our beliefs. All our actions are the products of the activity of our brains."[3]

All our actions? Really? Well, yes, says philosopher Patricia Churchland, but she insists she's okay with that. In an article titled "The Benefits of Realising You're Just a Brain," she tells the interviewer, "Gosh, the love that I feel for my child is really just neural chemistry? Well, actually it is. But that doesn't bother me."[4]

This philosophy is broadly categorized as *physicalism*.[5] Some physicalists, such as Daniel Dennett, believe consciousness is merely an illusion. Other physicalists believe consciousness exists but is wholly a product of the brain, having emerged naturally as humans evolved to become highly complex. However, nobody has been able to propose any credible mechanism for how consciousness could have emerged.

"How can mere matter originate consciousness? How did evolution convert the water of biological tissue into the wine of consciousness?" asks philosopher Colin McGinn. "Consciousness seems like a radical novelty in the universe, not prefigured by the after-effects of the Big Bang, so how did it contrive to spring into being from what preceded it?"[6]

Dualism, the idea that humans are a composite of a physical body and an immaterial mind or soul, does seem intuitive; in fact, it has been believed by "most people, at most times, in most places, at most ages," said philosophers Mark Baker and Stewart

Goetz in *The Soul Hypothesis*. "Such a belief is attested in almost all known human cultures."[7]

Dualists—people who believe we have both a body and a soul—include such thinkers as Augustine, Aquinas, Descartes, Leibniz, Locke, and Kant, as well as scientists Newton and Galileo. They're joined by quite a few credentialed philosophers and scientists working today.[8]

There's even evidence that children start out as dualists. Psychologists studied youngsters who had been told about a mouse that was being eaten by a crocodile. Although four- and six-year-olds understood the mouse was no longer alive *biologically,* and therefore its brain could no longer function, they nevertheless believed it still lived on *psychologically,* so that it would continue to have thoughts and desires.[9] Have you ever noticed something like this with a child?

"In short, the Soul Hypothesis seems to be extremely natural, indeed almost inevitable, to the human mind and experience," Baker and Goetz said.[10]

Of course, there are examples throughout history where people have held beliefs that seemed intuitive, only to have scientific advancements prove them wrong. Now discoveries in neuroscience, including progress in mapping the brain, are prompting physicalists to triumphantly declare that dualism is dead.

"As neuroscientists associate more and more of the faculties once attributed to the mind or soul with the functioning of specific regions or systems of the brain it becomes more and more appealing to say that it is in fact the brain that performs these functions," said philosopher Nancey Murphy.[11]

Daniel Dennett is blunt: "This idea of immaterial souls, capable of defying the laws of physics, has outlived its credibility, thanks to the advance of the natural sciences."[12]

Not true, retort dualists. They're convinced such conclusions are overblown and—excuse the pun—wrongheaded. Said Baker and Goetz, "Reports of the death of the soul have been exaggerated."[13] But on what basis do they make that claim? Allegations are empty without evidence. I was determined to press onward in order to really understand the complexities of this pivotal issue: Is the soul real or merely an illusion?

The Spirit Lives On

The soul is considered to be the seat of our consciousness, the locus of our introspection, volition, emotions, desires, memories, perceptions, and beliefs. It's the ego—the "I" or the self. The soul is said to animate and interact with our body, though it is distinct from it. "When we speak of the soul, we speak of *our essential core*," said philosopher Paul Copan.[14]

The Hebrew words *nephesh* (often translated "soul") and *ruach* (frequently rendered "spirit"), as well as the Greek word *psyche* (generally translated "soul"), occur hundreds of times in the Bible. However, they are used in a variety of contexts, leading to differing interpretations by scholars. Fueling these debates is the fact that the Bible doesn't have any direct teaching specifically on the existence and nature of the soul.[15]

Nevertheless, both the Old and New Testaments seem to presuppose that the soul is real. Taken as a whole, anthropologist Arthur Custance said the Christian Scriptures indicate that human beings are "a hyphenate creature, a spirit/body dichotomy."[16] Indeed, Moreland, whose philosophy doctorate is from the University of Southern California, describes himself this way: "I *am* a soul, and I *have* a body."[17]

Moreland argues that the Bible "explicitly affirms the reality of the soul without attempting to teach its existence explicitly." He writes, "For example, in Matthew 10:28, Jesus warns us not to fear those who can only kill the body; rather, we should fear Him who can destroy both body and soul. The primary purpose of this text is to serve as a warning and not to teach that there is a soul. But in issuing His warning, Jesus implicitly affirms the soul's reality. And on other occasions, the Bible just assumes the commonsense view [of dualism]. For example, when the disciples who saw Jesus walking on water (Matt. 14:26) thought they were seeing a spirit, the Bible is merely assuming that we all know that we are (or have) souls that can exist without the body."[18]

Piecing together clues in Scripture, Moreland said it appears that our soul separates from our body at the point of death as we enter into a temporary intermediate state of disembodiment until the general resurrection of the body at the consummation of history.[19]

As evidence, Moreland points to Jesus, who told the thief being crucified next to him that he would be with Jesus immediately after his death and before the final resurrection of his body.[20] Also, between his death and resurrection, Jesus continued to exist as a God-man independent of his body.[21] The apostle Paul says that to be absent from the body is to be present with the Lord.[22] And Jesus and Paul agreed with the teaching of the Pharisees that at death, the soul departs into a disembodied existence until the general bodily resurrection.[23]

[For clarity, as this book unfolds I will be using the term *intermediate state* to describe this disembodied temporary existence between death and the final resurrection, and the word *heaven* to describe the new heaven and the new earth[24] where embodied followers of Jesus will live for eternity with God after judgment occurs.]

Is it reasonable to believe that our consciousness, or soul, continues to exist in an afterlife? Or are we simply physical brains that are snuffed into oblivion when our heart stops pumping and our brain waves flatten?

"The concept of the soul, though having a long and respectable history, now looks outmuscled and outsmarted by neuroscience," argues Patricia Churchland, professor emeritus of philosophy at the University of California at San Diego.[25]

Is that true? To find out, I decided to seek an interview with a neuroscientist who received her doctorate from Cambridge University and has conducted brain research in Britain and the United States.

Interview #2: Sharon Dirckx, PhD

As a child, Sharon Dirckx (rhymes with *lyrics*) was sitting by the window in her home in Durham, England, while watching the rain falling outside. Suddenly, she became aware of her own consciousness. Thoughts popped into her head: *Why can I think? Why do I exist? Why am I a living, breathing, conscious person who experiences life?*

These were deep reflections for a youngster of ten or eleven, and they propelled her on a lifetime quest for answers. The daughter of a policeman, she grew up in a religiously neutral household. She always wanted to be a scientist. When Sharon was seventeen, a teacher gave her a book by evolutionary biologist and atheist Richard Dawkins, which helped form her agnostic beliefs.

"I became convinced that a person couldn't become a scientist and believe in God at the same time—they're incompatible," she recalled.

During her first week at the University of Bristol, she attended a forum featuring a panel of knowledgeable Christians, and she summoned the courage to ask a question about science and faith being at odds. The response took her aback. "They made the case that of course a person can be a Christian and a scientist at the same time," she said. "It rocked my world."

She ended up spending the next eighteen months investigating Christianity, coming to faith at twenty, and going on to earn her undergraduate degree in biochemistry. Her fascination with neuroscience prompted her to get her doctorate in brain imaging at Cambridge University, and she subsequently spent another seven years conducting neuroimaging research at both the University of Oxford and the Medical College of Wisconsin in Milwaukee.

Today, she and her husband, Conrad (they met in the brain imaging lab—"Very romantic," she quipped), live in Oxford with their two children, Abby and Ethan. She is currently a senior tutor at OCCA (Oxford Centre for Christian Apologetics). She lectures internationally on science, theology, mind and soul issues, and other topics, and she appears regularly on British radio programs, sometimes debating secular thinkers.

Her first book, the award-winning *Why? Looking at God, Evil and Personal Suffering*, came out in 2013.[26] Then she turned her attention back to her passion for neuroscience, philosophy, and theology. The result was her 2019 book *Am I Just My Brain?* Said Ruth Bancewicz of the Faraday Institute for Science and Religion at Cambridge, "Sharon makes a compelling case for why the answer to her book's title (spoiler alert!) is 'No.'"

That's what prompted me to set up a face-to-face interview with her via the internet. She was upstairs at home in Oxford, casually dressed, her brown hair in a bob, and speaking with an altogether British accent. We ended up engaging in a lengthy discussion on this first building block in the case for life beyond death.

Yuri Gagarin versus Buzz Aldrin

I started with a question more whimsical than probing: "When Russian cosmonaut Yuri Gagarin—an atheist—became the first person in space, he remarked, 'I looked and looked, but I didn't see God.' You've used high-tech imaging machines to peer inside human brains. Did you see a soul?"

That evoked a grin. "Well, I wasn't looking for one," she

replied. "As a neuroscientist, I was studying things like the effects of cocaine addiction on the brain. That's what scientists do—we explore the physical world. That may be partly why a lot of scientists just assume the physicalist position, because theirs is the material world of nature.

"Some people assume science can do more than it really can," she added. "For instance, it's not designed to resolve the question of whether God exists. Of course, if God is real, there will be signs pointing in his direction—as I believe there are. But science deals with the natural world.

"By the way," she said, "for every Yuri Gagarin, there's a Buzz Aldrin. He took Communion before walking on the moon and asked for silence from NASA as he read Psalm 8: 'When I consider your heavens, the work of your fingers, the moon and the stars, which you have set in place, what is mankind that you are mindful of them, human beings that you care for them?'[27] There are scientists who doubt, but others who believe."

"You mentioned, though, that many scientists are physicalists. How pervasive is that view?" I asked.

"Quite pervasive," she replied. "For example, *Scientific American* reported on studies of how brain networks are correlated to different mental states. The headline on the cover read, 'How Brain Networks Create Thought.' Now, that is *not* a scientific statement. It's not what the data tell you. That's a worldview statement, based on the belief that everything is ultimately tied to the physical and therefore it must be the brain that creates our thoughts. This happens all the time in our field."

Science, she said, could never disprove God. "That would be like scientists figuring out how all the programming works on Facebook and then declaring, 'So this disproves the existence of Mark Zuckerberg.'"

Now it was my turn to smile. "You're saying that science can tell us many things, but we still need philosophy and theology."

She nodded. "The Bible says that God has made himself known in two ways—through the natural revelation of the physical world and the special revelation of Scripture. Science tells us a lot about the natural world, but we still need theology and philosophy to plumb special revelation—the Scriptures—and to give thought to questions that science cannot answer. Questions like 'Why can we *think* at all?'"

Pen in hand to take notes, I turned to the issue raised by the title of her book—Is there any scientific evidence that we are just our brains?

Describe the Aroma of Coffee

I began by asking fundamental questions: "Are the mind and brain the same thing? Can everything be explained by the firing of neurons?"

"Let me explain why the answer is no," she said. "Scientists can measure activities of the brain—for instance, we see networks light up when various thoughts are taking place. But those networks aren't necessarily the thoughts themselves; they're merely correlated with our thoughts. The problem is that scientists can't access a person's *actual* inner thoughts or *qualia* without simply asking them. A person's thoughts defy traditional scientific methods."

"*Qualia?*"

"That's the plural of *quale,* which philosophers use to describe a quality or property that someone experiences or perceives. For example," she said, raising her cup, "you and I are both drinking coffee as we chat."

I took a sip from my own mug to acknowledge that.

"If someone asked you to describe the smell of coffee, what would you say?" she asked.

I thought for a moment before realizing how vexing that really is. "I'm not sure where I'd begin," I said.

"We could give the chemical structure of caffeine, but that

wouldn't get us any closer to the smell of coffee," Dirckx said. "We might talk about the physiology of what's happening in our body as we drink it, but that doesn't capture the aroma. To understand what coffee smells like, you need to *experience* it. Life is full of *qualia* like that—for example, seeing the color red or tasting a watermelon.

"It's like the difference between reading a review of a concert and experiencing the event yourself. Think about how many times someone tried to describe to you something they've experienced, like a rock concert, only to finally give up and say, 'Well, I guess you really needed to *be* there.'

"As a neuroscientist, I've measured the electrical activity of people's brains, but I can't measure their experience in the same way. I can't measure what's in their minds. I can't measure what it's actually like to be *you*. Why not? Because the brain alone is not enough to explain the mind."

To illustrate further, Dirckx described a thought experiment.[28] What if Mary were a scientist who had detailed knowledge of the physics and chemistry of vision? She knew all about the intricate structure of the eye, how it functions, and how it sends electrical signals to the brain through the optic nerve, where they're converted into images. But what if she were blind—and then one day suddenly she was able to see?

"At the moment of receiving her sight, does Mary learn anything new about vision?" Dirckx asked.

My eyes widened. "Of course!"

"That means physical facts alone cannot explain the first-person experience of consciousness. No amount of knowledge about the physical working of the eye and brain would get Mary closer to the experience of what it's like to actually *see*."

"What's your conclusion?"

"That consciousness simply cannot be synonymous with brain activity."

"You're saying that although they work together, they're not the same thing. Consciousness—the mind, the soul—are beyond the physical workings of the brain."

"Correct. Philosophers such as Leibniz make an important point: If two things are identical, there would be no discernible difference between them.[29] That means if consciousness were identical with brain activity, everything true of consciousness would be true of the brain as well. But consciousness and brain activity couldn't be more different. So consciousness cannot be reduced to the purely physical processes of the brain."

She pointed toward me and smiled. "You, Lee, are more than just your brain."

That did seem clear-cut—but there have been objections. "The atheist Daniel Dennett gets around this by saying that consciousness is illusory," I said.

She replied simply. "Illusion still presupposes consciousness."

"Could you explain that?"

"Illusion happens when we misinterpret an experience or perceive it wrongly, but the experience itself is still valid and real. So that's a problem with what he's saying. Honestly, I think his view is absurd. By the way, it backfires. If what he claims is true, then his very argument can't be trusted."

"Why not?"

"Because it's just an illusion."

Going beyond the Physical Brain

Neuroscientist Adrian Owen spent more than two decades studying patients with brain trauma. In 2006, the prestigious journal *Science* published his groundbreaking research showing that some patients considered vegetative with severe brain injuries were actually conscious.

Said Owen, "We have discovered that 15 to 20 percent of people in the vegetative state, who are assumed to have no more awareness than a head of broccoli, are in fact fully conscious, even though they never respond to any form of external stimulation."[30]

"What does that tell you?" I asked Dirckx.

"It's additional evidence that human beings are highly complex, and the condition of our brains is only part of the story," she said. "Consciousness goes beyond our physical brain and nervous system. It can't just be boiled down to brain activity. *We* are more than our brains."

That triggered thoughts about experiments in the 1950s by Wilder Penfield, the father of modern neurosurgery, who stimulated the brains of epilepsy patients, creating all kinds of involuntary sensations and movements. But no matter how much he tried, he couldn't evoke abstract reasoning or consciousness itself.

"There is no place . . . where electrical stimulation will cause a patient to believe or to decide," Penfield said.[31] For him, this evidence for a nonphysical mind distinct from the brain convinced him to abandon physicalism.[32]

But could the brain, as it evolved in complexity, have somehow generated the conscious mind? I asked Dirckx about this view, which is popular among many scientists.

"If we're dealing with a closed system of nonconscious neurons, how did these come to generate conscious minds?" she replied, letting the challenge hang in the air for a few moments. "This has been the big hurdle. Nobody can give a coherent explanation for it in a materialist world. And if all that's needed is a physical brain to create the mind, why aren't animals conscious to the same degree as we are? The discontinuity between primates and people isn't one of *degree*; it's one of *kind*. Complexity, all by itself, wouldn't be enough to get us across that chasm. Of course, there are Christians who take an emergent view, but for them, the system is not closed. If God exists, extraordinary things are possible. Then that chasm can be crossed."

She paused and then continued. "I'll add another potential line of evidence that humans are more than molecules," she said. "If consciousness and the brain were the same thing, then when a person died, their consciousness would be extinguished—right?"

"That's right," I said.

"But," she asked, "what if near-death experiences [NDEs] show that we can still be conscious without a functioning brain? Again, that would demonstrate that human consciousness is more than just physical brain activity."

In her book, Dirckx tells the story of Pamela Reynolds, who in 1991 suffered a severe brain hemorrhage from an aneurysm. During her surgery, called a "standstill" operation, doctors cooled her body temperature, "flatlined" her heart and brain signals, and drained the blood from her head. Clinically, she was dead—but when she was resuscitated after surgery, she astounded everyone by recalling how she had been conscious the whole time.

Thousands of patients have told stories about being clinically deceased and yet floating out of their body and watching resuscitation efforts from above. Many have described traveling through long tunnels, seeing deceased relatives and experiencing an astoundingly beautiful realm beyond our world. In a study of 1,400 NDEs, cardiologist Fred Schoonmaker said fifty-five patients had their out-of-body experience during a time when they had no measurable brain waves.[33]

No measurable brain waves? Yet their consciousness continued? That would certainly put the possibility of an immaterial mind, or soul, on the table. Personally, I had never explored the question of whether NDEs are credible. I asked Dirckx, "Do you think NDEs can provide good evidence for a soul and an afterlife?"

"This has certainly gone beyond mere anecdotes," she replied. "There have been various studies conducted in the United States, the Netherlands, and elsewhere. Of course, some stories could have been fabricated, but with others there's very intriguing evidence."

"Corroboration?"

"That's the claim. I suspect we'll see more data as research continues. But think about it this way: all we really need is *one* documented case."

"What would that do?"

"It would deal another serious blow to the idea that consciousness resides entirely in the brain," she said. "It would also suggest that even the sciences point to evidence of an afterlife."

I pondered this for a moment and then jotted on my legal pad: *Find out if NDEs are credible.*

The Illusion of Free Will

Here's another problem with the idea that we're just our brain: many philosophers say this means we wouldn't have free will in any meaningful sense. For instance, atheist Sam Harris says that although we *think* we're acting freely, we're simply fulfilling what our genetics and environment compel us to do. Basically, our neurons fire and we obey—it's as simple as that.

"Free will is an illusion," declares Harris, who earned his doctorate in cognitive neuroscience from UCLA. "Our wills are simply not of our own making. Thoughts and intentions emerge from the background causes of which we are unaware and over which we exert no conscious control. We do not have the freedom we think we have."[34]

This is called "hard determinism." I wanted to know from Dirckx: Does this view stand up to scrutiny?

"Let me apply three tests used to assess the legitimacy of any worldview," Dirckx said.[35] "First, is hard determinism internally consistent? Not really. If all our thoughts are driven by nonrational, mechanistic forces, then they are not really our thoughts as such. They come from forces beyond our control and therefore are meaningless. The person expressing a hard deterministic view is asking you not to believe them!"

"Second, does hard determinism make sense of the world around us? Again, not really. If free will is an illusion, why do we continue to imagine it's real? Why do we strive for autonomy? Why do we seek control over our finances, our health, and our careers—are we free to shape our own lives and decide our own fate or not? Hard determinism creates confusion, not clarity.

"Third, can hard determinism be authentically lived out? Not really. We don't live as though our choices are just the mechanistic firing of neurons in our brain; we live as though our decisions really do mean something. In fact, under hard determinism we wouldn't be morally responsible for our actions, since we wouldn't really have a meaningful choice in what we do. That means society couldn't legitimately punish people for their crimes or reward them for their virtue. We can't live that way."

I found the seeming absurdity of hard determinism to be another reason it makes sense to believe we're not just our brains. We must have a distinct mind, or soul, that gives us the capacity to make *real* choices—to love or hate, to help or hinder, to engage with God or turn away from him.[36]

"I like the grid you use to test a worldview," I told Dirckx. "Could you use that criteria to assess the view that we are just our brains and nothing more?"

"Okay, sure," she said. "First, is it internally consistent? I'd say no. You see, the view that you are your brain can't even be expressed without first presupposing an inner life. It's like saying, 'My first-person perspective is that there is no first-person perspective.' To deny consciousness is itself a conscious act.

"Second, does it make sense of the world? Well, it doesn't explain what it means to be a person. Brains don't write books. Brains don't have longing and desires. Brains don't make plans. Brains don't experience disappointment. *People* do these things *using* their brain. There's a huge explanatory gap between the experience we have of this world and the view that you're just a bunch of cell voltages and neurotransmitters.

"And third, can it be lived? Truly, we don't live as though we're a walking pack of neurons. We live as though we each have a unique and valid perspective of the world. Besides, we want to treat others as though they're conscious beings. For example, we're outraged at human trafficking precisely because we believe that the people involved are not packs of neurons but are conscious human beings who experience suffering.

"The idea that we're just our brains fails all three of these tests," she concluded. "We're not machines. Our brain and our mind are fundamentally distinct, though they work together. The brain offers a third-person perspective; it's the mind that provides a first-person experience."

Are Electrons Conscious?

Before we moved on, I asked Dirckx about a different way that some philosophers try to explain consciousness. It's called *panpsychism*, from the Greek *pan*, which means "all," and *psyche*, which means "soul" or "mind."[37]

Explained Dirckx, "This is the idea that matter itself is conscious—that there's only one kind of substance in the universe, and all particles have both physical *and* conscious dimensions."

"*All* particles?" I asked.

"This view would say there are levels of consciousness in everything—in fact, there are conscious states in each atom and in inanimate minerals. These levels would grow as the systems increase in complexity. Obviously, humans would have the highest levels of consciousness."

"In other words, consciousness was baked into the system from the very beginning," I said. "That's clever, but it doesn't explain where it all came from, does it?"

"It doesn't. And it doesn't explain why humans are unique in their consciousness compared to the rest of the animal kingdom. Also, here's a big problem: it's impossible to confirm this theory. To verify consciousness, you need word-based language to express it, and the natural world doesn't have this ability."

"How far down does consciousness go in panpsychism? Are electrons conscious?"

"Philip Goff of Durham University would say there are unimaginably small levels of consciousness even at that level.[38] But, of course, that raises problems too. If electrons are conscious and we have trillions of them in us, how can we account for the unity with which we experience the world? We don't have trillions of separate conscious experiences; we have one. It's all integrated. How do you explain this unity of consciousness?"

I shook my head. "To be honest, panpsychism seems like a big stretch to me."

"I understand that reaction," said Dirckx. "On the positive side, though, at least they're taking consciousness seriously and trying to account for it."

The Ultimate Purpose of Consciousness

All of which brought us back to dualism and the issue of the soul. In ancient Greece, shortly before he drank hemlock in 399 BC, Socrates expressed a kind of dualism when he said, "When I am dead, I shall not stay, but depart and be gone . . . to a state of heavenly happiness."[39]

It was Socrates's student Plato who became renowned for philosophizing about the soul, which was a concept, by the way, that had already been a commonsense belief among ordinary people, write philosophers Stewart Goetz and Charles Taliaferro. They credit Plato and his pupil Aristotle as being "the most important ones in shaping the history of the soul."[40]

Nevertheless, the Hebrew concept of the soul goes back even

farther, Dirckx said. "The Christian faith also has a lot to say about the soul. The soul is that which makes us more than matter, more than advanced primates, more than simply our brains. The soul is the impenetrable core of a person, given by God."[41]

"Here's a key question," I said. "Are the findings of modern neuroscience compatible with the idea that God exists?"

"Yes, absolutely," she replied. "It's important to point out that the recent discoveries of neuroscience are *entirely* compatible with the existence of God. In no way does *any* discovery in brain research rule out God. That would be a complete misunderstanding of the data."

"What happens," I asked, "if you start out with the worldview that God does exist?"

"Well, then everything begins to make more sense."

"But is it rational to adopt that worldview?" I asked. "Do you believe there are solid, independent reasons to believe that the God of Christianity is real?"[42]

"I do. That helped bring me to faith and has helped me grow deeper ever since."

"Some philosophers say because God is conscious, it explains why we are conscious. Is that persuasive to you?"

"Yes, it is," she replied. "Genesis 1:1 says, 'In the beginning God . . .' Before there was anything physical, there was consciousness in the form of the Father, Son, and Holy Spirit—the Trinity. The unembodied mind of God, which has always existed, gave rise to everything else. The Bible also says that human beings were made in God's image.[43] Consequently, it makes sense to say that because God has a mind, we have a mind; because God thinks, we think; because God is conscious, so are we. That would explain a lot, wouldn't it?"

"To get there, though, a scientist would have to push beyond his or her materialistic worldview."

"Nobody is neutral," she said. "We can either shut off

explanations or explore possibilities, but the best scientists always remain open to new ideas. I'm convinced the Christian world-view is well-founded. And if it is, that explains where our value as human beings originates—we're made in God's likeness. It also explains why we sometimes long for more than this world. Human beings aren't temporary, but we are intended to live on for eternity.

"If the materialistic narrative is all there is, then we can throw meaning, purpose, and significance out the window. We're a blip on the landscape. The cosmos is billions of years old, and we appear in the last millisecond. We are utterly meaningless. People may try to achieve meaning through their accomplishments, but those ebb and flow.

"However, the existence of God provides a firm foundation for our meaning. We can't simply look to the age of the cosmos, nor is our value based on what we accomplish. It comes from God. We are created and loved by him. The reason all of us have a longing for eternity is that, indeed, we were made by God to live forever.

"God is relational, existing from eternity past as the Trinity, and so like him, we are relational beings. This means we can interact personally with God. He is someone to be encountered. He is a first-person experience, not a third-person observation. We can go beyond facts *about* God and really *know* him."

With that, she stressed her conclusion: "Actually, that's the ultimate point of consciousness: *so that we can know God.*"

Can the Immaterial Impact the Material?

Still, there are objections raised by physicalists. For example, I asked Dirckx how something immaterial like a mind or soul can have an impact on something physical like the brain? The question didn't faze her.

"We see examples of this all the time," she answered.

"For instance?"

"What happens when you're cyberbullied? You may lose your appetite, have panic attacks, lose sleep. What happens if the person you love asks you for a date? You may blush or have a spring in your step. What happens if you get bad news? It triggers a physical process in which salt water is released from the lacrimal glands in your eyes. You see, the immaterial impacts the material every day. So why not a nonphysical mind interacting with a physical brain?"

That response made sense to me. I turned to a second objection. "What about Occam's razor?" I asked, referring to the law of parsimony, which means that when considering competing hypotheses, we should opt for the simplest one. "Wouldn't Occam's razor suggest that the simplest explanation—that we are just our brain—should be preferred to a theory that adds another entity, like the soul?"

"At first glance, it may seem that the simplest explanation is that we're just our brains. But as we've seen, people have to jump through hoops to try to explain the human person purely in terms of neurons.

"If we look at how other areas of science have developed, we see they haven't led to simpler explanations. Instead, we've seen increasing complexity, leading to deeper knowledge. Take, for example, the human cell. Two hundred years ago, scientists thought the cell was simple—just a homogenous blob. Now we can peer inside and see the complexity of Golgi bodies, a nucleus, DNA, RNA—incredible structures and micromachines.

"Look at physics, with Newton's laws giving way to a deeper understanding of very small things in terms of quantum physics. If someone thinks they understand quantum physics, they don't—it's too complex. As we've gone deeper and deeper into exploring reality, things have not become more and more simple, but they've become more and more complex and beautiful. Complexity isn't the enemy of truth.

"Human beings are highly complex," she added. "The implication that we are just our brains is incredibly limiting. It diminishes humans to this one dimension, even though we actually have many dimensions. We don't just have a brain. We have a personality, we have genetics, we experience trauma, we have a certain upbringing—all kinds of things shape our minds and who we are. Overly simplistic explanations don't do justice to the question, 'What is a person?'"

She thought for a moment and then concluded. "Although I could answer this question in another way too."

"How so?"

"I could put Occam's razor to use. I could posit the position that humans are conscious because God is conscious. That's simple and straightforward—though it actually has more explanatory power than physicalism."

Made for Another World

For me, the case had been made. I am more than just my body. My soul is distinct from my brain. To paraphrase J. P. Moreland, I *am* a soul, and I *have* a body. That opens the door to the possibility that when my body takes its last breath in this world, I can actually live on.[44]

After Dirckx and I exchanged some final pleasantries, I thanked her for her time and expertise. Our transatlantic internet connection blinked off. She went back to Abby and Ethan, who were baking downstairs in the kitchen. Life goes on—as it will for a while. Hopefully, for a long, long time. But eventually, ultimately, what happens in the afterlife will be of supreme importance for each of us.

Dirckx closes her book this way: "If you are just your brain, then you were made only for this world, and the only mantra to live by is to live well and make the most out of life while you have it. Christianity says you are more than your brain—you are made for eternity. One way or another, there will be consciousness in eternity, either with Christ or apart from him. Live today with eternity in mind."[45]

The first building block in our case for an afterlife was in place: death does not have to mean the end of human beings. Still, there was other evidence to consider. What about the issue Dirckx raised concerning near-death experiences—could they really shed light on what happens after we die? There are scholars who think so. Prominent Christian philosopher Paul Copan from Palm Beach Atlantic University believes there is "very strong evidence" for NDEs or out-of-body experiences.[46]

I lowered the screen on my laptop. Time to pursue more answers.

CHAPTER 3

Near-Death Experiences

A Peek into the World Beyond?

The evidence of near-death experiences points to an afterlife and a universe guided by a vastly loving intelligence.

PHYSICIAN AND NDE RESEARCHER JEFFREY LONG, *EVIDENCE OF THE AFTERLIFE*

As a Harvard neurosurgeon and an agnostic, Eben Alexander believed we are just our brains, nothing more.

"If you don't have a working brain, you can't be conscious," he said. "This is because the brain is the machine that produces consciousness in the first place. When the machine breaks down, consciousness stops . . . Pull the plug and the TV goes dead. The show is over, no matter how much you might have been enjoying it."[1] In short, no afterlife, no heaven, no existence of any kind beyond the grave.

Then came November 10, 2008, when a rare brain infection crashed his entire neocortex, the part of the brain that makes us human. "During my coma my brain wasn't working improperly—it wasn't working *at all*," he would say later.[2] While his brain wasn't functioning, he still found himself fully conscious, but now in a "brilliant, vibrant, ecstatic, stunning" new world[3]—a place fueled by an exhilarating sense of unconditional love.

There he encountered the face of a beautiful girl who gazed at him with an enigmatic smile. He had no idea who she was, but she radiated a beautiful love toward him.

Miraculously, the physician emerged fully healed from his near-death experience. He had been adopted as a baby, and after reconnecting with his birth family, he was sent a photograph—it was a picture of a sister named Betsy whom he had never known anything about and who had died years earlier.[4]

The photo floored him. This was the girl with the mysterious smile who had exuded such love to him in the world beyond.

"My experience showed me that the death of the body and the brain are not the end of consciousness, that human experience continues beyond the grave," he now declares. "More important, it continues under the gaze of a God who loves and cares about each one of us."[5]

Let's face it: we all want that to be true—but is it really?

In the previous chapter, Sharon Dirckx offered persuasive reasons to believe that we each have a soul or consciousness that is distinct from our physical brains. But is there any evidence to suggest that my consciousness would actually survive my physical death? Even as someone who has faith in Jesus, when I was hospitalized, I couldn't help but feel uncertainty—even anxiety—about what would happen if death were to clench me. What evidence is there that we will experience an afterlife? Do near-death experiences shed light or sow confusion over this issue?

Is There Life after Life?

Raymond Moody, a physician with doctorates in philosophy and psychology, coined the term "near-death experience" (NDE) in his 1975 book *Life after Life*, which has sold thirteen million copies and has been translated into a dozen languages.[6] Moody's interviews with 150 people who experienced NDEs inspired Kenneth Ring, a longtime professor of psychology at the University of Connecticut, to become a prominent NDE researcher and founding editor of the *Journal of Near-Death Studies*.

"The stories Moody's respondents told were so captivating and enthralling and depicted the experience of dying in such radiantly glorious language that people reading and hearing about it could scarcely believe that what they had always feared as their greatest enemy, when seen up close, had the face of the beloved," Ring said.[7]

"And more—when Moody's interviewees attempted to describe the experience of dying, they often mentioned a light of unceasing, supernatural brilliance that exuded a feeling of pure, unconditional, *absolute* love and was associated with such an overwhelming sensation of peace that they could only liken it to 'the peace that passeth all understanding.'"[8]

It's no wonder that the public was thrilled with Moody's writings and subsequent books by others about after-death experiences. "It seemed clear evidence," Ring wrote, "that what our Western religions, at least, taught was true: that life continues after death, that heaven is no fantasy, and that those who die do, indeed, see the face of God."[9]

Many scholars remain dubious. "The big question is, 'Do NDEs provide a proof of heaven? Or hell?' I don't think so. None of the arguments is persuasive," said John Martin Fischer, a philosophy professor at the University of California–Riverside.[10]

Wrote New Testament scholar Scot McKnight, "The differences among the various stories over the course of history are so dramatic it makes me skeptical that they are reporting what Heaven or the afterlife is like."[11]

According to a 2019 study, as many as one in ten people across thirty-five countries have undergone some sort of NDE.[12] But could these experiences be explained away? When I was hovering near death in the hospital, might my traumatized brain have manufactured hallucinations that I would have mistaken for reality? Maybe if I had been deprived of oxygen, I would have entered an imaginary world that actually had no more substance than a dream.

Or might these near-death experiences be fraudulent—after all, one youngster fabricated his account in a bestselling book,[13] and journalists have sought to undermine Eben Alexander's credibility as well.[14] Is there any corroboration to support claims of a post-death existence?

Fortunately, I knew where I could get answers. A long-time friend of mine—himself a former spiritual skeptic—has researched more than a thousand cases of near-death experiences and had recently written a book on the topic that was climbing the *New York Times* bestseller list. An email message yielded an appointment with him. Leslie and I packed our suitcases at our Houston home, got in the car, and headed west toward Austin.

"I Knew in My Heart This Was God"

After stopping for a barbecue lunch in the quaint town of Brenham, we pulled back onto US-290 and continued driving toward my interview with John Burke, a former colleague of mine at a Chicago church and now pastor of the burgeoning Gateway Church in the state's capital.

Along the way, Leslie began reading to me from Burke's book *What's after Life?* which opens with the NDE account of a single mom in London, England, who had been admitted to Memorial Hospital with severe bleeding:

> As the blood drained from my body so did my will to live. I heard a "pop" sound and suddenly the pain stopped . . . I had a very clear view of my body as they ferociously worked on me,

hooking up a transfusion and other tubes. I recalled thinking that I just wished they would stop . . .

The fact that I was having these thoughts from within inches of the ceiling didn't bother me or confuse me . . . I was totally conscious even though I had heard a nurse, the only one in a blue smock, tell the doctors I had lost consciousness soon after entering the emergency room. I was very aware of every detail of the events and the room. I was aware of a tunnel which appeared suddenly, and I was being pulled into it. I was happy to be away from that tense scene below. I floated toward the tunnel and passed right through a ceiling fan and then the ceiling . . .

I gained speed heading for a bright light far in the distance. As I proceeded at a faster rate, I felt there was a presence with me that kept me calm and emitted both love and wisdom. I didn't see anyone, but I felt the essence of my grandpa who had died when I was thirteen . . .

I finally came to the end [of the tunnel] and floated into a place which was overwhelmed by a radiant white light that seemed to embody all the concepts of love. A love which was unconditional and like a mother has for a child . . . I knew in my heart that this was God. Words can't describe my awe in this presence . . . I could tell He knew my every thought and feeling.

The next thing I knew I was seeing a sleeping baby I knew to be me. I watched with fascination as I saw the highlights of each stage of my life . . . I felt every good or bad deed I had ever done and its consequences upon others. It was a difficult time for me, but I was supported by unconditional love and weathered the painful parts. I was asked telepathically about whether I wanted to stay or return . . .

Suddenly, I was popped back into my body and searing pain tore through my lower body. The same nurse in the blue smock was giving me a shot and telling me to relax [and] that the pain medication would soon begin to take effect. It seemed as if I had not been unconscious for more than a few minutes yet my visit to the "Other Side" seemed to last [for] hours.

While I was out of my body in the ER, I noticed a red label on the side of the blade of a ceiling fan facing the top of the ceiling . . . I finally convinced [a nurse] to get a tall ladder and see for herself the red sticker whose appearance I described in great detail on the hidden side of the emergency room ceiling fan. The nurse and an orderly saw the sticker, confirming all the details of its appearance I described.[15]

Leslie closed the book. "Pretty compelling," she said.

"Yeah," I replied. "The part about the sticker gives it a certain credibility. But it does raise a lot of questions."

Leslie opened the book again. "I'll say this—it grabbed my attention."

I agreed. "The whole subject is fascinating," I said. "I just read an article about research showing that 40 percent of patients who survived a cardiac arrest were aware during the time they were clinically dead and before their hearts were restarted.[16] John has been studying NDEs for more than three decades. Honestly, I can't wait to get to the bottom of this."

In my view—echoing something similar to what neuroscientist Sharon Dirckx told me during our interview—all that's needed would be just one well-documented case of a near-death experience. For me, that would constitute strong evidence that our consciousness continues even after clinical death.

Just *one* case.

Interview #3: John Burke

John Burke was sixteen years old when his father, an engineer for an oil company in Houston, was dying of cancer. One day, John noticed a book on his dad's nightstand—it was Raymond Moody's groundbreaking report on NDEs. Curious, John picked it up and quickly read it from cover to cover.

"At the end—I'll never forget—I was sitting on my bed with tears streaming down my face," he recalls. "I was an agnostic at the time, but I remember thinking, *Oh my gosh, this Jesus stuff might be true—and if he's real, I want to be with him.*"

Shortly afterward, a friend led him in a prayer of commitment to Christ. John went on to get his engineering degree at the University of Texas, worked for a couple large oil companies, and then completed his master's level work in theology and philosophy at Trinity International University near Chicago. He and his wife, Kathy, ministered on college campuses and in Russia after the collapse of the Soviet Union.

I met John when he was executive director of ministries at the church in suburban Chicago where I was a teaching pastor. In 1998, he and Kathy left to start Gateway Church in Austin, which has grown from four people meeting in a home to more than five thousand attenders. John fosters a "come as you are" atmosphere that attracts skeptics, doubters, spiritual strugglers, and seekers. His nonprofit Gateway Leadership Initiative helps pastors and ordinary Christians love, serve, and engage the broader culture.

Over the years, John has written several influential books, including *No Perfect People Allowed*, *Soul Revolution*, and *Unshockable Love*. A father of two and grandfather to little Sophia, John has spoken in twenty-seven countries on leadership and spiritual development.

His curiosity about NDEs, sparked by Raymond Moody's book, has only increased through the decades. In 2015, Burke's research resulted in the bestseller *Imagine Heaven*, which has sold nearly a million copies. Said philosopher J. P. Moreland, "In all honesty, this is now the go-to book on Heaven and NDEs."[17]

While Leslie took a tour of the Gateway campus, John and I settled into a conference room at the church. He was casually dressed, his dark brown hair a bit tousled. He is athletic (an amateur sailor and soccer player) and quick-witted, with an easy smile and enthusiastic voice.

What NDEs Hold in Common

"In all of your research," I asked, "what was your most surprising discovery about near-death experiences?"

"First, I'm not particularly fond of the term near-death experiences," he began. "As one survivor said, 'I wasn't *near* dead; I was *dead* dead.' Some of these cases involve people with no heartbeat or brain waves. There are instances where doctors had already declared them dead. They may not have been *eternally* dead, but many were certainly *clinically* dead."

"Okay, good point," I said.

"Now, let me answer your question," he continued. "What surprised me the most is that even though they vary a fair amount, these accounts have a common core—and incredibly, it's entirely consistent with what we're told about the afterlife in the Bible."

"Yet a lot of Christians associate NDEs with the occult or New Age thinking," I said.

"Not all Christians think that way. Many take the approach of the late theologian R. C. Sproul, who tried to keep an open mind about NDEs and encouraged more research and analysis.[18] Christian philosophers J. P. Moreland and Gary Habermas have been writing about the implications of NDEs as far back as the early 1990s."[19]

"Why is there such a wide variation in how people describe their NDE?"

"Well, I noticed that there's a difference between what people *report* they experienced and how they *interpret* it," he said. "The interpretations vary, but when you dig down to what they actually experienced, there's a core that's consistent with what Scripture tells us about the life to come."

I cocked my head. "As a pastor, you're not basing your theology about heaven on these NDEs, are you?" I asked.

"Not at all. I'm basing my beliefs on the Bible. That's our most reliable source. I'm merely saying that the Bible contains black-and-white words about the afterlife, and these NDEs tend to add color to the picture. They don't contradict; they complement."

"What do NDEs hold in common?" I asked.

"Three-quarters of people experience the separation of consciousness from the physical body," he replied.

"An out-of-body experience."

"That's right. About the same number have heightened senses and intense emotions."

"Positive ones?"

"Generally, yes. Two out of three encounter a mystical or brilliant light, and more than half meet other beings, either mystical ones or deceased relatives or friends. More than half describe unworldly or heavenly realms. A quarter say they undergo a life review. A third say they encounter a barrier or boundary, and more than half were aware of a decision to return to their physical body."

"Isn't it true that many people find it difficult to describe the experience?"

"For sure," he said. "A girl named Crystal said, 'There are no human words that even come close.' A guy named Gary said nothing could adequately describe the divine presence he encountered."[20]

"More Brilliant Than the Sun"

"Tell me about that so-called divine presence," I said. "What do people typically say about him?"

"They talk about a brilliant light—brighter than anything they've ever seen," Burke said.

Then he told the story of an atheist named Ian McCormack

from New Zealand, who went scuba diving off the coast of Mauritius in the Indian Ocean and was stung four times by box jellyfish.

I cringed when he said that. I knew from my travels that these jellyfish are often called the world's most venomous creature. One sting can result in cardiovascular collapse and death in two to five minutes.[21] And Ian was stung *four* times.

"Ian was dying," Burke said. "He saw visions of his mother, who had told him to call out to God if he ever needed help. He was in utter darkness and felt terrified. He prayed for God to forgive his sins—and a bright light shined on him and literally drew him out of the darkness. He described the light as 'unspeakably bright, as if it was the center of the universe . . . more brilliant than the sun, more radiant than any diamond, brighter than a laser beam. Yet you could look right into it.'

"He said this presence knew everything about him, which made him feel terribly ashamed. But instead of judgment, he felt 'pure, unadulterated, clean, uninhibited, undeserved love.' He began weeping uncontrollably. Ian asked if he could 'step into the light.' As he did, he saw in the middle of the light a man with dazzling white robes—garments literally woven from light—who offered his arms to welcome him. He said, 'I knew that I was standing in the presence of Almighty God.'"[22]

Burke paused and then continued. "Remember the transfiguration? In Matthew 17:2, it says Jesus' face 'shone like the sun, and his clothes became as white as the light.'" He smiled. "Reminds me of that."

"But if Ian had been a Hindu, might he have encountered a god from that faith?"

"In all my research, I've never read of people describing anything like Krishna, who has blue skin, or Shiva, who has three eyes, or descriptions of the dissolving of the individual self in the impersonal supreme Brahma, which is the ultimate Hindu reality. In fact, two researchers studied five hundred Americans and five hundred Indians to see how much their cultural conditioning may have affected their NDE."

"What did they find?"

"That several basic Hindu ideas of the afterlife were never portrayed in the visions of the Indian patients. No reincarnation. They did describe encountering a white-robed man with a book of accounts. To them, that might vaguely suggest Karma, or the record of merits and demerits. But again, that's an interpretation, because it's also very consistent with what we find in the Bible. Bruce Greyson, who studied cross-cultural NDEs, agreed that it's not the core experience that differs, but the ways in which people interpret what they have experienced."[23]

"Everything Is Exposed"

I asked Burke to elaborate on the life review that so many people go through during their near-death experience.

"It occurs in the presence of the Being of light, and it often begins with him asking something like, 'What have you done with the life I gave you?' It's said not in judgment, but in love, to prompt reflection and learning.

"Everything is exposed from a person's life—every thought, every motive, every deed. Nothing is hidden. What's interesting is that the focus isn't on your accomplishments or trophies or résumé, but on how you loved others. It's all about relationships. People actually see and feel how their actions—even small, seemingly insignificant ones—ripple through the lives of other people, even four or five steps down the road, in ways they never knew.

"Through it all, there's no judgment. What happens is that people tend to judge themselves. One man said he was so ashamed by his cruel and selfish behavior that he begged them to stop the review.[24] Yet here's the thing—Jesus continued to communicate only unconditional love for him."

"Do people from different cultures experience this review differently?"

"Actually, it's pretty consistent. Steve Miller studied non-Western, non-Christian NDEs and said, 'In my non-Western sample, I saw no significant difference in life reviews compared to Western life reviews.'[25] And remember that Jesus said in the Bible: 'There is nothing concealed that will not be disclosed, or hidden that will not be made known.'"[26]

I put up my hand to stop him. "Wait a second," I said. "This is what concerns a lot of Christians. The Bible says God will judge each of us, but that doesn't sound like what these life reviews are about. It sounds more like universalism—everybody is saved, regardless of how they lived or ever sought forgiveness through Christ."

Burke's response was a smile. "That's based on a big misunderstanding," he answered. "First, Jesus himself said, 'For by your words you will be acquitted, and by your words you will be condemned.'[27] That's what people experience—God loves them and they judge themselves. Plus, the Bible talks about two judgments. One determines whether we've accepted or rejected God's free gift of love, forgiveness, adoption, and salvation; the other is to reward his followers for how they lived.[28]

"But this life review isn't either of those," he said. "Hebrews 9:27 tells us that 'people are destined to die *once*, and after that to face judgment' [italics added]. Remember, these people are not *irreversibly* dead; they may be *clinically* dead, but they will be returning to life at some point. This life review seems to be a clarifying reminder that God knows everything about us, and that we all one day will give an account. Keep in mind that the Bible teaches there's no judgment at all until human history comes to its conclusion."[29]

"So you don't see any conflict between these life reviews and Christian doctrine," I said, the words coming out more as a statement than a question.

"No," he said. "I really don't. Throughout my book *Imagine Heaven*, I cite chapter and verse for how the core of NDEs track with the Christian faith."

Descending into Hell

Most near-death experiences involve positive encounters—but not all. Twelve different studies involving 1,369 subjects revealed that 23 percent reported NDEs ranging from disturbing to terrifying or despairing.[30] In fact, a 2019 study by the European Academy of Neurology Congress of 1,035 people across thirty-five countries showed that one out of ten people had undergone a near-death experience—and 73 percent of them rated it as having been "unpleasant."[31]

I said to Burke, "In the early days of NDE research, very few people reported having a hellish experience. Why is that?"

"Embarrassment. Wanting to suppress the memory. Fear of social ostracism. Some suffer long-term psychological trauma. Today people are more willing to talk about it, like Howard Storm, who has become a friend of mine."

Storm was a professor of art at Northern Kentucky University and an avowed atheist when he "died" from a stomach ulcer that had perforated his duodenum. Oddly, he found himself standing up next to the bed, feeling better than ever. He began to follow some mysterious but friendly visitors who beckoned him down the hallway. This turned into a trek of miles, with conditions getting darker and darker.

Suddenly, the strangers who had greeted him so warmly became rude and hostile. Now it was pitch-black and Storm felt stark terror. They began pushing, hitting, pulling, kicking, biting, and tearing with their fingernails and hands as they laughed and swore at him. He fought back as best he could, but he was mauled—physically and emotionally—in the struggle.

"There has never been a horror movie or book that can begin

to describe their cruelty," he recalled. "Eventually, I was eviscerated. I definitely lost one of my eyes, my ears were gone, and I'm lying on the floor of that place.

"So now I have eternity—time without measure—to think about my situation . . . Because I had lived a garbage life, I had gone down the toilet. And I realized, this is the horrible part: that the people who had met me were my kindred spirits. They denied God, they lived for themselves, and their lives were about manipulation and control of other people. My life was devoted to building a monument to my ego. My family, my sculptures, my paintings— all of those were gone now, and what did they matter? I wasn't far from becoming like one of my own tormentors for all eternity."

Eventually, Storm called out for help. "I yelled into the darkness, 'Jesus, save me!' I have never meant anything more strongly in my life."

A small light appeared—"way brighter than the sun"—and hands and arms came out. "When they touched me, in that light, I could see me and all the gore. I was roadkill. And that gore began to just dissolve and I came back whole."

He felt a love far beyond words. "If I took all my experience of love in my entire life and could condense it into a moment, it still wouldn't begin to measure up to the intensity of this love that I was feeling. And that love is the foundation of my life from that moment on."

So transformational was this experience that when Storm was healed of his medical condition, he resigned his tenured professorship and chairmanship of the university's art department to become the pastor of a small church, where he serves to this day.[32]

"Sometimes," Burke said to me, "people suggest that NDEs are merely hallucinations of some sort. But hallucinations are typically scattered and confused, while NDEs are lucid and cohesive. Besides, I don't see people completely changing the direction of their life based on a mere hallucination. Often, though, people who've gone through an NDE are changed forever.

"Like my friend Howard."

The Boy Who Didn't Come Back

In 2010, the inspiring book *The Boy Who Came Back from Heaven* described how young Alex Malarkey was critically injured in a traffic accident and met Jesus in heaven during a near-death experience.[33] It became an instant hit in Christian circles, with more than a million copies sold, and was the basis of a television film.

Later, Malarkey made a startling confession: "I did not die. I did not go to heaven. I said I went to heaven because I thought it would get me attention."[34] The scandal rocked the Christian publishing industry. The lesson was clear: it was remarkably easy for someone to fabricate claims of an NDE.

I recapped that incident to Burke and asked, "Isn't this an ever-present danger in researching NDEs?"

"No question about it, but I've tried to guard against it in my research," he said.

"How so?"

"By focusing on stories from people who lack a profit motive. These are orthopedic surgeons, oncologists, bank presidents, cardiologists, commercial airline pilots, professors, neurosurgeons. They don't need the money and, frankly, they risk having their credibility tarnished if they make up wild tales. Very few of the more than a thousand people studied have written a book. Plus, think about the fact that around the globe—in all kinds of culturally diverse places—basically the same story is emerging from NDE survivors. There's no way everyone conspired together to concoct something."

"How convinced are you that there are no physiological or

neurological explanations for NDEs?" I asked. "A lot of theories have been put forth over the years."

Burke shrugged. "I just don't think any of them explain everything away," he replied. "For example, it's been shown that when you try to induce experiences, you don't completely replicate an NDE."

He picked up his book and flipped to its conclusion. "Pim van Lommel is a Dutch cardiologist who did a large-scale prospective study into NDEs that was published in the respected British medical journal the *Lancet*," Burke said.

He scanned the text for its relevant portions and then quoted them to me. "After examining possible alternate explanations for NDEs, van Lommel conceded that although 'various physiological and psychological factors could all play a role, none can fully explain the phenomenon.' His bottom line was that these theories 'fail to explain the experience of an enhanced consciousness, with lucid thoughts, emotions, memories from earliest childhood, visions of the future, and the possibility of perception from a position outside and above the body.'"[35]

"There's still controversy about NDEs though—isn't that right?"

"Certainly the debate continues," Burke said. "An increasing amount of research is being done. More than nine hundred articles have been published in scholarly journals. But many skeptical researchers have now concluded that NDEs give us a peek into the afterlife. None of the alternative explanations make as much logical sense as the straightforward conclusion that there really is life after death."

The Errant Tennis Shoe

Personally, I was hungry for further corroboration. I can't verify that Eben Alexander encountered a "brilliant, vibrant, ecstatic, stunning" new world; that Ian McCormack stood in the presence of Almighty God; or that Jesus rescued Howard Storm from torment. On the positive side, I have their testimony, their changed lives, and the evidence of similar encounters reported around the globe. All of that is intriguing. But, of course, I don't have independent eyewitnesses who can vouch for what happened. The investigative journalist in me wanted something that could be checked out.

"I was impressed by the case in which the dying woman left her body, drifted toward the ceiling, and was able to see a red sticker on the hidden side of the fan blade," I said. "Her description of the sticker was later confirmed to be correct. That kind of independent corroboration is helpful. Are there other cases like that?"

"Oh, sure," came his reply. "Quite a few."

"Give me some examples."

"There are many cases where NDE patients leave their body, watch doctors try to resuscitate them, and are able to later describe the exact procedures and tools the doctors used. Cardiologist Michael Sabom was a skeptic until he investigated those kinds of cases. For instance, his patient Peter Morton underwent cardiac arrest and yet described the resuscitation efforts in such precise and accurate detail that Sabom said he could have used the tape to train other physicians."

"Hold on," I said. "Couldn't the patient have been guessing? Maybe he was simply recalling what he had seen on medical shows on television."

"That's been investigated," Burke replied. "Dr. Penny Sartori did a five-year study and found that patients who claimed to be out of their bodies were 'surprisingly accurate' in their observations. She compared that with patients who were asked to guess what happened during their resuscitations."

"How did those folks fare?"

"Not well. She said they all had errors and misconceptions

of the equipment used and incorrect procedures were described. For example, she said many guessed that the defibrillator had been used when, in fact, it had not."[36]

"Interesting," I said.

"One of the most famous cases comes from researcher Kimberly Clark Sharp, who describes the out-of-body experience of a heart-attack patient named Maria. During the time Maria was unconscious, she drifted through the ceiling and outside the hospital. When she did, she saw a tennis shoe on the hospital's third-story window ledge."

"How did she describe it?"

"A man's shoe, left-footed, dark blue, with a wear mark over the little toe and a shoelace tucked under the heel. Sharp investigated, and sure enough—she eventually found the shoe, exactly as Maria had described it."[37]

I pondered the story for a moment. "Well, that's impressive," I said. "How often does this kind of corroboration occur?"

"Janice Holden studied ninety-three NDE patients who claimed to make multiple verifiable observations while out of their physical bodies. She said a remarkable 92 percent of the observations were 'completely accurate.' Think of that—nearly everyone was totally correct. Another 6 percent contained just 'some error.' Only 2 percent were 'completely erroneous.'"[38]

I had to concede. "That's a pretty amazing track record."

And the Blind Can See

I gestured toward Burke to continue with examples of corroborated cases. He thought for a second and then began rattling them off, occasionally picking up his book and flipping through it for details to refresh his recollection.

"The *Lancet* published an account of a patient who was brought into the hospital comatose and not breathing after cardiac arrest. A male nurse removed the man's dentures and tucked them into the drawer of a crash cart. A week later, in another room, the patient regained consciousness. When the nurse came in, the patient recognized him, saying, 'You took my dentures out of my mouth,' and he proceeded to precisely describe how the nurse had put them in the bottom drawer of a specific cart.

"The nurse said, 'I was especially amazed because I remembered this happening while the man was in a deep coma and in the process of CPR. When I asked further, it appeared the man had seen himself lying in bed, that he had perceived from above how nurses and doctors had been busy with CPR.'"

In another case, a seven-year-old girl named Katie was found floating facedown in a swimming pool. She was profoundly comatose, with massive brain swelling and no measurable brain activity. She didn't have a heartbeat for nearly twenty minutes. She was hooked up to an artificial lung to keep her breathing. Somehow, though, she made a miraculous recovery in just three days—and stunned doctors by saying, "I met Jesus and the heavenly Father."

Intrigued, the doctors questioned her at length. In fact, they had her draw a picture of the emergency room, and she succeeded in correctly placing everything. Then she said that in her out-of-body state, she followed her family home one night. She was able to give specific details about what she observed, including what her father was reading, how her brother was pushing a toy soldier in a Jeep, and her mother was cooking roast chicken and rice. She even knew what clothes each family member wore that night.

"Everything checked out," said Burke.

What's more, he added, there are cases where congenitally blind people can see during their NDE. For example, Vicki had never visually seen anything in her twenty-two years. Then she was in a car accident and found herself looking down on the crumbled vehicle, and later she watched doctors working on her body as she floated toward the ceiling.

After going down a tunnel to a wondrous place, Vicki

encountered two schoolmates who had died years before. Though mentally disabled in life, they were now fully healthy. She then saw a playback of her earthly years. She was later able to provide various accurate observations, including about her childhood friends, which she could not have witnessed at the time but claimed to have seen in the life review.

Among the conclusions of Kenneth Ring, who interviewed twenty-one blind people who reported NDEs, are that "blind and visually impaired descriptions of the experience show visual, or 'visual-like' perceptions, and some of these reports have been validated by outside witnesses."[39]

A *Parade of the Improbable*

The more I investigated NDEs, the greater the number of documented cases of corroboration I found, including several reported by J. P. Moreland and Gary Habermas:

- A woman registered an absence of brain waves, had no vital signs, was declared dead, and was being wheeled to the morgue when she regained consciousness. She accurately described the exact resuscitation procedures used on her by doctors, repeated a joke one of them had told to relieve tension, and even recalled the designs on the doctors' ties.
- A young woman on her deathbed left her body and went to another room at the hospital, where she overheard her brother-in-law say he was going to wait around to see if she was going to "kick the bucket." She later embarrassed him by telling him what she had heard.
- Five-year-old Rick was comatose with meningitis before he was taken by ambulance to the hospital. He remained unresponsive for several days. Yet he described leaving his body and seeing grief-stricken relatives during that time— and he even watched as a twelve-year-old girl was moved

out of the room he was to occupy. His specific observations were confirmed by others.

- On her deathbed, a woman named Eleanor began calling out the names of deceased loved ones she was seeing. Suddenly, she saw a cousin named Ruth. "What's she doing here?" Eleanor blurted out. It turns out that Ruth had died unexpectedly the week before, but Eleanor, because of her illness, had never been told.

- Another girl, who had an NDE during heart surgery, said she met her brother in the afterlife—which surprised her because she didn't have a brother. When she later recovered and told her father, he revealed to her for the first time that she did, indeed, have a brother, but he had died before she was born.[40]

- A five-year-old Dutch girl contracted meningitis and fell into a coma. In her NDE, she met a girl, about ten years old, who told her, "I'm your sister. Our parents called me Rietje for short." Rietje kissed her and said, "You must go now," and the girl returned to her body. She later shocked her parents by relaying the story. They confirmed she did have a sister named Rietje who had died of poisoning, but they decided not to tell the other children until they were old enough to understand.[41]

Head-scratchers, all of them. And just the tip of the iceberg. I'm not surprised that NDE researcher Jeffrey Long, a seasoned radiation oncologist, concluded, "NDEs provide such powerful scientific evidence that it is reasonable to accept the existence of an afterlife."[42]

The Culmination of What We Seek

Fair or not, there are stereotypes about engineers—for instance, that they're relentlessly rational rather than syrupy or sentimental, and that they favor facts and logic over feelings and emotions. I live in a Houston neighborhood populated by oil company engineers, and frankly, those perceptions aren't far off the mark. And I did detect some of these traits in Burke—until we came toward the end of our conversation.

The exchange began with a rather innocuous question. "What do you want people to walk away with from reading your book *Imagine Heaven*?" I asked. I anticipated a perfunctory answer.

Burke thought for a few moments. "I want them first to fall in love with Jesus, and to see"—his voice caught, then he halted. His eyes flooded. Emotions overwhelmed him. "I'm sorry," he muttered as he fought to regain his composure.

"It's all right," I assured him.

He took a breath. "It's just that"—he stopped to gather himself before he resumed. "It's just that I want people to see that Jesus is everything we want. He's the culmination of all we seek," he said finally.

"Many people I've interviewed try to describe the astonishing beauty they've seen in heaven," he continued. "Scenery that takes your breath away. A fragrance so gentle and sweet. Colors like nothing on earth. One person said, 'The colors seemed to be alive.'[43] But then they say, 'Yes, it was amazing, but I didn't even care about it.' I'd ask why. And they would say, 'Because I couldn't take my eyes off Jesus. He's beyond beautiful. He's everything I've ever longed for.'"

Burke's eyes met mine. "That helped crystalize something that has profoundly changed me."

"What is it?"

"That everything I've ever enjoyed in life—the beauty of the outdoors, the love of a parent, the laughter of a child, the fulfillment of marriage—all of that is just a speck compared to the greater reality that's found in him."

Now *my* eyes moistened. I clicked off my recorder.
Enough said.

A Peek into the Afterlife

That evening, Leslie and I sat across from each other in a booth
as we ate dinner at an Austin seafood restaurant. I described my
interview with Burke at length, giving her all the salient details.

"What's your conclusion?" she asked.

I put down my fork. "These descriptions of an afterlife are
fascinating," I said. "And John's right—a lot of these core experiences do match up with biblical accounts of what happens after
we die. Still, there's quite a variation among the stories."

"And," Leslie added, "there's really no way to verify all these
details about heaven and hell."

"True," I said. "But are they making this stuff up? So many
people have had NDEs that it's hard to believe they could all
be fabricated. What are these accounts, really? Are these people
sincerely describing an experience like a dream or hallucination
that's been produced by some medical phenomenon, like oxygen
deprivation? Well, no alternate explanations have been able to
account for all the features of NDEs. But let's set aside these
descriptions of the afterlife and just focus on what we can know
for sure."

"And what's that?" Leslie asked.

"At a minimum, these cases demonstrate convincingly that
consciousness really does continue after clinical death. For how
long? The evidence doesn't establish that. But we have corroboration of a lot of things that people could never have otherwise
known unless they'd had an authentic out-of-body experience."

I let that statement stand for a while as we ate. "I guess what
I'm saying," I added, "is that the best explanation for the totality
of the evidence is that there is a postmortem existence of some
sort. After our brain stops working, after our heart stops beating,

after the doctors declare us dead—we still live on. Our conscious-ness survives. *We* survive."

Leslie let that soak in and then asked, "How can we deter-mine for sure what the afterlife is like? Christians say one thing; Islamic theology says another."

I smiled at her. "Honey, when's the last time you visited Indiana?"

"Why? Are you saying it's a slice of heaven?" she asked with a chuckle.

"Not exactly. But I have another old friend up there who I think can help settle this."

Leslie put down her napkin. "I'll check on flights first thing in the morning," she said.

The Pyramid to Heaven

Why Trust Christianity on the Afterlife?

I want atheism to be true and am made uneasy by the fact that some of the most intelligent and well-informed people I know are religious believers.

PHILOSOPHER THOMAS NAGEL,

THE LAST WORD

Chad Meister, a young electromechanical engineer who had grown up questioning the reality of God, was sitting in his apartment in Tempe, Arizona. He was holding a gun. Mired in depression, he was on the verge of pulling the trigger.

In the midst of his anguish, he called out, "God, if you're there, please show me, because I don't want to live anymore. And if you're not there, life's not worth living." With that, he instantly had a vision. Everything went dark, and all he could see were black-and-white letters spelling out "Acts 14:22."

"I had no idea what that was," he recalled later. "I thought maybe it had something to do with the Bible, but I'd never read the Bible, although I had heard of some of the books in it."

Putting down the gun, he went out, got a Bible, came back to his apartment, and searched until he found the chapter and verse, in which Paul and Barnabas tell the disciples, "We must go through many hardships to enter the kingdom of God."

That sentiment registered deeply with Chad. As he thought back on the travails of his life, he realized for the first time that God had been there all along, pursuing him, but Chad had repeatedly pushed him away and walked in the other direction.

His depression lifted. Right there in his apartment, Chad committed his life to God. He vowed, "I'm going to follow you wherever that leads."

Sure enough, his life changed. He married a Christian accountant named Tammi, and they moved to Minneapolis, where they attended a church that encouraged congregants to tell others about Jesus. He decided to do just that—but his efforts backfired.

He was getting ready to go on a four-hour car trip with his boss, a well-educated Hindu. *Okay, this is terrific,* Chad thought. *There's one Christian going out on this trip, and there'll be two Christians coming back.*

Instead, this sincere and articulate Hindu extolled the beauty and wonder of his religion so eloquently that he was influencing Chad. Since Chad had never really studied why he was a Christian, he became disoriented. "My head was spinning," he said.

That same week, a Mormon colleague shared her beliefs with Chad. A friend who had been studying with a cult challenged Chad's understanding of the Trinity. Another engineer who was part of a fringe sect attacked Chad's beliefs. At a meeting of Toastmasters, a public speaking organization, Chad heard a woman give a passionate speech about the New Age movement and how everyone is part of Mother Gaia, this glorious flower of a universe.

"I was so confused," Chad said. "I didn't know what to believe anymore. I began rethinking that vision I had. Maybe it was from Allah or Brahman or some other divine reality. My faith drained away, and I became an agnostic."

He began to seek answers. On business trips to Rochester, Minnesota, he would stop at L'Abri Fellowship, started by Christian thinkers Francis and Edith Schaeffer. Instead of pushing Christianity, the people there gently encouraged Chad to carefully analyze differing worldviews. Which is reasonable? Which is logical? Which is livable? Which one has evidence on its side?

"I started at square one by asking the question, 'What is truth?'" Chad said. "I ended up researching worldviews for a year and a half. At the end, the conclusion was clear: Christianity is the most reasonable, the most livable, the best supported evidentially, and it matched my own personal experiences of God. So I recommitted my life to Christ."

So exhilarating was his spiritual investigation that Chad decided to leave his engineering career and to study theology and philosophy instead. Today, he is a highly respected and widely published scholar—which is what brought Leslie and me to Mishawaka, Indiana, where Chad is chair of the religion and philosophy department at Bethel University.

I wanted to know: with so many different theories about an afterlife in various religions, why should people trust what Christianity teaches about the world beyond?

Interview #4: Chad V. Meister, PhD

If anyone looks like a philosophy professor, it's Chad Meister. His dark hair, tinged with silver, is short and neatly parted on the side; his mustache and goatee are a distinguished gray. He wears conservative glasses with thin rims. Add a tweed sports coat with patches at the elbows, and he's straight out of central casting.

With his incisive mind, gentle humor, and warm personality, Meister is among the most popular professors at Bethel, where he began teaching in 1998. He received his master's degree with honors from Trinity Divinity School and his doctorate with honors from Marquette University. He also has been a visiting research scholar at the Oxford Centre for Hindu Studies—ironic in light of the conversation with his Hindu boss that once helped derail his faith.

Meister has authored, coauthored, or edited more than twenty books, including *Philosophy of Religion*; *Evil: A Guide for the Perplexed*; *Contemporary Philosophical Theology*; *The Cambridge Companion to Religious Experience*; *Debating Christian Theism*; and *The Oxford Handbook of Religious Diversity*. He and Charles Taliaferro are general editors of a six-volume series called *The History of Evil*. Meister and apologist William Lane Craig edited *God Is Great, God Is Good*, which won *Christianity Today's* 2010 book award.

However, I was there to discuss Meister's first book, *Building Belief: Constructing Faith from the Ground Up*, released in 2006.[1] The story behind this book involves—well, me.

When Meister was a student at Trinity, he attended a church where I was a teaching pastor and my colleague Mark Mittelberg was director of evangelism. Mittelberg recruited Meister to be the volunteer leader of the church's apologetics ministry, a role in which Meister flourished.

One Sunday after giving a sermon on the resurrection, I was greeting visitors while Chad sat nearby. A man approached me and said, "I just want you to know that I'm an atheist. A friend invited me here. What you presented was interesting. I'd like to pursue more; in fact, would you be able to meet with me this week?"

I told him that, unfortunately, I would be traveling for the next three weeks. "But that guy there—he'll meet with you," I said, pointing toward Meister.

Meister perked up. "Sure, I'd love to meet with you," he told the skeptic.

The atheist agreed to come to Meister's apartment for dinner. In the meantime, Meister prayed about how he could help this skeptic—and into Meister's mind popped what has become known as the "apologetics pyramid," a visual depiction of how a quest for the truth about Christianity can be logically and systematically pursued.

An outgrowth of Meister's own spiritual journey, the pyramid assumes nothing extraordinary at the outset, starting with the broadest question and then narrowing the issues as you get toward the peak. Its goal isn't absolute proof, but to show that the most reasonable understanding of the evidence is to conclude that Christianity is true.

The atheist came over for dinner. At 7:00 p.m., they ate. Then they worked through the pyramid. By 2:00 a.m., the doubter was a believer.

I wanted Meister to walk through the six layers of evidence that constitute his pyramid. We met in his book-choked office on the third floor of the Huffman Administration Building on Bethel's campus. Francis Schaeffer always urged Christians to begin with common ground, and so we started at the base of the pyramid, with the fundamental laws of logic and reality.

Level 1: Truth—Why Can't Everyone Be Right?

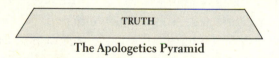

TRUTH

The Apologetics Pyramid

I began by saying, "Pontius Pilate famously asked, 'What is truth?'[2] If you were asked that today, how would you respond?"

Meister cleared his throat. "Even before Pilate lived, the ancient Greeks thought carefully about this," he replied. "Plato said in his book the *Sophist* that a true claim states things the way they are, and a false claim states things differently from the way they are.[3] His student Aristotle says something similar in *Metaphysics*.[4] And they were onto something.

"This is the correspondence theory of truth. A claim or proposition is true if it corresponds with a fact. If I make the claim, 'Your rental car is in the parking lot outside,' this would be true, because my statement corresponds with or matches reality. That would mean truth is absolute and universal."

"Seems like common sense," I said.

"Yes, it's the way we all approach life every day."

"Of course, people try to exempt religion," I said. "They say religious truth isn't absolute but relative."

Meister wasn't buying it. "If I said, 'My truth is that your rental car *isn't* in the parking lot,' that wouldn't be accurate just because I say it's *my truth*; instead, that claim would be false. It doesn't match reality. Opinions and beliefs are subjective and personal, but facts aren't. Besides, there's a logical problem with relativism."

"What's that?"

"To say there are no absolutes is to make an absolute claim. It's self-refuting," he said. "Think of it this way: if a member of the Flat Earth Society did not agree that the earth was round, you wouldn't say, 'Well, truth is relative. His belief in a flat earth is *his* truth—it works for him or it coheres with his other beliefs.' No, you'd say, 'He's flat-out wrong.'"

"But," I interjected, "isn't religion different? Some say religion shouldn't be understood as being true or false, since we don't have a God's-eye view of things. They say a religious claim can *become* true as it informs the lives of those who believe it."

"All major religions make truth claims that are absolute," said Meister. "And they fundamentally contradict each other. They can't all be true, because they assert opposite things—for example, the Bible says Jesus is the Messiah, who gave his life as a sacrifice for sin. Other religions deny this claim. Both *can't* be true. That's the law of non-contradiction.[5] To say all religious claims are true may sound magnanimous, but it's logically absurd. Our task is to discover what's true and what isn't."

"Still, isn't it intolerant to say truth is absolute?"

"Truth can't be bigoted, but people certainly can be—whether they're Christians, atheists, Hindus, or Muslims. Truth is truth, but how we communicate it can be narrow-minded and arrogant. We need to follow the examples of Jesus and Gandhi, who taught in a humble though passionate way."

The foundation of the pyramid was established. Truth isn't relative—that is, determined by what we believe—but truth is whatever is *consistent with reality*. Our job is to figure out what's true by continuing to climb the pyramid. Said theologian John Stackhouse, "Religion is fundamentally about truth: trying to figure out what is real and how best to represent it."[6]

Level 2: Worldviews—The Clash of the Three Isms

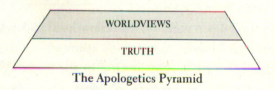

The Apologetics Pyramid

The next layer of the pyramid examines the three major worldviews. "A worldview is a collection of beliefs and ideas about the central issues of life," Meister explained. "It's the lens through which we view the world, whether consciously chosen or not. Broadly speaking, every religion or ideology can be found within one of three categories—*theism, atheism,* or *pantheism*. But, of course, their core assumptions contradict each other, and therefore only one of them can be true."

"How do you analyze their differences?" I asked.

"There are five fundamental questions that each worldview must address," he said. "First, is there a God, and what is God like? Second, what is ultimate reality? Third, how is knowledge obtained? Fourth, where is the basis of morality and value found? And fifth, who are we as human beings?"

"Okay," I said, "let's ripple through the three *isms*."

"I'll have to speak broadly, of course," Meister said. "First, there's *theism*, or belief in a personal God separate from the world. For the major theistic religions—Judaism, Christianity, and Islam—there is one God, creator of all, who is all-knowing, all-powerful, all-present, and all-good.

"The ultimate reality in theism is God, who is beyond the physical realm of existence. We acquire knowledge through our five senses and other means, including the revelation in Scripture. The basis of morality is God. Right, wrong, good, evil—they're all based on the nature of the infinite, personal God who created everything. Finally, what does it mean to be human? We're not on a par with God, though we're on a higher plane than the rest of the animal kingdom. We're unique, and we have an immaterial soul that lives on in eternity."

I was jotting down notes on my yellow legal pad as he spoke. "Good summary," I said. "What about atheism?"

"*Atheism* means disbelief in God or the gods. What's the universal reality? As astronomer Carl Sagan put it, 'The Cosmos is all that is or ever was or ever will be.'[7] There's no supernatural domain or existence beyond this physical world. How do we acquire knowledge? Since the physical world is all that exists, any knowledge we have must be about it and it alone. We're limited to empirical knowledge, with the scientific method being the gold standard."

"What about morality?" I asked, keeping track of the five fundamentals in my notes.

"Generally, atheists don't consider morality to be objectively true. Instead, they typically say it emerged through evolution. In other words, humans—or our genes—invented the idea of morality because it improved our chances for survival, so morality can vary from place to place and time to time. Now, some atheists are uncomfortable with that. One prominent atheist said morality doesn't come from God or evolution, but that 'it just is.'[8] Frankly, that doesn't really explain much.

"Finally, on the question of humans, atheism says we're electromechanical machines—animals that have grown in complexity over the eons thanks to evolution. As biologist Richard Dawkins says, 'We are . . . robot vehicles blindly programmed to preserve the selfish molecules known as genes.'[9] There's no soul or immaterial aspect to people. We live, we die, we decay—that's all there is."

"That doesn't sound very encouraging! How about pantheism?"

"*Pantheism* doesn't have a single form; there are both philosophical and religious aspects to it. Generally speaking, there are no ultimate distinctions in the universe—all is changeless, all is one, and all is God—or Brahman in Hinduism. In short, God is one with the universe.

"As for the ultimate reality, it's God—indistinguishable and indescribable. All distinctions are *maya*, or illusions. Animals, plants, insects, rocks, you, me—everything is one and the same ultimate reality. For pantheists of this sort, knowledge is acquired not through rational inquiry but through meditation and other practices intended to empty the mind. Chanting and various other techniques are used for altering consciousness and experiencing a unity with all that is.

"Also, objective good and evil are illusory. The pantheist Mary Baker Eddy, who founded Christian Science, said, 'Evil is but an illusion, and it has no real basis. Evil is a false belief.'[10] Finally, who are humans? For pantheists, we are God. We are spiritual divinity; we are one with the universe. But unfortunately we're under universal illusion, and as a result we don't realize our divine nature. Thus, our goal is to recognize this truth and win release from this illusion so we can see and experience the God that we really are."

I let all of this soak in for a few moments. "Three worldviews—all contradictory to each other," I said. "How can anyone determine which is true?"

"Ah," said Meister with a grin, "we need to press onward."

TESTING ATHEISM AND PANTHEISM

Meister proposed two tests for which worldview is most plausible: logic and livability. A worldview is false if its core beliefs are internally contradictory or incoherent, and a worldview should be rejected if it cannot consistently be lived out.

"Let's start with atheism," I said. "Is there any objection that invalidates it?"

"Well, there's the logical problem of good," Meister replied.

"The problem of good? Are you saying atheists can't live decent lives?"

"Not at all. I'm saying that if morality is a survival mechanism, then it's a mere illusion 'fobbed off on us by our genes,' as atheist philosophers Michael Ruse and Edward Wilson admit.[11] So it's no more rational to believe in morality than in Santa Claus. Even if morality isn't rooted in genetics but is just a social construct, again it's subjective and relative, not absolute and universal.

"And if there's no objective morality, the atheist can't logically affirm that there are such things as objective good, evil, right, or wrong. An atheist can't even really claim that the murder of innocent children is objectively, morally evil. She could say she's offended by it, but that's a preference; she can't consistently affirm it's really wrong. If this view of morality were actually lived out, chaos would ensue. As the atheist Jean-Paul Sartre said, 'Everything is indeed permitted if God does not exist.'[12] While some atheists have attempted to establish a kind of universal right and wrong, these arguments are also problematic."

"Crystalize your argument a bit more for me," I said.

"Okay. First, if objective moral values exist, then atheistic materialism must be false. Yet objective moral values *do* exist—and we all know it. Therefore, atheistic materialism must be false. On top of that, atheism fails the livability test. Frankly, atheists can't consistently live out the view that morality is merely illusory or relative. Is the statement 'Torturing babies for fun is evil' objectively true or just an opinion? If someone claims that doing this is okay, nobody would accept that. Why? Because we know it is really and truly wrong. You remember what the notorious serial killer Ted Bundy said?"[13]

"What?"

"He said that given his enlightened view of the world, there is no God, no transcendent reality—we're just molecules in motion. He said there's no such thing as objective morality. We can decide for ourselves what to do, because morality is personal and relative. Fortunately, few people really live that way. Even if someone claims they don't believe in moral absolutes, they act as though they do."

"Your conclusion, then, is that atheism isn't plausible," I said.

"That's right."

"What about pantheism?"

"Pantheists have a problem with right and wrong as well," he said.

He told me about having a spaghetti dinner with a pantheist, who told him, "Everything is God and everything is one. There are no distinctions." Meister replied to her, "But if there are no distinctions, then there is ultimately no right and wrong, no distinction between cruelty and noncruelty, or between good and evil." With that, he took a pot of boiling water from the stove and held it over her head, pretending he was going to spill it on her. "Are you *sure* there's no distinction between right and wrong, cruelty and noncruelty?" he teased.

She acknowledged the gesture with a smile, saying, "Well, I guess there *does* seem to be a distinction between right and wrong!"

"Of course," continued Meister, "pantheists can *say* there's no distinction between good and evil and that suffering is just an illusion, but they can't really live that way. People live as though there *are* moral absolutes.

"Besides," he added, "pantheism seems to be logically incoherent. In pantheism, I am God and ultimately impersonal. I am the changeless All. Yet I'm encouraged to discover this fact about myself. Through meditation, I need to realize I am one with the Divine. But there's a problem."

"What's that?"

"First, under pantheism we are one with God. Second, God is the changeless All. Third, we—God—need to move beyond our ignorance and become enlightened by realizing our own divinity. Those statements are logically incoherent."

"How so?"

"To come to know something is to change from a state of ignorance to a state of enlightenment, and I can't be changeless and at the same time change in order to realize that I am changeless.

"Also," he added, "the universe is supposed to be impersonal—but I'm a person with hopes, dreams, thoughts, and feelings, all of which pantheists say are illusions. Somehow the universe coughs up illusory and deceived people, which are really nonpersons, and now they need to get back to the impersonal self that they really are. But how can impersonal me be deceived into believing I am a personal being who needs to recognize my true, impersonal nature? How can something impersonal be deceived, anyway? It makes no sense."

I knew how pantheists would respond. "Wouldn't they say you need to get beyond rationality and open up to a mystical awareness of your unity with the cosmos?" I asked.

Meister's look turned sour. "To argue against reason is to use reason in an attempt to deny reason—again, incoherent. Let's face it, if you want to be logical and consistent in your views, pantheism isn't the worldview you want."

WHAT ABOUT THEISM?

All of this left an obvious question: Does the existence of evil and suffering invalidate theism? Isn't it a contradiction to say there's a God who's powerful and loving, yet there is evil that exists in the world he created?

"That's a serious problem. I don't pretend it isn't," Meister replied. "In fact, it's so serious that I've published ten books on this subject. But it's not unique to theism. All worldviews wrestle with the issue of evil and suffering. However, I don't believe it's a contradiction for theism; in fact, I'd say Christians have the most plausible response."

"In what way?"

"For one thing, it's at least logically plausible to say that if there is a God, he gave people free will."

He collected his thoughts and then continued. "As you know, I was once a robotics engineer. I remember hearing about a large robotic device that crushed a worker. But the robot wasn't charged with a crime. Why? It wasn't culpable. There was no intentionality. It lacked free will. So it seems the very notion of moral responsibility and the ability to do good requires freedom. Even love requires the freedom to choose *not* to love—which is why robots can't fall in love. They can only do what they're programmed to do.

"God could have created a world where people were like robots, but then we could never experience the highest value in the universe, which is love. We couldn't truly be doing good and moral actions. And where there's freedom, it necessarily entails the freedom to turn against the good. That's a plausible explanation for why we have moral evil in the world."

Meister described how he once received a note from a woman at church who was very effective at helping others struggling with pain in their past. She disclosed to him how she herself had gone through a traumatic experience while growing up.

A few weeks earlier, Meister and his wife had baked a cake. Meister decided to taste every ingredient individually. Baking powder—*disgusting*. Raw eggs—*ugh*. Vanilla extract—*yuck*. But once they were mixed together and baked, the result was a flavorful chocolate cake.

"I shared this story with the woman, and she was in tears," Meister recalled. "She realized God didn't want those bad things to happen to her. He didn't cause them. And yet in his omniscience and omnipotence, he is able to take even the bad stuff that happens and turn her into a beautiful person with a big heart for helping those who suffer.

"Now, we can resist God and become hardened against him, but that's not what he wants. Sometimes it takes trials and tribulations to make us into mature, spiritual human beings. The Bible talks about how hardship develops character and perseverance.[14] We all know that if we raise a child in a totally sheltered way, they won't fully mature."

"You're saying that creating a mature individual must necessarily involve some hardship?" I asked.

"Yes, that's plausible. There's no contradiction in God existing and evil existing if God has a good and sufficient reason for allowing them to exist. As I've shown, it's at least logically possible that God does have such reasons.

"Actually, Augustine wrote an entire book on how freedom allows for the possibility of the free agent choosing evil over good.[15] He argued that it's a good thing that God gave us freedom, but with this freedom came the danger that people would use this good gift for the wrong reasons—even malicious ones. And this is what happened—humankind turned against their maker.

"But we can see why God might allow evil to exist. A serious difficulty or even a tragedy can cause people to acknowledge God and their need for salvation. As C. S. Lewis famously said, 'God whispers to us in our pleasures, speaks in our conscience, but shouts in our pains: [evil] is His megaphone to rouse a deaf world.'"[16]

I said, "Your bottom line, then, is that while pantheism and atheism are disqualified because of logical contradictions, incoherence, and unlivable claims, theism survives."

"Correct," came his response. "There's so much more to be said—I've written a lot on this. We're just scratching the surface here. But my conclusion is that, given all of this, theism in general—and Christianity in particular—is the most plausible worldview."

Level 3: Theism—The Fingerprints of God

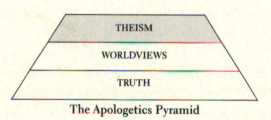

The Apologetics Pyramid

I was interested in Meister's assessment of the positive evidence for theism, so I offered him a challenge: "Give me three affirmative reasons that theism is true."

"Just three?" he replied. "Okay, sure." He leaned forward and said, "First, there's the fine-tuning of the universe. A life-permitting universe is extremely unlikely. Scientists have discovered that if you were to slightly alter the fundamental laws of the cosmos or any of the dozens of basic constants of physics, it would make life impossible.

"Things like the gravitational constant, the strong nuclear

force constant, and the relative masses of elementary particles are just a few of the fifty or more examples from physics that are calibrated on a razor's edge so that life can exist. The probability of this occurring by undirected natural causes or chance is virtually zero."

I was conversant with this argument. A few years earlier, I interviewed physics professor Michael Strauss of the University of Oklahoma. To give just one example of the universe's fine-tuning, he said, "Shortly after the big bang, the amount of matter in the universe was precisely tuned to one part in a trillion trillion trillion trillion trillion—that's a ten with sixty zeroes after it! In other words, throw in a dime's worth of extra matter, and the universe wouldn't exist." His conclusion: "I think the most plausible explanation is that the universe was designed by a Creator."[17]

But skeptics have an escape hatch, which I posed to Meister: "What if there's an infinite number of universes, and therefore, when you randomly spin the dials of physics enough times, one universe will come up with the lucky numbers by chance—and it's ours?"

"There's no experimental or physical evidence to support the many-universe theory," Meister replied. "Though personally, it wouldn't surprise me if there were many universes."

His answer surprised me. "Why?"

"The principle of plenitude says goodness desires to share more goodness. If God is infinite goodness, then God would want to share his goodness—so perhaps he created many universes in which to share it. But as physicist and philosopher Robin Collins points out, an infinite number of universes must be produced by some sort of many-universe generator, which itself would need an intelligent designer. You're back to theism."[18]

"Okay, what's your second argument for theism?"

"The beginning of the universe points powerfully toward a Creator," he replied. "As philosopher William Lane Craig says, whatever begins to exist has a cause; virtually all scientists now agree the universe began to exist at some point in the past; therefore, the universe must have a cause.[19] Given that *universe* means time, space, matter, and physical energy, this cause must itself be timeless, spaceless, matterless, and powerful enough to create all the physical energy that exists. That describes God."[20]

"Who created God?"

"Nobody," Meister said flatly. "By definition, he is the uncaused cause, so to ask what caused God is incoherent."

I pursued another angle. "Maybe an impersonal force brought the universe into being rather than a personal God."

"If there was an impersonal force, something would need to trigger it, so there would need to be a prior cause, and that would need a prior cause, and on and on ad infinitum.[21] And an actual infinite series of causes and effects is logically impossible. In contrast, a personal cause can freely choose to bring the universe into existence, which makes more sense."

"All right, what's your third reason for theism?"

"It's the moral argument I raised earlier. First, if there are objective moral values, then God exists. Objective moral values are precepts that are universally binding on all people at all times and places, whether they follow them or not. Second, we know that objective moral values *do* exist—for example, it's objectively evil to torture a baby for fun. Therefore, God exists."

"But how do you explain moral disagreements from society to society?" I asked.

"Just because a society doesn't live according to a particular moral precept doesn't mean the precept doesn't exist," he replied. "Given the global malady of sin, that's what we should expect. Christian theism says all people use their free will to act against what's right and good.[22] And besides, you can find fundamental moral precepts—such as adultery is wrong—in virtually all societies in world history."

Meister had quickly summarized three of the arguments he develops in far greater detail in his books. His conclusion flowed naturally: "For these and many other reasons, Lee, I'm convinced that theism is the most plausible worldview—by a long shot."

That did, indeed, seem logical. But which species of theism rings true? That brought us to the next level of the pyramid.

Level 4: Revelation—Has God Spoken to Humankind?

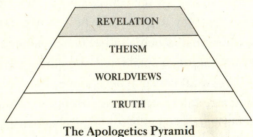

The Apologetics Pyramid

Every major religion believes its scriptures are authoritative and divinely inspired. Christians see no conflict between their Bible and the Jewish scriptures contained in the Old Testament, since Christians regard their faith as being the fulfillment of Judaism.

However, there are irreconcilable differences between the Bible and other sacred texts. For example, the Qur'an explicitly contradicts biblical teaching about the Trinity, the death and resurrection of Jesus, and the teaching that Jesus is God's unique Son.[23] Consequently, if it's plausible to believe that the Bible is reliable, it would rule out the claims in the Qur'an that contradict those in the Bible.

I wanted to focus on the New Testament, because it contains the starkest contrast with Jewish and Islamic beliefs. Meister proposed three tests for whether it's plausible to believe that the New Testament can be trusted.

"First, there's the bibliographical test," he said, "which refers to whether we can trust the transmission of the text through history. It's no exaggeration to say the evidence for the New Testament text is staggering. We have more than 5,800 ancient Greek manuscripts and fragments, some of which date back to fewer than a hundred years after the originals. That swamps other ancient writings. While this doesn't prove that the New Testament is true, it does offer good reason to believe we have a reasonably accurate representation of what was originally written."

I spoke up. "Yet there are a lot of variances between the copies."

"True, but the vast majority are minor spelling differences, and no cardinal doctrine of Christianity is at stake," he replied.[24]

"Next," Meister continued, "there's internal evidence. Several New Testament documents refer to their authors as *being* eyewitnesses to the events, *mentioning* eyewitnesses, or *interviewing* eyewitnesses. For example, the author of Luke's gospel talked with eyewitnesses and notes he 'carefully investigated everything' to establish 'the certainty' of what occurred.[25] Peter says he was personally an eyewitness to the events he described.[26] Paul notes there are hundreds of witnesses to what he claimed about Jesus and his resurrection.[27] No other religious text has this level of eyewitness authentication. This gives the New Testament special credibility.

"Then there's external evidence, which looks at whether outside sources provide any corroboration. Over and over again, archaeological discoveries have confirmed—and never disproven—core New Testament references. Plus, there are ancient writings outside the Bible that corroborate the basic outline of Jesus' life."

"Are you saying, then, that the New Testament's reliability has been proven?"

"All I'm trying to establish is that it's plausible to believe in the reliability of the Bible. I know I don't have to convince you,

Lee—you've written hundreds of pages on this topic in your books. I'm merely saying any reasonable person would be justified in rendering the verdict that the Bible is essentially trustworthy."

Level 5: Resurrection—Did Jesus Rise from the Grave?

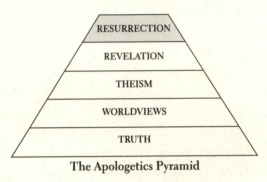

The Apologetics Pyramid

The final category of evidence for Christianity, said Meister, is the resurrection of Jesus, which vindicated his claim to being the Messiah and God's only Son.[28]

Historian and philosopher Gary Habermas analyzed 2,200 expert sources on the resurrection. Out of this study, he compiled several "minimal facts" that are strongly evidenced and considered historical by the large majority of scholars, including skeptics.

They are (1) Jesus was killed by crucifixion; (2) the disciples believed he rose and appeared to them; (3) the church persecutor Saul was converted; (4) the skeptic James (Jesus' half brother) was converted; and (5) Jesus' tomb was empty.[29]

"I'll focus on just two facts," Meister said to me. "First, Jesus' tomb was vacant.[30] This is reported in the gospel of Mark, the first gospel written, which comes too quickly for an elaborate legendary story to have developed. In fact, all four gospels report that the tomb was empty, and it's clearly implied by Paul.

"And this is highly significant: Even Jesus' enemies conceded the tomb was empty. Instead of disputing it, they merely tried to explain it away. All they needed to do to squelch this new religious movement would be to produce Jesus' body, which they never did. Skeptical historian Michael Grant of Cambridge said that 'the evidence is firm and plausible' that the tomb was vacant.[31]

"Second, Jesus' followers believed that the risen Jesus appeared to them. All four gospels reference this. Again, these are early sources—as scholar William Lane Craig says, 'Legends do not arise significantly until the generation of eyewitnesses dies off.'[32] Also, Peter confirmed that he was an eyewitness to the resurrected Jesus.[33] And Paul reported that he encountered the risen Christ, transforming him into a follower of Jesus who became an apostle and ended up writing much of the New Testament.[34]

"The most persuasive evidence, though, comes from a letter Paul wrote roughly twenty years after Jesus' death, in which he recounts a creed of the earliest Christians that cites groups and individuals who were eyewitnesses to the resurrected Jesus, including five hundred people at once.[35] Prominent historian James D. G. Dunn says 'we can be entirely confident' that this creed was actually formulated within *months* of Jesus' death.[36] Think of that," Meister said, his eyebrows rising. "That's a historical news flash!"

Actually, I have written extensively on this issue. We have many facts that we accept from ancient history based on one or two sources, and yet we have no fewer than *nine* ancient sources, inside and outside the New Testament, confirming and corroborating the conviction of the disciples that they had encountered the resurrected Jesus.[37] In addition to the creed, the four gospels, and Peter's words,[38] we have Paul affirming that he and the disciples were saying the same thing about the risen Christ.[39]

What's more, we also have two strong nonbiblical sources

who knew some of the eyewitnesses. First, there's Clement. The early church father Irenaeus reports that Clement conversed with the apostles, and Tertullian says Clement was ordained by Peter himself. Second, there's Polycarp. Irenaeus says Polycarp was instructed by the apostles, and Tertullian confirms that John appointed Polycarp as a bishop. Both Clement and Polycarp specifically confirm that it was the actual resurrection of Jesus that motivated the disciples.[40]

"A very common objection by skeptics," I said to Meister, "is that the disciples were merely hallucinating."

He shook his head. "These couldn't have been hallucinations. Psychology professor Gary Collins says that 'by their nature only one person can see any given hallucination at a time.'[41] Yet Luke and John report group appearances, and the earliest report of all, the creed I mentioned, says Jesus appeared to five hundred people at once."

"Maybe it was something more subtle, like a vision," I said.

"Again, that's not plausible—the disciples talked with Jesus, ate with him, and touched him," replied Meister. "Besides, Paul and James were skeptics—they weren't psychologically primed for a vision. On top of that, if these were visions or hallucinations, there is still an empty tomb to be explained.

"Look," he said, "many books have been written to refute the naturalistic explanations that skeptics have put forward. The historical facts, in my opinion, are clear and convincing—Jesus rose from the grave, and in doing so, he demonstrated his divine nature.

"And this clinches Christianity as the worldview that makes the most sense to me. It's plausible and it's livable. As the pyramid demonstrates, it's built on a solid foundation that can be trusted. In fact, through the years a lot of people who started out as doubters have become believers after studying the evidence."

I slipped my hand up. "Including me," I said.

Level 6: The Gospel—Opening the Door of Heaven

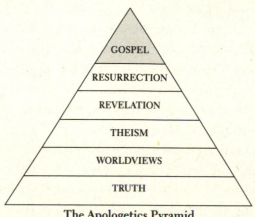

The Apologetics Pyramid

That brought us to the summit of the pyramid: the good news of the gospel. Logic and evidence had narrowed the reasonable alternatives down to this single option. If the building blocks of the pyramid are solid, which they appeared to be, then Christianity has been established as the most rational viewpoint among many. In other words, it's thoroughly reasonable to take the Bible's teachings on the afterlife with the utmost seriousness.

Suddenly, what sounds like the most outrageous assertion ever made by Jesus is now imbued with credibility because of his resurrection credentials. "I am the way and the truth and the life," he said. "No one comes to the Father except through me."[42]

"I am," Jesus declared, "the resurrection and the life."[43] His promise of a never-ending home in heaven for his followers is explicit: "My sheep listen to my voice; I know them, and they follow me. I give them eternal life, and they shall never perish; no one will snatch them out of my hand."[44]

Jesus said in Luke 4:43, "I must proclaim the good news of the kingdom of God . . . because that is why I was sent." A kingdom is a place where a king reigns. Explained one theologian, "At the heart of this theme is the idea of God's messianic kingdom. It is a kingdom that will be ruled by God's appointed Messiah, who will be not just the Redeemer of His people, but their King."[45]

As the story of Jesus unfolds in the New Testament, he is revealed to be the Messiah who was unjustly killed in payment for our sins, was resurrected in triumph over death, ascended to the Father, and is coming back to rule. We can spend forever with him in his kingdom if we receive his freely offered gift of grace.[46] *That's* the good news of the gospel.

Meister told me about a movie he had seen about a mythical place called Camelot. "The idea is that you have this amazing kingdom where the king loves his people and the people love and serve the king. He provides for them and cares so much for them. That's the notion of a kingdom—a kingdom is the place where the good king rules.

"And Jesus says he's opening God's kingdom to us. The Bible makes it clear that the kingdom of God is where God rules in a perfect way—he loves his people, provides for them, cares for them—and we gratefully love and serve and worship him in return. He invites everybody to enter—and in his kingdom, we are transformed.

"The New Testament says that the fruit of the spirit—love, joy, peace, patience, kindness, goodness, faithfulness, gentleness, and self-control—are manifestations of a life surrendered to the king.[47] The more we surrender, the more we experience what life was meant to be. It's the life we've always wanted. It's everything we desire. We can enter God's kingdom now and experience it forever."

Meister was probably wondering why his words brought a smile to my face. I couldn't help but remember that all of this was coming from a man who had once been mired in despair and mere moments away from suicide.

Meister's unique heaven pyramid had provided a sturdy foundation for trusting what Jesus taught about eternal life. Do we want to know the truth about the afterlife? In short, Jesus is the most trustworthy source.

So what will heaven be like? As comfortable as a mansion with many rooms, Jesus assured his followers.[48] A place where "'there will be no more death' or mourning or crying or pain, for the old order of things has passed away."[49] A wonderland where we will dwell with God in perpetuity.[50]

But there was so much more to uncover in our investigation. What will happen during our first hour in heaven? Will some people receive special rewards for the way they've lived? Is there a way station of purification, called purgatory, that must be endured before we reach our final destination in eternity?

Personally, I couldn't wait to dig deeper—and I knew just where to go for more information. I needed to reach out to a prominent New Testament scholar who has written movingly about what he calls "the heaven promise."

CHAPTER 5

Heaven: A Guide

How Followers of Jesus Will Spend Eternity

Joy is the serious business of heaven.

C. S. LEWIS, *LETTERS TO MALCOLM*

God made this world of space, time, and matter; he loves it, and he is going to renew it.

N. T. WRIGHT, *SIMPLY GOOD NEWS*

The Star Wars movies, the original *Star Trek*, and the TV program *Cosmos* captivated the imagination of Sarah Salviander as she was growing up in Canada. "By the time I was nine years old, I knew I would be a space scientist someday," she said.

Soon Salviander turned into an atheist like her parents. Though she had never read the Bible, she thought Christianity was "philosophically trivial" and made people "weak and foolish." Ultimately, she earned her doctorate in astrophysics. But there were unexpected twists. For instance, her early physics professors were Christians, and their influence tempered her antipathy toward the faith.

Then as she was studying deuterium abundances in relation to the big bang, she was "completely and utterly awed" by the underlying order of the universe and the fact that it could be

99

explored scientifically. "Without knowing it," she said, "I was awakening to what Psalm 19 tells us so clearly: 'The heavens declare the glory of God; the skies proclaim the work of his hands.'"[1]

After that, a physicist and theologian convinced her that the Bible's creation account was "scientifically sound and not just a 'silly myth' as atheists believed."[2] And if Genesis is true, what about the Gospels? That led her to investigate the life of Jesus. Like Albert Einstein, she became "enthralled by the luminous figure of the Nazarene."[3]

It was, in short, an intellectual journey similar to climbing the pyramid that philosopher Chad Meister described in the preceding chapter. Based on her cerebral analysis of the evidence, Salviander put her trust in Christ. And yet it was a subsequent personal tragedy that truly solidified her faith.

Her first child, a girl named Ellinor, was stillborn—a heartbreaking experience for Salviander and her husband. Nurses allowed them to stay in the hospital room most of the day to hold their deceased baby.

"I bonded with Ellinor during that time," Salviander told me. "Sadly, though, what I had bonded with was a tiny lifeless body. Grief does a lot to twist our thinking, and as awful and crazy as it sounds, I felt like it was my motherly duty to be buried with Ellinor."

What rescued her from this morbid impulse? It was nothing less than the reality of heaven. If the evidence was sufficient to convince Salviander that Christianity is true, then its teachings about heaven aren't based on wishful thinking but are truly grounded in reality—and that meant Ellinor would be parented by none other than her heavenly Father himself.

"Knowing she was safe in a realm of indescribable love, joy, peace, and beauty—and that this would be the place in which we would eventually be reunited—I was finally freed from despair," she said. "I experienced a vision of Ellinor's body being gently taken from my arms by God and carried up to heaven, and that was the precise moment I had peace. There was no better place for her to be, and as a mother, that was the only way I could really let her go."[4]

Her confidence in the existence of heaven made all the difference for Salviander. But how much can we really know in advance about what our experience in eternity will be like? As it turns out, the Bible provides precious few concrete details. In fact, it actually declares, "No eye has seen, no ear has heard, and no mind has imagined what God has prepared for those who love him."[5]

As Martin Luther said, "As little as children know in their mother's womb about their birth, so little do we know about life everlasting."[6] J. Todd Billings, a Christian theologian suffering from incurable cancer, said that although we know that Christ "will be the center of the life to come," nevertheless "the *information* we have about life everlasting is tiny, minuscule."[7]

As a result, myths and misconceptions abound. "Nearly every Christian I have spoken with has some idea that eternity is an unending church service," said author John Eldredge. "We have settled on an image of the never-ending sing-along in the sky, one great hymn after another, forever and ever, amen. And our heart sinks. *Forever and ever? That's it? That's the good news?* And then we sigh and feel guilty that we are not more 'spiritual.' We lose heart, and we turn once more to the present to find what life we can."[8]

Yet there are some facts we *can* know about heaven—and that's what drew me to a modest Anglican church in the northern suburbs of Chicago on a balmy summer afternoon. I was anxious to have a discussion with a noted New Testament scholar whose book on heaven debunks several popular myths about the afterlife and sets the record straight, based on what we can responsibly glean from the biblical accounts.

Interview #5: Scot McKnight, PhD

Scot McKnight is a highly influential and prolific New Testament scholar, with particular expertise in historical Jesus studies, the Gospels, early Christianity, and contemporary issues involving the church. Having grown up as the son of a Baptist deacon in Freeport, Illinois, he came to faith in Christ as a youngster and later had a transformative experience with the Holy Spirit at a church camp.

Asked about his career in theology, he told me, "That's all I ever wanted to do my whole life."

He earned his master's degree from Trinity Evangelical Divinity School and his doctorate from the University of Nottingham, where he studied under the eminent scholar James D. G. Dunn. After serving as a professor at Trinity and North Park University, he now teaches at Northern Baptist Theological Seminary in Lisle, Illinois.

McKnight has become a force in Christian culture through his highly successful blog, Jesus Creed; through media exposure on television and in such magazines as *Time* and *Newsweek*; and through his lectures in places around the world, including South Korea, Australia, and South Africa.

Among the more than eighty books he has authored are the award-winning *The Jesus Creed*; *The Blue Parakeet: Rethinking How You Read the Bible*; *The King Jesus Gospel*; commentaries on various New Testament books; texts on how to interpret the New Testament generally and the Synoptic Gospels specifically; and even a book on Jesus' mother called *The Real Mary*.

It was McKnight's book on the afterlife, called *The Heaven Promise*, that prompted me to get together with him near Chicago, not far from where he and his wife, Kristen, a psychologist who was his childhood sweetheart, have resided for years.

With a fringe of graying hair and wire-rimmed glasses,

McKnight has a professorial demeanor, though not in an off-putting way. His smile is quick, his eyes are inquisitive, and his manner is engaging and empathetic—in short, he seems like the kind of professor who would hang out with students at a coffee shop to chat about their lives outside of the classroom.

After recounting some of the evidence for heaven that I presented in the first part of this book, I decided to ask McKnight why he believes in an afterlife with God. Like any good theologian, he laid out his thoughts crisply and systematically, saying he had nine reasons in all.

"First," said McKnight, "I believe in heaven because Jesus and the apostles did. Jesus said, 'For my Father's will is that everyone who looks to the Son and believes in him shall have eternal life, and I will raise them up at the last day.'[9] Peter promised his churches they would 'receive a rich welcome into the eternal kingdom of our Lord and Savior Jesus Christ.'[10] As for John, he said, 'And this is what [God] promised us—eternal life.'[11] Paul talked about our frail bodies, saying, 'For we know that if the earthly tent we live in is destroyed, we have a building from God, an eternal house in heaven, not built by human hands.'[12] If all of them believed in heaven, then it's good enough for me."

"What's your second reason?" I asked.

"Because Jesus was raised from the dead—to me, that's the big one," he replied. "Not only was he resurrected, but people saw his body; they talked with him; they ate with him; and then he returned to the Father with the promise that he will come back to consummate history. This gives great credibility to an afterlife—and as N. T. Wright said, 'The resurrection of Jesus is the *launching of God's new world*.'[13]

"My third reason for believing in heaven is that the overall Bible believes in it."

"Wait a second," I said. "The agnostic scholar Bart Ehrman says the earliest biblical books don't teach anything about heaven, and he seems to suggest that the concepts of heaven and hell were simply made up over the centuries."[14]

"Well, let's look at some facts," responded McKnight. "It's true that there's very little interest in heaven or the afterlife in the Old Testament. It speaks of death—or *sheol*—the way that other Near Eastern and Mediterranean cultures did at the time, which is that death seems to be permanent. *Sheol* is a dark, deep, and miry pit. In fact, the Old Testament's only statements about the afterlife are found in its latest books.[15] It's the New Testament that ushers in a new hope for eternal life and heaven."

"Should that bother Christians?" I asked.

"Not in the slightest, because this is how divine revelation works. It unfolds over time," he explained. "The Bible's major themes develop and grow and expand and take us to the very precipice of eternity. It's like watching a play, where the whole story isn't clear until the end. Once we get to Jesus, and especially his resurrection, the Old Testament's images of *sheol* give way to his glorious teachings of immortality, eternal life, and the kingdom of God."

Beauty, Desire, Justice, Science

"What's your fourth reason for believing in heaven?" I asked McKnight.

"Because the church has taught it consistently," he said.

I knew this was significant, because if the church had ever wavered on its teachings about eternal life or significantly altered them, this might indicate that the relevant biblical passages are ambiguous and can be legitimately interpreted in a variety of different ways.

"Christian theology from the very beginning has believed in an afterlife, especially because of the resurrection," McKnight told me. "There has never been an era in which the church hasn't believed in heaven.

"Then there's my fifth reason for believing in heaven—because of beauty."

That sounded intriguing. "How so?"

"Even atheists get awestruck by the grandeur of the world—visiting the Grand Canyon, strolling among the California redwoods, hearing Bach, or seeing a painting by Van Gogh. These point us toward something beyond. You see, many of us believe in heaven because we see in the present world a glimpse of something far grander—the world as we think it *ought* to be. Where do we get that sense of *ought*? Could it indicate a future reality—a new heaven and a new earth? If God made a world this good, doesn't it make sense he would make a world where it will all be even better?"

McKnight let that question linger for a minute. Then he moved on to his next reason for believing in heaven—namely, because most people do. He cited statistics showing that 84 percent of Americans believe in some kind of heaven, with nearly seven out of ten convinced that it's "absolutely true."[16]

Indeed, Todd Billings points out that even a third of those who *don't* believe in God *still* believe in life after death. In fact, he said, "belief in the afterlife appears to be on the rise" over recent years in America.[17] Said Jean Twenge, a researcher at San Diego State University, "It was interesting that fewer people participated in religion or prayed but more believed in an afterlife."[18]

McKnight told me, "Essentially, humans down through history and across the spectrum of religions and philosophies have always believed in an afterlife. Why is that? Is there something inherent in humans, a kind of innate intuition from God, that there's life beyond the grave? The Bible says God has 'set eternity in the human heart.'[19] I believe the history of human belief in heaven is an argument for believing it's true."

"What's your seventh reason?"

"Because of desire," he replied. "C. S. Lewis said, 'If we are made for heaven, the desire for our proper place will be already in us.' He said this is a desire that 'no natural happiness will satisfy.'[20] Elsewhere he explained, 'If I find in myself a desire which no experience in this world can satisfy, the most probable explanation is that I was made for another world.'[21] As philosopher Jerry Walls put it, 'A good God would not create us with the kind of aspirations we have and then leave those aspirations unsatisfied.'[22]

"I believe that the ongoing lack of fulfillment in possessing what we desire—the love of another, family, beauty, work—indicates there is a true home that will ultimately satisfy all our desires fully—and that home is heaven. In other words, the fleeting satisfactions of this world point beyond us toward a place of final and lasting fulfillment."

With that, McKnight went on to his eighth reason for believing in heaven—the desire for justice to be done.

"This world reeks of injustice. We've been told since childhood that life isn't fair." He gestured in the direction of the city of Chicago. "Not far from here, innocent kids in the inner city are getting shot. Sexual abuse and exploitation flourish around the world. When I was in high school, I thought racial discrimination would end in my generation, but it obviously didn't. We seem to have an innate sense of what's right and wrong, and we long to see justice done.

"I believe in heaven because I believe God wants to make all things right. He wants justice to be finally and fully established. That means victims of injustice will someday sit under the shade tree of justice and know that God makes all things so new that past injustices are swallowed up in the joy of the new creation."

"And what's your final reason?"

"Because science doesn't provide all the answers. We have an empirical mindset today. A lot of people believe scientific knowledge is superior to any other form of knowledge. But that's simply

106

not true. Science can tell us how the world works and behaves, but it can't probe meaning and purpose. It can map brain function, but it can't explain love."

I interrupted to observe, "Even the statement that 'science is the only form of knowledge' is self-refuting, because that statement itself can't be confirmed by the scientific method."

"Right," he said. "The point is that science can't prove heaven, but not everything has to be subjected to scientific scrutiny. For instance, we have excellent historical evidence for Jesus' resurrection, and that ought to be sufficient to point toward the reality of an afterlife with God."

A New Heaven and a New Earth

Among the misconceptions about heaven is that it's an ethereal existence, up in the clouds somewhere, a purely spiritual place where we are ghostly souls who spend every waking hour singing hymns to God. When I asked McKnight to respond to those ideas, his eyes widened. "Well, there's a lot to set straight there," he said.

"Let's start at the beginning."

"Okay," he said. "We need to see heaven as being in two phases. First, there's the present heaven, which is where we go when we die. This is a temporary situation—I liken it to a dormitory where students don't expect to stay forever. Eventually, they'll move into a more permanent condo or house."

"This would be the so-called 'intermediate state,'" I said.

"Correct. Jesus said to the thief on the cross, 'Today you will be with me in paradise.'[23] When Stephen was being stoned to death, he looked up to heaven, or paradise, and saw the glory of God.[24] We don't have a lot of information to go on, but in this intermediate state we will be consciously present with God."

I said, "When Jesus talks about the death of his friend Lazarus, he says Lazarus has 'fallen asleep.'[25] Doesn't that mean the intermediate state is a place of slumber where we're unaware of what's happening?"

"No, Jesus used that term to suggest Lazarus was in a place of rest in the presence of God. This was a temporary situation, as sleep is. Ultimately, this present heaven is going to give way to a new heaven and a new earth. That's the second phase."

"So in the end heaven isn't some far-off place, but it's *here*," I said.

"Right. It's the complete renewal of our world, a very earthy, physical place, not just for spirits or souls, but for resurrected bodies designed for the kingdom of God. John says in Revelation, 'Then I saw "a new heaven and a new earth," for the first heaven and first earth had passed away, and there was no longer any sea. I saw the Holy City, the new Jerusalem, coming down out of heaven from God, prepared as a bride beautifully dressed for her husband.'"[26]

"Does that suggest that the new heaven will be situated over the current Jerusalem?"

"Some people think so, and also that God will dwell in the reconstructed temple. But I think that's too wooden of an interpretation. The Bible says this is a *new* Jerusalem. In other words, this world will resemble our present earth, but it will be a transformed place for transformed people. There will be no temple, because John tells us that 'the Lord God Almighty and the Lamb are its temple.'[27]

"We're talking about a glorious redemption and restoration of all creation," he continued, his voice getting more animated. "Jesus described it as a place with multitudes of rooms for his followers.[28] God will dwell with us, and we will dwell with God. We will actually see God's face. Can you imagine that? All of creation will be set free and turn to God in praise. It will be creation on steroids, the way it was designed to be. The Hebrew word for *good* is *tov*. So whatever is truly *tov* about our world today will be enhanced in the new heaven and the new earth. It will be a place of celebrations, music and songs, festivals and festivities." He winked as he added, "And the Cubs will always win the World Series."

That *did* sound extraordinary!

"How will all of this unfold?" I asked.

"Paul says in 1 Corinthians 15 that first is the resurrection of Jesus, after which he will return to triumph over the powers of evil that are at work in the world. Then he will conquer death itself before he hands over the kingdom to the Father. With that, the mission of history is accomplished. Paul ends with the expression 'so that God may be all in all.'[29] That's the goal of history. God is the Alpha and Omega—he is the beginning and end of all existence and at the center of all its meaning."[30]

Theocentric versus Kingdom-Centric

"According to the Bible, what will our bodies be like in this new heaven and new earth?" I asked.

"Our souls will be reembodied, only this time our bodies will be transformed and imperishable," McKnight explained. "In fact, whatever can be said about Jesus' resurrected body could be said about ours. Our bodies will be perfected for a new kind of existence in eternity."[31]

He patted his bald head. "I'll even have hair in heaven," he added with a chuckle.

"How old do you think we'll be in heaven?" I asked.

"There have been long debates about that. Some think it will be the age of Jesus at his resurrection, but we don't really know. I think we'll age without aging; in other words, we won't degrade over time, but we'll continue to grow and expand intellectually as we learn and develop further. It's important to note that this isn't a *new* body; it's a transformation of our *current* body. There's a one-to-one correspondence, or continuity, between the two.

People in heaven will recognize us. They'll say, 'Hey, it's Lee Strobel. I'm surprised he made it!'"

Which of course evoked a hearty laugh.

McKnight continued. "Paul says we are 'sown a natural body' and 'raised a spiritual body.'[32] By that, he meant we'll have a body made for a perfectly Spirit-driven world. In one sense, our body will be ordinary. When the disciples met Jesus on the road to Emmaus, for example, they didn't see anything weird about him. It was a body that needed food and had marks from his earlier life. But in another sense, our body will be extraordinary—it can appear in a room without opening the door or even glow with the glory of God."[33]

I said, "Americans tend to be pretty individualistic, and our tendency is to see the final heaven as a place where we'll have a singular experience with God. But it's much more than that, isn't it?"

"Yes, Christians tend to go to one of two extremes in thinking about heaven," came his answer. "Some people see heaven as purely *theocentric*, or God-centered, focusing on individuals worshiping him and bringing him glory. He will be fully exalted, but that can come from more than just an endless and ecstatic worship service. God is glorified when we're caring, when we're being good parents, when we're nurturing our garden. Sometimes this theocentric view pictures heaven as a spiritual experience rather than an embodied one.

"On the other side is a *kingdom-centric* view of heaven, which stresses the community aspect of the afterlife. Here, the emphasis is on God and his people, on worship and fellowship, on justice and peace, on social engagement. It's an embodied existence where relationships flourish amid our total devotion to God."

"Do you think this view can get carried too far as well?"

"Yes, the descriptions of heaven can become almost too mundane," he said.

Indeed, I had seen examples in which the afterlife is painted as if it's not much more than one big, friendly neighborhood block party. One person complained about too much emphasis on the social aspects of heaven by saying, "Who wants a parade and a barbecue every day?"[34]

"The answer, it seems to me, is in the middle," McKnight concluded. "We need a balance between the two views. Heaven will be a place of both worship *and* fellowship. It will be a glorious union of delight in God *and* delight in one another. We have a king *and* we will be citizens of his kingdom, who are in a flourishing society together."

"How will people in heaven enjoy themselves," I asked, "if they know there are others, perhaps even relatives, who are suffering in hell?"

McKnight acknowledged the question with a nod. "That issue has spurred a lot of debate through the years," he said. "A bunch of theories have been offered. We don't know how God will do it, but somehow he will deal with this. We can have confidence in that. C. S. Lewis said that God won't allow hell to have veto power over people rightfully enjoying themselves in eternity with him."[35]

The Heavenly Veranda

For me, the community aspect of heaven has been especially intriguing. I asked McKnight to elaborate further.

"The final heaven will be a global village," McKnight said. "It's a place designed for those who want to be in relationship with God and in fellowship with others. After all, what happened after Jesus rose from the dead? He immediately renewed fellowship with his disciples. In the eternal heaven, God will be on his throne, but at the same time the new creation will be filled with loving relationships among his people."

McKnight paused to remind me that the Bible doesn't give

111

us a high-resolution picture of heaven. Rather, it uses metaphors and images to stoke our imagination by suggesting what eternal life with God will be like. One such picture is that Jesus is preparing rooms for us in heavenly homes.[36]

"When I use my imagination," McKnight said, "I picture our homes as having a veranda for fellowship and a garden for retreat."

"A veranda?" I asked.

"Yes, it's a sign of hospitality," he replied. "A church leader studied the history of architecture in New Zealand and found that before World War II, homes were built with verandas, where people would sit in the evening with their family to greet passersby and invite them to stop and chat. But verandas tended to disappear after the war. They were replaced by gardens in the back of the property, where people would retreat from the rest of the world."[37]

Interestingly, Leslie and I had been spending our spare time looking at houses to downsize, and one of our priorities has been a roomy front porch where we can sit and interact with neighbors. I was surprised that even in so-called retirement communities, few homes offer such a feature.

"I like the vision of the veranda," I said to McKnight.

"Me too," he replied. "When I was growing up, we didn't have air-conditioning, so after dinner we'd go out in the front yard to cool off and neighbors would come up and chat and hang out. It was great. I believe heaven will strike the perfect balance of privacy and devoted love of God, as well as fellowship and devoted love of family and others.

"And there will be parties—oh, will there be parties!" he added. "The Bible uses the metaphors of banquets and feasts—in fact, the first image of the kingdom of God in the final vision of Revelation is a wedding celebration of love and friendship and community.[38] Heaven will be a fellowship of differents—everyone reconciled and forgiven, all relationships characterized by trust and joy, and everyone with a story to tell—one that all of us will want to hear."

The First Hour in Heaven

If there will be an authentic—indeed, transcendent—sense of community among people in the final heaven, what about all of the petty conflicts, testy arguments, and relational quarrels that exist between us in this world? Won't they carry into eternity and frustrate God's plan for us to live in harmony forever?

"That's a good question," McKnight said. "And that brings me to what I believe will transpire in our first hour of heaven."

"What's that?"

"Reconciliation," he replied. "I believe we will have face-to-face meetings with everyone we've been in conflict with—and there will be truth telling, confession, honesty, and repentance. No equivocation, no excuses, no pretending. Friendships will be repaired; relationships will be set right. We'll lock arms and slap backs and give hugs and shed tears of relief and joy."

"You really think so?"

"How else can we carry on in peace and harmony if these rifts aren't healed?" he asked. "Obviously, I don't know the mechanics of how this will take place. Maybe it will be instantaneous. But take place it must. And we will *want* it to happen. God will fill us with the desire and ability to reconcile with each other. Tutsis will sit down with Hutus; unfaithful husbands will sit down with their wounded wives; rebellious children will settle up with their parents."

That last comment triggered a personal thought. My father and I had a rocky relationship. He told me at the height of an argument on the eve of my high school graduation, "I don't have enough love for you to fill my little finger." We never really reconciled after that; instead, we swept our conflict under the rug.

I believe my father, who died in 1979, was a genuine believer and that we will meet again someday in heaven. In recent years, through prayer and introspection, I've come to grips with the many ways my own rebellion, dishonesty, and selfishness contributed to the schism between us. I've longed to admit all this to him and express my regret and repentance. I've wanted to get past the ill will we both harbored for so many years.

I mentioned this briefly to McKnight, who listened with the patience of a counselor. "Well," he said, "I do think that your father is already more conscious of these things than you are."

"Really?"

"He has the perfect desire to reconcile. I'm guessing he has already repented of his side in the conflict. And one day, your relationship will be healed. It will be a beautiful moment for the both of you. Think of it—after that, you'll spend forever with him in the kind of father-son relationship that both of you have always wanted."

I smiled and reached down to check the recorder as if to make sure it was still working properly. It was a ruse, of course. I didn't want McKnight to see that my eyes were glistening.

Seeing the Face of God

Scripture has several references to the hope of seeing God face-to-face in eternity, often called the *beatific vision*, a doctrine that has inexplicably faded in much of contemporary Protestant theology.

Scholar Hans Boersma, in tracing the beatific vision through Christian tradition, said, "We are true to the way God has made us when we make the vision of God our ultimate desire."[39] Andrew Louth, professor emeritus at the University of Durham, said that "the 'beatific vision,' gazing on God in utmost joy, is the ultimate goal of Christian living, the fulfillment of our Christian discipleship."[40]

In the Psalms, David wrote, "One thing I ask from the LORD, this only do I seek . . . to gaze on the beauty of the LORD and to seek him in his temple."[41] Paul said that although we see things dimly now, someday in eternity "we shall see face to face."[42] Jesus said in the Sermon on the Mount, "Blessed are the pure in heart, for they will see God."[43]

"This seems confusing," I said to McKnight. "The Bible says God told Moses, 'You cannot see my face, for no one may see me and live.'"[44]

"Yes, the Bible says people cannot gaze on God and survive his glorious brilliance," McKnight said. "But while God's full presence is unendurable for humans here and now, in eternity all of his followers will get face time with him. The apostle John specifically confirms that all those in heaven 'will see his face.'[45] When we're there, we won't merely be able to *survive* his glorious presence, but we will *revel* in it forever."

He pointed out that Jesus said, "Anyone who has seen me has seen the Father."[46] At one point, Jesus was transfigured before his disciples, and "his face shone like the sun." Even his clothes "became as white as the light."[47]

"They saw him as he manifested his essential glory—the resurrected body—and the book of Revelation opens with John catching a glimpse of this same glorious Jesus," McKnight said. "When we see God in eternity, it will fill us to overflowing with happiness and joy. We will be fully alive, with a profound relational knowledge of the Almighty."

McKnight said that when his children were young, they enjoyed "Magic Eye" books, where you stare at a bundle of dots until they morph into a three-dimensional picture, all while you lose peripheral vision. In a sense, you enter into the scene as your eyes adjust and are transformed for the image.

"Being with God will be like that, except greater. Our everyday life of devotion to God is like that bundle of dots—sometimes it's wonderful, sometimes it's not," he said. "When we encounter God fully under the power of a transformed body, all the dots will suddenly make sense—and we will have been absorbed into the depth of who God is. Saint John of the Cross called God's presence a 'living flame of love'[48]—that means our dwelling with God will be a wonderfully warm and intimate encounter."

He pursed his lips. "We're not ready for that yet," he said, a hint of longing in his voice. "Someday, yes. Then the veil will be torn away, and we will have the capacity to experience God face-to-face. You see, Lee, that's what heaven is for. Heaven will exist for those who long to gaze upon the luminous and beautiful face of God."

In the words of the towering eighteenth-century theologian Jonathan Edwards, "How good is God, that he has created man for this very end, to make him happy in the enjoyment of himself, the Almighty."[49]

Charles Spurgeon couldn't contain himself at the thought: "The very glory of heaven is that we shall see him, that same Christ who once died upon Calvary's cross, that we shall fall down, and worship at his feet, nay more, that he shall kiss us with the kisses of his mouth, and welcome us to dwell with him forever."[50]

"No man hath seen God at any time," says the King James Version of John 1:18. "The only begotten Son, which is in the bosom of the Father, he hath declared him." In the original Greek, the idiom "in the bosom" describes the closeness of God and his Son.

In effect, says Michael Reeves in his book *Delighting in the Trinity*, John is painting a picture of Jesus as being eternally in the lap of the Father. "One would never dare imagine it," said Reeves, "but Jesus declares [John 17:24] that his desire is that believers might be with him there."[51]

Go ahead—for just a moment, *dare*.

Trustworthy and True

It's a staggering thought—heaven will be *here*, in this world, a re-created and renewed environment free from sin and decay, a bustling place full of commerce and friendships and beautiful nature, all focused on the community of God's people glorifying their triune Creator.

As the apostle John wrote in Revelation 21:5, "He who was seated on the throne said, 'I am making everything new!' Then he said, 'Write this down, for these words are trustworthy and true.'"

Wrote author John Eldredge, "If God were wiping away reality as we know it and ushering in a new reality, the phrase would have been, 'I am making all *new things*!' But that's not what he says."[52] Rather, he said he is making "everything new." "The early Christians," said N. T. Wright, "believed that God was going to do for the whole cosmos what he had done for Jesus at Easter."[53]

We can trust that God's words are "trustworthy and true," but what about all of the implications? Our curiosity is piqued. Questions proliferate. Debates have raged through the centuries. There's a temptation to go beyond the text and untether our imaginations completely, but I was intent on resisting that impulse.

I pulled a yellow legal pad out of my satchel. "I've got seven questions about heaven that I'm especially curious about," I said to McKnight.

He motioned for me to continue. "I'll do my best," he replied.

CHAPTER 6

Seven on Heaven

Top Questions about Eternal Life with God

> *In a day when speculation about heaven runs rampant, I've found it both exciting and refreshing to carefully examine what Scripture says.*
>
> RANDY ALCORN, "5 CURIOUS
> QUESTIONS ABOUT HEAVEN"

When the topic is heaven, questions proliferate. The image of a new heaven and a new earth stimulates our imagination, piques our curiosity, spurs us to search the Scriptures, and makes us hunger all the more for that day when the Lord "will wipe every tear" from our eyes and "there will be no more death or mourning or crying or pain."[1]

And since I had unfettered access to a world-class biblical scholar like Scot McKnight, the journalist in me couldn't resist exploring seven nettlesome questions about what lies beyond this world. With McKnight's consent, I flipped my legal pad to a fresh page and, pen in hand, resumed our conversation in the comfortable lounge of a small suburban Chicago church.

But I didn't start with the most theologically significant issue—or the most profound or even the most consequential. Instead, I began with the question that almost always comes up when talking to any audience.

Question #1: Will There Be Pets in Heaven?

For McKnight, it was a black Labrador named Sam. For me, it was a giant poodle named Nikki. Childhood pets are warm and wonderful companions—but will we see them again in heaven?

"Sam used to go on my paper route with me," recalled McKnight. "But he had the instinct of a retriever, so at first when I'd throw a paper, he'd run after it and bring it back to me."

Whether it's a kitten or a hamster, a chinchilla or a parakeet, most families have a furry, feathery, or scaly friend that endears itself to kids and parents alike. Our hearts say we'd love to see them again in eternity, but what do the biblical facts say? Is the title of the animated film *All Dogs Go to Heaven* a theologically correct assertion?

"As far as animals in general, yes, I believe the new heaven and new earth will be populated by all sorts of wildlife," McKnight told me. "Predators and prey will be at peace. Isaiah says that 'the wolf will live with the lamb, the leopard will lie down with the goat, the calf and the lion and the yearling together; and a little child will lead them.'[2] What God makes, God perfects. And what God has made for our world today, he will perfect in the world to come."

"But what about my dog and yours?" I asked. "Will specific pets greet us in the final heaven?"

Popular opinion seems to say yes. A survey of the oldest pet cemetery in America, where seventy thousand animals are buried, showed that before the 1980s almost no inscriptions mentioned any hope of heaven for Fido. But since the 1990s, gravestones often "express the owner's belief in an afterlife for the pets, as well as the expectation, or at least the hope, that owners and pets will be reunited in the afterlife."[3]

McKnight's response was a smile. "When the theologian Rich Mouw was a kid, he asked his mom whether pets will be in heaven—and when Mouw was a father, his son asked him the same question. In both cases, the answer was, 'Well, dogs don't have souls, you see. But anything is possible with God. He will do what is best for us.'[4]

"And he *will* do what's best for us," McKnight said. "I'm convinced that heaven will not be a duller place than this world, and I think the world would be duller without pets. While our focus in heaven won't be on pets, I believe it would be just like God to have our dogs there for us."

"But no cats," I stressed.

"Absolutely. No cats. That goes without saying."

Scrappy and Scupper

Though kidding about kittens, McKnight's cautious optimism on the topic is the same assessment of many Christian thinkers. Asked about pets in heaven, philosopher Peter Kreeft playfully replied, "Why not?"[5] He pointed to Psalm 36:6, which some scholars translate, "You save humans and animals alike, O LORD."[6]

Said Kreeft, "We were meant from the beginning to have stewardship over the animals; we have not fulfilled that divine plan yet on earth; therefore it seems likely that the right relationship with animals will be part of Heaven . . . And what better place to begin than with already petted pets?"[7]

What about Joni Eareckson Tada's pet schnauzer, Scrappy? "If God brings our pets back to life, it wouldn't surprise me," she said. "It would be just like him. It would be totally in keeping with his genuine character . . . Exorbitant. Excessive. Extravagant in grace after grace. Of all the dazzling discoveries and ecstatic pleasures heaven will hold for us, the potential of seeing Scrappy would be pure whimsy—utterly, joyfully, surprisingly superfluous."[8]

Hank Hanegraaff, the longtime Bible Answer Man, points out that animals populated the Garden of Eden, "thus there is a precedent for believing that animals will populate Eden restored, as well."[9] While he said we can't know for certain if specific pets will be resurrected for eternity, "I for one am not willing to preclude the possibility."

Absent specific biblical teaching on the topic, theologian Alan Gomes is more circumspect. "Some verses and biblical themes imply that there may well be animals in the ES [eternal state]," he said. However, he added, "If there are animals on the new earth, it is unlikely that they would be the same animals that existed on this earth. That is, God would create new animals, not resurrect previously existing ones."[10]

However, Gomes admitted that he lacked personal interest in the issue, since he's only "modestly fond" of his pet parakeet, Scupper. "Emotionally speaking," he said, "I really do not have a dog in this fight."[11]

Philosopher J. P. Moreland offers both good and bad news. The good news is that although our pets don't have complex souls like humans, who are uniquely made in God's image, there is biblical evidence that they do possess some sort of rudimentary soul.[12]

The bad news: "I don't think the animal soul outlives its body. I could be wrong, but I think the animal soul ceases to exist at death."[13]

I hope he's wrong—for Sam and Nikki's sake. Oh, and Scrappy. And even a marginally appreciated parakeet named Scupper.

Question #2: Will There Be Marriage in Heaven?

When Leslie and I got married in 1972, we pledged to love and care for each other "as long as we both shall live." That's standard verbiage in wedding vows, but does it suggest our marital relationship will end abruptly at the grave?

Well, yes, say many Christian thinkers. They teach that there will be no marriage or families in the final heaven. For example, Colleen McDannell and Bernhard Lang summarize Augustine's teaching this way: "All special attachments [marriage, family, friendships] will be absorbed into one comprehensive and undifferentiated community of love."[14]

Randy Alcorn, whose book *Heaven* is a mega bestseller, put it this way: "In heaven, there will be one marriage, not many. That marriage will be what earthly marriage symbolized and pointed to, the marriage of Christ to his bride [the church]. So we will all be married—but to Christ."[15]

From scholars to popular authors, the issue of whether there is marriage in heaven often gets an unambiguous reply. "Fortunately, the Son of God himself answered this question as clearly and simply as anybody could. And his answer is a resounding, 'no,'" said Alan Gomes, a professor at Talbot School of Theology.[16]

Mark Hitchcock, pastor of an Oklahoma church and author of several books, couldn't agree more: "Jesus clearly stated that marriage as we know it here on earth will not carry over to the hereafter."[17]

I mentioned this conclusion to McKnight, and I watched as a skeptical look slowly spread over his face. He cleared his throat. "Well," he said, "I respectfully disagree."

I settled deeper into my chair, wishing I had some popcorn. *This is gonna get interesting*, I mused.

"For They Are like the Angels"

Everything hinges on a passage recorded in all three Synoptic Gospels.[18] The Sadducees, a religious sect that didn't believe in the resurrection, was trying to put before Jesus a conundrum that would cast doubt on the resurrected life.

As usual, Jesus beat them at their own game. He quoted from their Torah to affirm the resurrection. In response to a question about marriage that the Sadducees were attempting to trick him with, Jesus responded, "When the dead rise, they will neither marry nor be given in marriage; they will be like the angels in heaven."[19]

"That seems pretty clear-cut to a lot of people," I said to McKnight.

McKnight held up his hand. "Hold on a minute," he replied. "If Jesus had wanted to teach that there would be no marital life in heaven, he could have said it more clearly. He could have said, 'Read my lips: No marriages or families in heaven.' But he didn't. He said people 'will neither marry nor be given in marriage.' The first part—'will neither marry'—refers to the groom, and the second part—'be given in marriage'—refers to the bride being given away.

"What is he really saying? He's saying there won't be *weddings* or *new marriages* in heaven. He doesn't say anything about whether people who are married now will remain in a married state in the final heaven. He's just saying there won't be any *new* marriages there. Why? He says because 'they will be like the angels in heaven.'"

I interrupted. "Some commentators say angels don't have a gender, so this fits with the idea of no marriages in heaven."

McKnight picked up his Bible and opened it to the gospel of Luke. "Luke's account adds an important clue. Jesus is quoted there as saying that people in heaven 'can no longer die; for they are like the angels.'[20] Jesus is emphasizing that angels live forever. A major reason for marriage is procreation to continue one's lineage, but in heaven people are eternal, so no one will need to procreate in order to continue the family line. Thus, there won't be a need for *new* marriages in heaven."

He closed the Bible and continued. "This is the key text people cite against marital relationships in heaven, but as you can see, it doesn't say that marriages and families from this world won't stay intact in the final heaven. Consequently, I believe marriages and families *will* exist in heaven—and like everything else, they will be so much better than they are now."

McKnight offered much to ponder. As someone whose marriage for almost fifty years has been wonderful and fulfilling, I would certainly look forward to continuing in a marital relationship with Leslie forever in the world to come.

But even if Alcorn, Gomes, and Hitchcock are correct that marriage itself won't continue, that wouldn't diminish the joy of heaven. "Couples who shared the closest intimacy on earth will continue to know, treasure, and appreciate each other in the life of the Lord forever," Hitchcock said. "I plan to spend all of eternity with my wife, Cheryl, in a relationship that goes far beyond anything we have experienced here on earth."[21]

Concluded Gomes, "God takes nothing away from us in the eternal state except to replace it or enhance it with something better. In this instance, it is not that we will love our earthly spouse any less in the eternal state than we do now, but that we will love *everyone* in the eternal state to a degree unfathomable and unattainable at present."[22]

Question #3: Will There Be Rewards in Heaven?

Will everyone be equal in heaven, or will some Christians be more rewarded than others? How should we understand the Bible's references to rewards or "crowns" earned in this life? Entry to heaven is only through God's grace, but will "good deeds" by Christians in this world impact the *quality* of their afterlife?

Many Christians think so. "We may reasonably conclude that all of God's servants in one sense receive the same reward, which is everlasting life," said Alan Gomes. "That said, we also see indications that 'within the realm of salvation' the Lord indeed rewards his servants variously."[23] Other theologians, though, aren't so sure.

"I remember as a kid being motivated to memorize Bible verses because of the rewards I'd get in the form of recognition from teachers," McKnight said to me. "But the first place I'd go to explore this issue would be to a parable told by Jesus."[24]

In that story, an estate owner hires laborers early in the morning, promising a denarius to work in his vineyard. Later that morning, he hires more laborers, saying he will pay them "whatever is right." He does this again at noon, at midafternoon, and at 5:00 p.m.

At day's end, those hired last and who worked only an hour were given a denarius. Those hired earlier got the same amount, prompting them to grumble. The landowner replied, "I am not being unfair to you, friend. Didn't you agree to work for a denarius? Take your pay and go. I want to give the one who was hired last the same as I gave you. Don't I have the right to do what I want with my own money? Or are you envious because I am generous?"

Said one commentator, "Almost everyone agrees that Jesus is teaching about a fundamental equality here among those who are truly his disciples. All are rewarded alike."[25] Said another, "In the kingdom of God the principles of merit and ability may be set aside so that grace can prevail."[26]

McKnight spoke up. "The landowner's actions are seen as outrageous and even unjust. But God's ways aren't our ways," he told me. "In God's kingdom, the correlation between work and reward seems out of whack. We're exacting, but God is lavish. A key line is this: 'Or are you envious because I am generous?' God's generosity is the opposite of human envy. We crave hierarchy and status, but he is gracious. In heaven, we'll all be gazing equally at God in *his* glory—not ours."

Crowns, Rewards, Equality

But, I asked McKnight, what about passages concerning rewards and "crowns" that Christians earn in this life?[27] Second

Corinthians 5:10 reads, "For we must all appear before the judgment seat of Christ, so that each of us may receive what is due us for the things done while in the body, whether good or bad."

"Doesn't this contradict this parable?" I asked.

"First," said McKnight, "all the talk about rewards shouldn't distract us from focusing on God's glory and his promise that we will all experience fulfillment forever in heaven. Second, look at John's last visions of heaven in Revelation 20–22. There are no gradations there. Nobody is more important than anyone else. Third, I think it's wise to see the language of reward as God's way of motivating us to be faithful.

"And fourth," he said, "in the final heaven, all God's people will be full of joy—and you can't get fuller than full. God's generosity will overwhelm any sense of correlation between what we did on earth and any reward in the afterlife. Notice that in Revelation, it says the saints will 'lay their crowns before the throne.'[28] That's a good picture for us—any crowns deserve to be thrown at the feet of the God of grace."

New Testament scholar Craig Blomberg's article that analyzed the passages about rewards concluded, "I do not believe there is a single NT [New Testament] text that, when correctly interpreted, supports the notion that believers will be distinguished one from another for all eternity on the basis of their works as Christians."[29]

Most commentators, he said, agree that the texts about crowns "are not at all talking about degrees of reward in heaven but simply about eternal life."[30] He added, "Several NT texts warn believers that they must give an accounting to the Lord for every deed performed (Rom. 2:6; Rev. 22:12) and word uttered (Matt. 12:36; Luke 12:2–3), but nothing in the contexts of any of those passages suggests varying degrees of reward or the perpetuating of distinctions beyond the Day of the Lord. The purpose of Christians' standing before God's bar of justice is to declare

127

them acquitted, not to embarrass them before the entire cosmos for all their failings."[31]

An Enhanced Experience?

In his writings, theologian Millard Erickson noted another parable in which ten servants are each given one mina by their master, eventually returning different amounts and being rewarded in proportion to their faithfulness.[32] Erickson acknowledged, though, that biblical peeks at heaven show "no real difference" between people there—"all are worshiping, judging, serving."[33]

He said if rewards in heaven were to involve some people getting a visible perk, such as a larger room, this would reduce the joy of others and be an eternal reminder of their shortcomings. Instead, he speculated that rewards might come in people's subjective experience in heaven.

"Thus, all would engage in the same activity, for example, worship, but some would enjoy it much more than others," he said. "Perhaps those who have enjoyed worship more in this life will find greater satisfaction in it in the life beyond than will others."

As an analogy, he said the same sound waves fall on the ears of all concert attenders, but those who have deeply studied music have a greater experience than those around them. In heaven, he said, "no one will be aware of the differences in range of enjoyment, and thus there will be no dimming of the perfection of heaven by regret over wasted opportunities."[34]

I offered that analogy to McKnight. "Will some have an enhanced experience in heaven?" I asked.

"That's a pretty common view in the history of the church. Is it possible? Maybe, I don't know. In another sense, if we're all fully redeemed, aren't we all going to have a fully enhanced experience?" he asked. "In the end, I see the talk of rewards as being motivational language to encourage us. It certainly motivates me—although, ultimately, shouldn't we joyfully serve God purely out of gratitude for his grace?"

Question #4: Is Purgatory Biblical?

"There's no ducking the fact that *purgatory* is a fighting word," said philosopher Jerry Walls—and he speaks from experience.[35] As one of the few Baptist university professors who endorses the doctrine, Walls has received plenty of vociferous pushback from other evangelical thinkers.[36]

Opposition to purgatory was forcefully expressed by the Reformer John Calvin, who declared in the sixteenth century, "We must cry out with the shout not only of our voices but of our throats and lungs that purgatory is a deadly fiction of Satan."[37]

Yet many Christians are surprised to learn that no less of an evangelical icon than C. S. Lewis wrote unambiguously, "I believe in Purgatory."[38] Today, Walls said, "some Protestant thinkers have recently shown a willingness to reconsider the doctrine."[39]

As Walls points out, all theologians need to account for two realities. First, heaven is a place of perfection, and Hebrews 12:14 reads, "Without holiness no one will see the Lord." Second, most Christians, if not all, are far from perfectly holy when they die. They are forgiven through Christ and have presumably made some progress in pursuing holiness, but they haven't completed that journey.

Faced with these two facts, evangelical Christians respond by saying that at the moment of death, God in his grace instantly perfects believers by an act of glorification. The other alternative is purgatory, a way station between this world and the final heaven.

There is the *satisfaction* model of purgatory, in which the individual undergoes retributive punishment until God's justice is fully satisfied. Then there's the *purification* model, where "God will continue the sanctification process after death with our free cooperation until we are fully and completely perfect," to use Walls's description.[40] "Purgatory is the successful end of the pursuit of that holiness without which no one can see the Lord," he said.[41]

As for C. S. Lewis, he recognized the difference between these two approaches and only endorsed the purification model. "Our souls *demand* Purgatory, don't they?" he asked.[42]

A *Testing by Fire*

My question to McKnight was whether any biblical texts support purgatory, particularly a commonly cited passage in which Paul talks about testing by fire. The Greek word for *fire* is *pur*, from which we get the word *purgatory*, or "perfected by fire."

McKnight was ready with an answer. "In that passage, Paul seems to be saying that either at death or thereafter, the things we've done in our lives will be tested by fire, with whatever survives being eternal. This means that, yes, the image of a fire that purges is definitely there. But, no, the passage doesn't support the doctrine of purgatory."

"Explain why not."

"Listen to the text carefully," he said, opening his Bible and reading from 1 Corinthians 3:11–15:

> For no one can lay any foundation other than the one already laid, which is Jesus Christ. If anyone builds on this foundation using gold, silver, costly stones, wood, hay or straw, their work will be shown for what it is, because the Day will bring it to light. It will be revealed with fire, and the fire will test the quality of each person's work. If what has been built survives, the builder will receive a reward. If it is burned up, the builder will suffer loss but yet will be saved—even though only as one escaping through the flames.

McKnight pointed to the page. "You see, it isn't *people* being tested and approved, but it's their *works*," he said. "There's no sense in which there's a postmortem experience where people work off their sins under God's disciplinary hand. When the Bible talks about purging, it's referring to life now—and it's an act of God, not something we join him in. This text reveals that at death or judgment, God judges our works and purges or sanctifies us from our corruptions so we will be fit for his presence."

Alan Gomes comes to the same conclusion about the passage. "In context," he said, "Paul is discussing the different rewards that believers will receive for their service to Christ. It has nothing whatever to do with paying for the temporal penalties for one's sins, nor with one's purification through purgatorial fire."[43]

I asked McKnight, "Are there any other passages that would support purgatory?"

"No, there really aren't," he said, closing the Bible. "Some people cite 2 Maccabees, where soldiers pray for the souls of the dead so they might join in the final resurrection.[44] But Protestants don't accept that book as canonical, for various reasons. Besides, when you study the passage closely, you can see there's no evidence there for believing in purgatory anyway."[45]

With that, McKnight leaned forward for emphasis. "Frankly, Lee, I don't see *any* biblical basis for purgatory," he said. "We have to be very careful not to diminish what Christ has done for us through his freely offered grace. That's the real danger with believing in purgatory."[46]

Question #5: Should Christians Be Cremated?

Urn or casket? More and more people these days are opting for cremation rather than burial. Today, more than 55 percent of Americans say they prefer cremation—a number that is projected to increase to 70 percent by 2030.[47] The biggest reasons are economic (it's cheaper) and environmental (it saves land).

Although he doesn't condemn cremation as heretical, N. T. Wright writes negatively about the practice, noting that cremation classically belongs to Hindu or Buddhist theology. "When people ask for their ashes to be scattered on a favorite hillside or in a well-loved river or along a shoreline, we can sympathize with the feeling," he wrote. "But the underlying implication, of a desire simply to be merged back into the created world, without any affirmation of a future life of new embodiment, flies in the face of classic Christian theology."[48]

Hank Hanegraaff agrees: "Scripture clearly favors burial over cremation . . . While burial points to resurrection, cremation in its Eastern permutations highlights escape from the body."[49] When asked for his advice, Billy Graham also leaned against cremation: "We should honor the earthly tent of our dwelling when it is in our power to do so, for the physical body is the work of [God's] hands."[50]

As I questioned McKnight about cremation, it emerged that his main concern centers around the intent behind it. "Generally speaking, I don't have any problem with cremation," he told me. "The Bible says, 'For dust you are and to dust you will return.'[51] Ecclesiastes 12:7 says, 'The dust returns to the ground it came from, and the spirit returns to God who gave it.' All that cremation accomplishes is to speed up our inevitable return to dust, from which God will remake us into our resurrection bodies designed for the final heaven."

"Certainly, God would have no problem resurrecting the cremated," I observed.

"That's right. A person who is buried eventually ends up as thoroughly annihilated as someone who is cremated. It just takes longer. Someone eaten by a wild animal or killed by a nuclear blast can be reconstituted by God and resurrected, so cremation doesn't present any insuperable problem for him."

"Do you have any hesitations about cremation at all?"

"Actually," he said, "I would be concerned if someone chooses cremation out of the wrong motivation."

"For instance?"

"If it's motivated by a negative attitude toward the body, I wouldn't endorse it. That's not Christian. Our bodies are God's creation; they're the temple of the Holy Spirit and highly valued in the Bible. It's not appropriate to want to incinerate it out of a negative view of self. Or if someone sees cremation as a way of liberating their soul from their body as quickly as they can, that's not Christian theology; that's Greek philosophy. Nowhere does the Bible teach that our souls are trapped in our bodies and are in need of being set free."

Otherwise, he said, if the motivation is based, say, on a desire to honor God's creation by not taking up space in a cemetery, he has no concerns with cremation.

"My advice to pastors," he said, "would be to wisely discover why someone wants to be cremated to make sure it's not based on some theological misunderstanding."

Question #6: What about Children Who Die?

In his book *The Heaven Promise*, McKnight tells the poignant story of a woman who had an abortion as a teen and later went on to get married and have several children. When the children got old enough, she and her husband sat them down to tell them the story. "They were shocked, of course. Cried a bunch. As I did. I asked their forgiveness, since, after all, this was a half-sibling of theirs."

Later that day, two of them handed her a sheet of paper. "We came up with a name for our baby," they said. The children had taken a letter from each of their names and created the name: Kasey.

"Oh, how I wept as those girls handed me that! And I've wept several times since," she said. "I believe the day will come when I will meet the child named Kasey. I believe that as well about babies that are miscarried or stillborn. Whether we give that baby a name or not, God has given that child a soul."[52]

"That's obviously a heartfelt hope all mothers would have," I said to McKnight. "But is it a biblical belief?"

"The Scriptures don't come right out and explicitly say what happens to infants or children," he said. "When you piece together the clues—not just some verses, but the overarching teachings about God's nature—many theologians conclude that, yes, they will be in heaven. That includes such well-known Christians as Charles Hodge, B. B. Warfield, John Stott, and Billy Graham."

In support of that conclusion, many theologians point to Romans 1:20, which declares that unbelievers are without excuse because of the evidence for God in creation. Youngsters, on the other hand, don't experience creation as adults do. Therefore, they can't logically be held accountable for failing to draw the conclusion that God exists.

Other Christian thinkers believe in the salvation of children because of the verse in which David says of his stillborn child, "I will go to him, but he will not return to me."[53] Another commonly cited passage is where Jesus said, "Let the little children come to me, and do not hinder them, for the kingdom of heaven belongs to such as these."[54]

"What's your own position?" I asked McKnight.

"I start with the fact that God is loving, good, and just," he said, "which leads me to conclude that God wouldn't send infants or young children into eternal darkness. Rather, I believe that children will be resurrected and will grow to maturity, to the delight and joy of their parents. As the theologian Graham Twelftree said, 'We have no alternative other than to leave the matter in the hands of a God we have come to trust as fully just and totally loving.'"[55]

"That's reassuring to a lot of parents like me, who have gone through the experience of a miscarriage," I said.

"We went through one too, though it was very early," he said. "I remember talking about this issue one day with a woman who had gone through an abortion, and she started to weep. That showed her yearning for what was done to be made right."

I brought up another perspective. "Some theologians say that God, in his omniscience, will judge infants based on how he knows they would have responded if they had been told the gospel."

"Yes, that's the Molinist position, which has some attraction.[56] Of course, we don't know for sure," replied McKnight. "But I believe in an expansive heaven, where these children will grow to full maturity and flourish for eternity. So when people ask me where their child or infant is after a premature death, I simply tell them, 'In the hands of our good God.'"

Question #7: Who Will Be in Heaven?

I thought my question was straightforward, and McKnight did give me a simple answer—but it ended up requiring a more elaborate explanation.

"Who will be in heaven?" McKnight asked, echoing my inquiry. "That's easy. The Bible says it clearly: *Jesus.*"

"Uh, yeah, I know that," I replied. "But how do people get there?"

"Ah," he said, "that's the way we tend to look at things, right? We want to know what we have to do to get into heaven. And the answer, again, is Jesus. He's the one who lived, who died, who was raised into the presence of God, and who will be the center of the kingdom forever. Everything begins with him. He told his followers he was going to prepare a place where they would dwell with him forever.[57] So the answer is, those who are *in Christ* will be in heaven. Heaven is for Jesus and his people.

"You see," he continued, "when we put the focus on *us* and what *we* need to do to get to heaven, we take our attention away from *him*. We don't have to *do* anything to get into heaven—we don't have to practice a lot of religious rituals or live up to a long list of demands or accomplish a bunch of good deeds. We simply have to look to Jesus, turn to him, believe in him, and let *his* life, death, and resurrection be *our* life, death, and resurrection. The question we need to ask is, 'Are you in Christ?'"

"How would you explain the gospel?"

McKnight took a deep breath. "Well, we need to look at what the New Testament specifically calls the gospel. In 1 Corinthians 15, Paul says *this* is 'the gospel' and 'by this gospel you are saved'—namely, 'that Christ died for our sins according to the Scriptures, that he was buried, that he was raised on the third day according to the Scriptures, and that he appeared to Cephas [Peter], and then to the Twelve.'[58] *That's* the gospel, Paul says.

"Toward the end of his life, Paul wrote: 'Remember Jesus Christ, raised from the dead, descended from David. *This* is my gospel.'[59] In other words, remember that Jesus is the Messiah—that's the reference to him descending from David—and remember that he rose from the dead.

"So the earliest Christian gospel was to tell the story of Jesus—he was the Messiah; he died unjustly at the hands of sinners; God overturned his death and raised him; he ascended; and he's coming back to rule. At Pentecost, Peter told the story of Jesus.[60] When he met with Cornelius, Peter told the story of Jesus—and the Holy Spirit came down on everyone there, and they spoke in tongues and got baptized.[61] This story of Jesus, says Paul, is the gospel that saves.

"First and foremost, then, I don't think we should focus on how we can be happy when we die. We should focus on the story of Jesus. It's a redeeming story. Through it, we encounter the hero to this greatest true tale ever told. We meet the one who loves us so much that he endured the cross to pay for our sins. Who will be in heaven?" McKnight asked in conclusion. "The answer is Jesus and his people."

That means Jesus is the only route into God's kingdom—a claim that rankles many people. "Dare we patronize Him?" asks Boston College philosopher Peter Kreeft. "Dare we pat Him on the head and say, in our superior way, 'There, there, now; we know you have to exaggerate a bit to put the fear of God into the uneducated peasants of your unfortunate, benighted era. But we know better. We are The People . . . We know there *must* be other ways. Everyone says so. How dare we put all our eggs in one basket—your basket—as you demand? It's not a reasonable investment.'"[62]

To which Kreeft responds: "No. It is not. One does not get to Heaven by making reasonable investments . . . One does not fall in love by making reasonable investments. One falls in love by giving one's all. That is what He demands. Love will not settle for anything else . . . His claim is total on our life because He claimed not just to show the way but to *be* the Way. Remember where all human ways lead: into the valley of the shadow of death. How can we expect to endure *that* way alone? Only One has passed that way and lived: the One Who uttered the heart-stoppingly incredible claim, 'I am the Life.'"[63]

Heaven and Its Alternative

I emerged from that stone church after my interview with McKnight and sat alone in my car for quite a while. We had covered a lot of ground in a short time. I was almost giddy at the picture of heaven as a glorious re-creation of our world, transformed into everything we could ever want it to be—and more. And at its center, on its throne, exalted and lifted high—our leader, our Savior, our Lord, our King, our closest Friend, our All in All, Jesus Christ. More than ever, I wanted to keep my eyes on him. His story alone points the way to eternal life.

Sadly, other ways lead to a dead end. As unsettling as it is, I knew I couldn't avoid the subject of hell. I picked up my cell phone and scrolled through the directory for the phone number of one of the few philosophers I knew who could bring a balanced biblical perspective to such a vexing topic.

CHAPTER 7

The Logic of Hell
Do the Traditional Teachings Make Sense?

I can conceive of no more powerful and irrefutable argument in favor of atheism than the eternal torments of hell.

UKRAINIAN PHILOSOPHER NIKOLAI A.
BERDYAEV, *DREAM AND REALITY*

Those who desire to be rid of eternal punishment ought to abstain from arguing against God.

AUGUSTINE, *THE CITY OF GOD*

On the night before Good Friday in the year AD 1300, thirty-five-year-old Italian poet Dante Alighieri descended into hell, guided by the ghost of the ancient Roman poet Virgil. At least, that's the story depicted in Dante's 14,233-line epic poem *The Divine Comedy*, his allegorical trek through *Inferno* (hell), *Purgatorio* (purgatory), and *Paradiso* (heaven), considered one of history's greatest works of literature.

Dante describes entering the gates of hell, beyond its inscription carved in stone:

I AM THE WAY INTO THE CITY OF WOE.

I AM THE WAY TO A FORSAKEN PEOPLE.
I AM THE WAY INTO ETERNAL SORROW . . .
ABANDON ALL HOPE, YE WHO ENTER HERE.[1]

He and Virgil encounter hell's nine concentric circles of torment deep within the earth, where various forms of punishment reflect poetic justice. For instance, fortune tellers who used forbidden means to peer into the future are now consigned to walk eternally with their heads on backward, making it impossible to view what's ahead. For the king who built the Tower of Babel out of which various languages sprang, all speech is forever meaningless to him and his own words are "simply gibberish" to others.[2]

The first circle of hell is limbo, reserved for virtuous non-Christians. The second circle is for sinners who succumbed to lust. The third is for gluttons; fourth, the greedy; fifth, the wrathful; sixth, the heretics; seventh, the violent; eighth, the frauds; and the ninth circle is for those guilty of treachery.

At hell's core is an anguished Satan, whose ultimate sin is treachery against God. He is depicted as having three faces, each mouth gnawing eternally on a notorious traitor from history, including Judas Iscariot, who is described as "that soul that suffers most."[3]

As Dante and Virgil proceed through the fiery and putrid circles, the torments become increasingly horrific. The impenitent are variously buffeted by storms with fetid rain, trapped in flaming tombs, immersed in rivers of boiling blood, consumed by clawed birds, scorched by flames falling from the sky, mercilessly whipped by demons, steeped in excrement, attacked by snakes and lizards, and hacked by swords.

And this is surprising: though most people associate Dante's account with the imagery of unquenchable fire, he actually depicts hell's final circle as a frozen lake where sinners guilty of treachery are entombed in ice, symbolizing their rejection of the warmth of God's love.[4]

Witnessing all of the suffering evokes grief in Dante. "I felt my senses reel and faint away with anguish," he says. "I was swept by such a swoon as death is, and I fell, as a corpse might fall, to the dead floor of hell."[5]

Dante's depiction of hell has influenced countless authors and artists through the centuries, coloring how many people view what happens to those who are barred from heaven. But how much does his metaphorical tale reflect what hell is actually like? How does Scripture describe the fate of people who refuse to accept God's free offer of salvation?

Two things are certain: the Bible teaches that there is a place called hell—and beyond that, the specifics are open to controversy. In other words, said author Preston Sprinkle, "The Bible is arguably less clear on the nature of hell than on the existence of hell."[6]

Indeed, Jesus spoke more about hell and judgment than anyone else in the Bible, referring to it as *Gehenna* (transliterated, *Geenna*), or the Valley of Hinnom, located just south and west of Jerusalem.[7] Once thought to have been a smoldering garbage dump during Jesus' time, Gehenna is now recognized by scholars as having been "actually far worse: a place where the most horrible things take place, such as the willful sacrifice of children," said pastor and professor Mark Jones.

"Evil at its worst is associated with Gehenna," Jones added. "Hell is a place of pure evil, a place as scary as it is destitute of all hope. And it is an everlasting place."[8]

The Church's "Crazy Uncle"?

"Hell, as traditionally conceived, has few friends, it seems," said Steve Gregg in his book, *All You Want to Know about Hell*.[9] And certainly that's true. Hell is not a topic that typically comes up in polite conversation—or even in many sermons these days. Maybe that explains why just a bare majority (58 percent) of Americans believe in hell (down from 71 percent in recent years),[10] and only 2 percent believe they'll end up there,[11] even though Jesus warned that "wide is the gate and broad is the road that leads to destruction, and many enter through it."[12]

Under Christianity's traditional teaching about hell, the impenitent endure eternity in conscious torment and separation from God—a truly horrifying prospect. Harvard-educated church historian John Gerstner said there's "one essential reason" that evangelicals hold tenaciously to this doctrine: "God's Word teaches it."[13]

But does it *really*? Or is the issue more nuanced than many Christians suppose? "The word *hell* conjures up an image gained more from medieval imagery than from the earliest Christian writings," said scholar N. T. Wright, the former bishop of Durham in the Church of England.[14]

In the view of Bible teacher Grady Brown, "The doctrine of 'endless punishment' has for centuries been the 'crazy uncle' that the Church, with justifiable embarrassment, has kept locked in the back bedroom."[15] Said Canadian theologian Clark Pinnock, "Everlasting torture is intolerable from a moral point of view because it makes God into a bloodthirsty monster who maintains an everlasting Auschwitz for victims whom He does not even allow to die."[16] Opined British atheist Bertrand Russell, "I do not myself feel that any person who is really profoundly humane can believe in everlasting punishment."[17]

In recent years, an increasing number of professors and preachers are opting for alternatives to the traditional understanding of hell. Some maintain that the unrepentant are simply eradicated by God after a limited period of suffering. Others believe "love wins," meaning everyone will be saved in the end— including, presumably, Hitler, Pol Pot, and Chairman Mao. So if hell does exist, eventually it's going to be vacant.

I'll consider these theories in the next chapter. In the meantime, I wanted to listen with an open mind to an adherent of the conventional view that hell involves eternal conscious suffering—and where better to find such an advocate than in Florida in the depths of summer, where the sweltering heat is often likened to Hades itself—not unreasonably, it seems to me.

Interview #6: Paul Copan, PhD

Soft-spoken and sincere, mild-mannered and unfailingly polite, philosopher Paul Copan comes off as a consummate gentleman and the kindly father of six. While all of that is accurate, he is also a rigorous scholar with an incisive mind who is not afraid to wade boldly into controversial waters. For example, his provocatively titled 2011 book *Is God a Moral Monster?* followed by *Did God Really Command Genocide?* have become go-to resources for his penetrating analysis of troubling Old Testament texts.[18]

Copan, who descends from Eastern European stock (his mother was born in Latvia, his father in the Ukraine), earned his doctorate at Marquette University. He has authored or edited nearly forty books, including such popular-level works as *"True for You, But Not for Me"*; *When God Goes to Starbucks*; and *"How Do You Know You're Not Wrong?"* as well as academic books such as *The Routledge Companion to Philosophy of Religion, The Naturalness of Belief*, and *The* Kalām *Cosmological Argument* (a two-volume anthology).

He is a professor and the Pledger family chair of philosophy of ethics at Palm Beach Atlantic University in West Palm Beach, and he has been a visiting scholar at Oxford University and served as president of the Evangelical Philosophical Society for six years. His speaking ministry has taken him around the planet, from Russia to Singapore and from Finland to India.

Copan writes about hell in one of his most recent books, the second edition of *Loving Wisdom: A Guide to Philosophy and Christian Faith*, which is what initially caught my attention.[19]

"You opened your chapter by saying the doctrine of hell has troubled both believers and unbelievers alike," I began. "Purely on an emotional level, do you personally find the traditional view of hell to be disquieting?"

Copan adjusted his glasses as he acknowledged the question with a slight nod. "Yes, at some level I do," he replied. "C. S. Lewis said he would love to discard the doctrine of hell, but if Christianity is the story of reality, then we can't pick and choose which bit of reality to believe and which to reject."

I was familiar with Lewis's words: "There is no doctrine which I would more willingly remove from Christianity than this, if it lay in my power. But it has the full support of Scripture and, specially, of Our Lord's own words; it has always been held by Christendom; and it has the support of reason."[20]

Copan continued. "The Bible says the judge of all the earth will do what is right.[21] So if it turns out that our understanding of hell is truly unjust, then we would have to reject it. The goodness and justice of God are more fundamental than our limited interpretations of hell, which are sometimes colored by centuries of tradition, going back to Dante's *Inferno*."

"All the more reason," I said, "to carefully sort out what's biblical and what isn't."

"That's right."

"We Can Do What We Wish"

"Do you think the traditional view of hell repels a lot of people from God?" I asked.

"To a certain point, yes, but that needs qualification," he said. "For some people, no matter what philosophical perspective we give about hell, their visceral rejection of it—perhaps based on caricatures or misunderstandings—will nevertheless prevail."

"Can you elaborate on that?"

"Sociologist Robert Bellah and educator Allan Bloom pointed out that freedom has become the new absolute and that relativism has become the default position in our culture.[22] So if this is the average person's worldview, it's not surprising that the doctrine of hell would offend them. Hell violates the 'absolute' of relativism, and to many in our culture, the existence of hell would undermine an individual's own freedom. More recently," Copan added, "we encounter another challenge in talking about hell, which Greg Lukianoff and Jonathan Haidt discuss in their book *The Coddling of the American Mind*."[23]

I chuckled. "That's an intriguing title."

"Intriguing, yes, and accurate," Copan replied. "They point out that a growing number of universities are protecting students from words and ideas they don't like, creating safety zones, and barring professors from uttering microaggressive statements, such as 'America is a land of opportunity.' The authors argue that universities are contributing to the infantilization of our culture by prohibiting any speech that causes offense or discomfort."

"And," I said, "hell is certainly a topic that can make people extremely uncomfortable."

"Exactly right."

"How would you push back against all of this?"

"First, by noting that Jesus is considered by many to be *the* outstanding moral and spiritual authority in history—and yet he taught extensively on hell. If God is the cosmic authority, we should expect his ways and standards to be infinitely more finely tuned than our own limited moral perceptions. Our perspective may be skewed by our own self-interest or because our cultural lenses cloud our notions of justice or fairness.

"Second, other cultures may not find the notion of hell morally problematic. So why are we imposing our individualistic Western judgment on those non-Western cultures?

"Third, the fact that God and hell both exist serves as a reminder that cosmic justice will ultimately be done. Human beings will not get away with evil but will be held accountable for their actions—and that's a good thing. I remember reading Romanian pastor Richard Wurmbrand's story of being imprisoned and tortured for his faith under the brutal dictator Nicolae Ceauşescu."

Copan paged through some notes to find Wurmbrand's words. "He wrote, 'The cruelty of atheism is hard to believe. When a man has no faith in the reward of good or the punishment of evil, there is no reason to be human. There is no restraint from the depths of evil that is in man. The Communist torturers often said, 'There is no God, no hereafter, no punishment for evil. We can do what we wish.'"[24]

"Wow," I said. "That's stark."

"And it's logical if there are no definitive consequences for evil. Finally, fourth, remember that if any view of hell truly diminishes the goodness and justice of God, then it must be rejected. That means we may need to hold certain conceptions of hell tentatively."

"For some people, hell might be a wake-up call," I observed.

"Right. Jesus said to repent or perish.[25] The doctrine of hell can remind us that there is an accountability before God, and the consequences of separating ourselves from him are, indeed, dire and miserable."

Flames, Darkness, Gnashing of Teeth

"The description of hell typically includes eternal flames," I said to Copan. "Some theologians see this as literal—in fact, John Walvoord, longtime president of Dallas Theological Seminary, said that 'the frequent mention of fire in connection with eternal punishment supports the conclusion that this is what the

Scriptures mean.'[26] Others, though, say the flames are metaphorical. What's your assessment?"

"I don't believe hell is a place of intense thermal output," came his answer. "These images of hell are metaphorical. John Stott and others have made the point that if two key images of hell—flames and darkness—were taken literally, they would cancel each other out. The flames would illuminate the place. Also, the flame imagery is associated with the lake of fire in Revelation 19 and 20, which is where the devil and his angels will be cast. Literal fire affects physical bodies with nerve endings, not spirit beings like them; so physical fire would be pointless."

I raised my hand to slow him. "Isn't the idea that the flames are metaphorical just a modern attempt to soften the picture of hell for those repulsed by it?"

Copan shook his head. "Not at all," he insisted. "Even the Reformers Martin Luther and John Calvin took this metaphorical view."[27]

"A metaphor always points toward a reality that it's trying to illustrate," I said. "What's the point of the imagery of the flames and darkness?"

"Both images represent existence away from the Lord's presence.[28] This is the real essence of hell: being cut off from our source of life and joy and separated from God's blessings forever. Darkness evokes this sense of separation and removal. The reference to flames represents severe, holy judgment. Even in a state of separation, God sustains in existence those who have chosen to separate themselves from him. To be away from the presence of the Lord—the 'great divorce,' as C. S. Lewis put it—is the worst loss possible for any human being. That's torment."

"Is hell a torture chamber for eternity?" I asked.

"There's a difference between *torture*, which is externally imposed, and *torment*, which is internally generated. Torment, in effect, is self-inflicted. It's because people have resisted the initiating grace of God that they end up having their own way forever. God isn't willing that any perish; hell is the result of humans freely separating themselves from him and his love."

"What's the nature of the torment?"

"Revelation 14:11 speaks of 'the smoke of their torment' and that they have 'no rest day or night' forever. To be tormented means not being at rest. Just two verses later, we see that this torment is the opposite of the 'rest from their labor' that's experienced by faithful saints."

"Seven times in Matthew and Luke we see references to 'gnashing of teeth,'" I said. "What's that imagery about?"

"New Testament scholar Craig Blomberg said this reflects anger at God. For example, those who were about to stone Stephen were gnashing their teeth in anger.[29] Again, this imagery is meant to warn us that hell is spiritual misery. This misery is a natural consequence of a life lived apart from God, as well as the punishment of those who don't want to be in God's presence. Indeed, God's presence would actually be *greater* misery for them."

"You mean they wouldn't *want* to be in heaven?"

"Right. They would have to repent in order to be in God's holy presence. That's why philosopher Dallas Willard said that 'the fires of heaven burn hotter than the fires of hell.'[30] They'd be much more content in their own self-absorbed misery away from God rather than face the discomfort of God's glorious presence."

I asked the question that arises in the minds of so many people. "Why would a good God send people to hell?"

"I think that question is framed incorrectly," Copan said.

"How so?"

"The operative word is *send*. Each choice we make in this life moves us closer to our ultimate destination—whether toward or away from God. We set our own spiritual and moral compasses. Thus, those who reject the rule of God *send themselves* to hell. Humans bring misery upon themselves by separating themselves from him. People consign themselves to hell—and God reluctantly lets them go. As the musician Michael Card says, God 'simply speaks the sentence that they have passed upon themselves.'"[31]

Dallas Willard agrees. "Some people not only want to hide from God, but want to be as far away from God as possible . . . The best place for them to be is wherever God is not, and that's what hell is," he wrote. "If their hearts are really set on seeing themselves as God and they are intent on running their own world, that will keep them away from God. This is like the teacher who finally sends the trouble-making student out of the classroom, as it were, and says, 'Okay, if you want to go away, you can go away.'"[32]

Copan added an illuminating illustration from a 1960 episode of *The Twilight Zone* called "A Nice Place to Visit." As Copan described it, "After petty criminal Rocky Valentine is shot and killed, he finds himself surrounded by that which he pursued during his earthly life—women, fame, wealth. But he eventually tires of them because they're not ultimately satisfying. He tells his 'guardian angel' that he wants to leave heaven to go to 'the other place.' The 'angel' asks him why in the world he should think he's in heaven. '*This* is the other place!' At the conclusion of the episode, the narrator Rod Serling refers to Valentine as a man who now 'has everything he's ever wanted—and he's going to have to live with it for eternity.'"[33]

Of Grasshoppers, Frogs, and Babies

For many critics, the everlasting nature of hell is a disproportionate consequence of a limited lifetime of wrongdoing. "Finite beings can perform only a finite amount of sin, and therefore a finite amount of suffering is sufficient to atone for it," contends John Stackhouse Jr., a professor of religious studies.[34]

Asks former pastor Rob Bell in his book *Love Wins*, "Have billions of people been created only to spend eternity in conscious punishment and torment, suffering infinitely for the finite sins they committed in the few years they spent on earth?"[35]

I posed the question to Copan, "Wouldn't infinite torment be an injustice that would be inconsistent with God's character?"

"The amount of time it takes to commit a sin isn't commensurate with the seriousness of the sin," Copan answered. "If I were to pick up a gun and kill you right now, how much time does that take? A few seconds? Yet the impact of that would be catastrophic and would reverberate through time, down the generations of your family. It might take many years for me to defraud you of your savings, siphoning off a little at a time from your bank account. But a murder committed in a flash would be the more serious offense and deserving of the greater punishment.

"You see," he continued, "everlasting hell is warranted for those who have deliberately rejected the infinite God—the infinite Good—and spurned the knowledge of God and the boundless gift of salvation he offers. God is more concerned with the direction of one's heart than the number of sins committed. People aren't consigned to be away from God because they committed a string of finite sins, but because they have spurned the greatest Good. Also, consider that people commit these sins against an infinite God—that's relevant too."

That reminded me of a parable told by conservative theologian Denny Burk. Imagine, he said, encountering a stranger on a bench who is pulling the legs off a grasshopper. You'd think this was odd, but you might not initiate a confrontation over it. What if he were pulling the legs off frogs? That would be a little more disturbing. What if it were a puppy? That would cross a line, and you'd probably call the authorities. What if he were holding a human baby and trying to tear her legs off? You would move heaven and earth to save that baby, intervening even at your own personal risk and demanding prosecution because justice would require it.

"In each of the scenarios above, the 'sin' is the same—pulling the legs off. The only difference in each of these scenarios is the one sinned against," Burk wrote. "The seriousness of sin—and thus of the punishment due to sin—is not measured merely by the sin itself but by the value and the worth of the one sinned against."

If God were like a grasshopper, he said, then "to sin against Him wouldn't be such a big deal" and "eternal conscious suffering under the wrath of God . . . seems like an overaction on God's part." However, Burk stressed, "To sin against an infinitely glorious being is an infinitely heinous offense that is worthy of an infinitely heinous punishment."[36] Too often, we have a diminished view of our sin—and thus of the judgment due for it—because we have a diminished view of God.

I mentioned the parable to Copan. "That's an apt illustration," he said. "Rejection of the greatest Good brings the consequence of being separated from that greatest Good everlastingly. The punishment fits the crime."

Centuries ago, Thomas Aquinas put it this way in his *Summa Theologiae*: "Now a sin that is against God is infinite; the higher the person against whom it is committed, the graver the sin—it is more criminal to strike a head of state than a private citizen—and God is of infinite greatness. Therefore, an infinite punishment is deserved for a sin committed against him."[37]

Copan added, "I'll mention one other factor as well."

"What's that?"

"It's the fact that the rebellion against God isn't just confined to a limited time on earth, but it continues unabated in hell—and therefore warrants ongoing judgment," he said.

"The prominent theologian D. A. Carson has written that the Bible doesn't suggest there will be repentance in hell,"

Copan said. He rustled through some notes before finding the quote from Carson: "Perhaps, then, we should think of hell as a place where people continue to rebel, continue to insist on their own way, continue societal structures of prejudice and hate, continue to defy the living God. And as they continue to defy God, so he continues to punish them. And the cycle goes on and on and on."[38]

Said Copan, "As we discussed earlier, the gnashing of teeth in hell reflects continued anger at God. And if people continue to resist and hate God, then continuing judgment is certainly warranted."

Hell Isn't "One Size Fits All"

Two decades earlier, when I was personally struggling to reconcile the doctrine of hell with the justice of God, I sought out philosopher J. P. Moreland and grilled him on the topic.[39]

One of his points that helped my understanding was that not everyone in hell will suffer the same way. Adolf Hitler won't have the same experience as my narcissistic neighbor who turned up his nose at God for his entire life but didn't murder anyone. As evidence, Moreland cited Matthew 11:20–24, where Jesus said certain cities would suffer more than others because they refused to repent despite miracles he had performed there.

Likewise, New Testament scholar Craig Blomberg said Luke 12:42–48 ranks "among the clearest in the entire Bible in support of degrees of punishment in hell."[40] This parable includes Jesus saying, "The servant who knows the master's will and does not get ready or does not do what the master wants will be beaten with many blows. But the one who does not know and does things deserving punishment will be beaten with few blows."

Augustine believed in degrees of punishment, saying in the fifth century, "We must not, however, deny that even the eternal fire will be proportioned to the deserts of the wicked."[41]

I asked Copan, "Do you agree that justice in eternity won't be 'one size fits all'?"

"Yes, absolutely, just as there are degrees of sin, so there are degrees of punishment. For example, Numbers 15 refers to intentional sins and unintentional sins. Jesus speaks of the blasphemy against the Holy Spirit, which won't be forgiven in the present life or the life to come, in contrast to any other sin or blasphemy, which can be forgiven.[42] Or consider the Jewish leaders of his day committing the 'greater sin,' whereas the sin of Roman authorities was a lesser one."[43]

"It makes sense to me that God's justice would be proportional," I said.

"Me too. The fact that the degreed nature of sin spills over into the afterlife—that each person is judged according to his deeds—does significantly address the challenge of hell's unreasonableness," he replied. "As I said earlier, the Bible asks, 'Will not the Judge of all the earth do right?'[44] And the answer is, yes, of course he will. In hell, the degree of misery will be correlated to the degree of responsibility."

From Sméagol to Gollum

Even so, Copan said, as people in hell continue to hate and resist God, over time the divine image in many of them may very well become eclipsed so that they turn into mere wisps and shadows of what they once were.

"Notice how Revelation reveals an irrational human hostility despite God's severe judgments," he said. "The text refers to people being 'seared by the intense heat,' the beast's kingdom becoming 'darkened,' and 'huge hailstones' falling from the sky. People 'gnawed their tongues because of pain.' And nevertheless—despite all this—they continue to curse and blaspheme God.[45] What's going on here could be called corrosivism."

"What do you mean by that?"

"I mean the end state of the unredeemed is the diminishing of their humanity, something akin to the deterioration of J. R. R. Tolkien's hobbit Sméagol. Over time, he turned into the diminished, corroded, corrupted, wisplike 'sub-hobbit' creature Gollum. In *The Great Divorce*, C. S. Lewis spoke of a grumbling woman who eventually, in a postmortem existence, resembled a grumble more than she did a woman. She ultimately turned into something machinelike.[46]

"Some theologians claim that unredeemed people who resist God to the end will eventually be extinguished from existence. In a way, this kind of diminished humanity bears some resemblance to that view. Who they were once has faded away."

Copan sorted through some papers until he found a quote from N. T. Wright:

> It seems to me . . . it is possible . . . for human beings to choose to live more and more out of tune with the divine intention, to reflect the image of God less and less, [such that] there is nothing to stop them finally ceasing to bear that image, and so to be, as it were, beings who were once human but are not now. Those who persistently refuse to follow Jesus, the true Image of God, will by their own choice become less and less like him, that is, less and less truly human. We sometimes say, even of living people, that they have become inhuman . . .
>
> I see nothing in the New Testament to make me reject the possibility that some, perhaps many, of God's human creatures do choose, and will choose, to dehumanize themselves completely.[47]

Copan put down the paper. His look was at once sober and sad. "And so," he said, "we end up not with human beings in hell, but with human 'remains,' as C. S. Lewis put it.[48] Human debris.

Subhuman creatures in whom the light of the image of God has effectively been extinguished. That's so very, very tragic."

"A Dreadful Torment"

Everything about hell is dreadful, I mused as Copan and I took a break in our conversation. The danger of saying that hell's flames and worms are metaphors is that some people might sigh with relief and conclude it might not be as bad a place as they had imagined. Actually, it's far worse than anyone can envision. That's why Jesus used metaphorical language. No literal description can adequately convey the horrors of hell.

Said the Reformer John Calvin, "These forms of speech denote, in a manner suited to our feeble capacity, a dreadful torment, which no man can now comprehend, and no language can express."[49]

In Jesus' parable of Lazarus and the rich man, he uses the imagery of fire to give a harrowing peek at an afterlife separated from God.[50] Lazarus, a beggar during his lifetime, is safely embraced by Abraham, but the ungenerous rich man is "in torment," pleading for Lazarus to "dip the tip of his finger in water and cool my tongue, because I am in agony in this fire." A chasm prevents that. The rich man begs for Lazarus to warn the man's five brothers "so that they will not also come to this place of torment." Abraham replies that they should listen to the prophets.

Granted, this is a story not about eternal hell itself, but about the intermediate state between death and the final judgment, or a place commonly referred to as Hades. We know this because the rich man's brothers are still alive. And the focus of the parable isn't to actually teach about the afterlife.

Nevertheless, it seems unlikely that Jesus would mislead his listeners about the ultimate fate of the unrepentant. It would make sense that the imagery he used would portray a foretaste of the suffering that awaits those in hell. While the fire in the parable must be metaphorical, since this is the disembodied state where there would be no nerve endings to feel physical pain, the misery is all too compellingly depicted.[51]

Said Randy Alcorn, "In his story of the rich man and Lazarus, Jesus taught that in Hell, the wicked suffer terribly, are fully conscious, retain their desires and memories and reasoning, long for relief, cannot be comforted, cannot leave their torment, and are bereft of hope."[52]

Nearly three hundred years ago, the eloquent Jonathan Edwards warned his congregation about the unending terror of hell in his famous sermon, "Sinners in the Hands of an Angry God." He declared, "It would be dreadful to suffer this fierceness and wrath of Almighty God one moment; but you must suffer it to all eternity. There will be no end to this exquisite horrible misery. When you look forward, you shall see a long forever, a boundless duration before you."[53]

In recent years, theologian Alan Gomes sought to paint a picture of a horrific afterlife divorced from God's presence. "There is . . . every reason to expect the wicked in hell to suffer great bodily pains there. This suffering will take place from the inside out, as it were. It will not arise from God boiling sinners in a cauldron or turning them over slowly on a rotisserie spit," he wrote.

"Rather," he continued, "they will suffer the natural consequences of rejecting God and his goodness toward them, in which they will experience the pain of complete abandonment, remorse unmingled with comfort, and the relentless torments of their own consciences, which will burn forever but never finally consume. This cup they will drink to the full, experiencing unmitigated pain in both body and spirit."[54]

And yet . . .

What if there were an escape hatch—a valid biblical alternative to the traditional view of hell? What if God cut short the torment of the unrepentant by snuffing them out and thus ending their suffering? Surely that kind of nonexistence would be preferable to an agonizing eternity. Or what if all of humanity were to personally benefit from God's provision of redemption? Then everyone headed for hell would take a detour to heaven.

I stretched my legs while waiting to resume my interview with Copan. He had offered a cogent case for the traditional view of hell. I wondered how he would handle these increasingly popular challenges of annihilationism and universalism.

CHAPTER 8

Escape from Hell

Are There Alternatives to Eternal Torment?

*When it comes to hell, we can't afford to be
wrong. This is not one of those doctrines where
you can toss in your two cents, shrug your
shoulders, and move on. Too much is at stake.
Too many people are at stake. And the Bible
has too much to say.*

FRANCIS CHAN AND PRESTON SPRINKLE,

ERASING HELL, ITALICS IN ORIGINAL

He was the closest thing to an evangelical pope in modern times. *Time* magazine called him one of the world's most influential people. The Cambridge-educated theologian was a leader in international missions, a pastor at a prominent London church, a chaplain to the Queen of England, and an author of more than fifty books.

Then in 1988, John Robert Walmsley Stott wrote six pages that prompted some scholars, including theologian John Gerstner, to question his very salvation.

Stott's sin? He challenged the traditional Protestant understanding of hell as being a place of eternal conscious torment for the unrepentant. Instead, Stott "tentatively" embraced the alternative view of *annihilationism,* or *conditional immortality,* which teaches that the unredeemed are snuffed out of existence

159

forever, perhaps after a limited period of punishment for their sins in hell.[1]

Concluded Stott, "I question whether 'eternal conscious torment' is compatible with the biblical revelation of divine justice."[2]

"Traditionalists, who make up most of evangelicalism, were shocked," said seminary professor Robert Peterson, author of *Hell on Trial: The Case for Eternal Punishment.* "Evangelicals have been debating the subject ever since, both sides producing books and articles defending their views and contesting the opposition."[3]

Stott's fellow Anglican John Wenham, part of an evangelical think tank at Oxford, was among the scholars who embraced annihilationism. "For more than fifty years I have believed the Bible to teach the ultimate destruction of the lost, but I have hesitated to declare myself in print," he said in his 1991 book *Facing Hell.* "Now I feel that the time has come when I must declare my mind honestly."

With that, he didn't mince words. "Unending torment speaks to me of sadism, not justice. It is a doctrine which I do not know how to preach without negating the loveliness and glory of God," he said. "It is a doctrine which makes the Inquisition look reasonable. It all seems a flight from reality and common sense."[4]

He wasn't finished. "I believe that endless torment is a hideous and unscriptural doctrine which has been a terrible burden on the mind of the church for many centuries and a terrible blot on her presentation of the gospel," Wenham declared. "I should indeed be happy if, before I die, I could help in sweeping it away."[5]

Annihilationists (or conditionalists) emphasize that humans are not intrinsically immortal, which is actually a view affirmed by Christian orthodoxy. They say God, who alone is inherently immortal, grants eternal life to those who embrace Jesus as their forgiver and leader.[6] Lacking immortality, the unsaved simply cease to exist when they die, or they are resurrected for the final judgment and then consigned to hell for a limited period of punishment, after which their lives are extinguished forever. Either way, there's no everlasting torment in unquenchable fires.

This view contradicts what Robert Peterson called the "impressive pedigree" of the traditional view. Tertullian, Lactantius, Basil of Caesarea, Jerome, Cyril of Jerusalem, Chrysostom, Augustine, Aquinas, Luther, Calvin, Edwards, Whitefield, and Wesley "all endorsed eternal punishment."[7]

Peterson said while embryonic forms of annihilationism are found in Justin Martyr and Theophilus of Antioch, Arnobius (died ca. 330) was the first to defend the idea explicitly. The Second Council of Constantinople (553) and the Fifth Lateran Council (1512–1517) both condemned annihilationism.

The Trend toward Annihilationism

There has been a resurgence of interest in annihilationism during the modern era.[8] "My prediction is that, even within conservative evangelical circles, the annihilation view of hell will be the dominant view in 10 or 15 years," said Preston Sprinkle, coauthor of *Erasing Hell*. "I base that on how many well-known pastors secretly hold that view. I think that we are at a time and place when there is a growing suspicion of adopting tradition for the sake of tradition."

He said that some pastors are reluctant to publicly declare themselves annihilationists because "we have a very fear-driven evangelical culture where if you don't toe the line, you get kind of shunned."[9]

As an annihilationist, Southern California pastor Gregory Stump said he has "often faced alienation and marginalization from peers who have vehemently disagreed with me, along with the potential of losing my job over the view of hell that I held."[10]

Despite the confidence of many Christians that the Bible teaches eternal conscious torment, Stump said he "found the biblical, theological, and philosophical evidence for this perspective to be weak and insubstantial."

In contrast, he said the case for conditional immortality is compelling. "This view seemed to be derived from the clear and consistent language of Scripture, it had an internal coherence that made sense of the overarching narrative of redemptive history, and it resolved philosophical and intuitive difficulties that have plagued generations of Christians and non-Christians alike for centuries."[11]

Stott's Arguments Summarized

Annihilationists are often accused of being motivated by sentimentalism, a charge they vehemently deny. "Emotionally," said John Stott, "I find the concept [of eternal conscious torment] intolerable and do not understand how people can live with it without either cauterizing their feelings or cracking under the strain." Nevertheless, he said, "our emotions are a fluctuating, unreliable guide to truth," and the only trustworthy resource is the Bible itself.[12]

Stott's arguments included the following:[13]

- **Language.** "The vocabulary of 'destruction' is often used in relation to the final state of perdition," he said. "It would seem strange, therefore, if people who are said to suffer destruction are in fact not destroyed."
- **Imagery.** The metaphor of fire is used to describe hell. "The main function of fire is not to cause pain, but to secure destruction, as all the world's incinerators bear witness," Stott said. While the Bible calls the fire "eternal" and "unquenchable," it would be "very odd if what is thrown into it proves indestructible."

Also, while Jesus contrasts "eternal life" and "eternal punishment" in the parable of the sheep and goats in Matthew 25:31–46, "he did not in that passage define the nature of either," said Stott. As for Jesus' parable of Lazarus and the rich man, Stott said it's "not incompatible . . . with their final annihilation."

He acknowledged that Revelation says those in the lake of fire "will be tormented day and night forever and ever." But he said this refers to the devil, the beast, and the false prophet, as well as "the harlot Babylon." Stott said they "are not individual people but symbols of the world in its varied hostility to God," and they cannot experience pain. "The most natural way to understand the reality behind the imagery is that ultimately all enmity and resistance to God will be destroyed," he said.

- **Justice.** Stott said biblical justice requires God to judge people according to what they have done, which implies a penalty commensurate with the evil committed. He asked, "Would there not, then, be a serious disproportion between sins consciously committed in time and torment consciously experienced throughout eternity?"

Stott also said that "the eternal existence of the impenitent in hell would be hard to reconcile with the promises of God's final victory over evil." He asked how God can reconcile all things to himself through Christ[14] and "'be everything to everybody'[15] while an unspecified number of people still continue in rebellion against him."

Wrote Stott, "It would be easier to hold together the awful reality of hell and the universal reign of God if hell means destruction and the impenitent are no more."

Are his arguments persuasive? Does the Bible affirm that the unrepentant will suffer the ultimate death penalty? To test these issues, I continued my conversation with philosopher Paul Copan, who adheres to the traditional view that hell involves eternal conscious torment.

Continuing Interview with Paul Copan

Seeking to take Copan's temperature on conditional immortality, I read him the closing words of Stott's chapter in *Rethinking Hell*: "I also believe that the ultimate annihilation of the wicked should at least be accepted as a legitimate, biblically founded alternative to their eternal conscious torment."[16]

"Is annihilationism heretical, or does it fall under the umbrella of orthodoxy?" I asked.

Copan put down his cup of water. "I believe it's a secondary issue," came his response. "It's not a major doctrinal deviation, even if I disagree with it. There's some precedent among a few early church fathers who held this view, and there are solid evangelical scholars who embrace it. When conditionalism is the position of someone as biblically sound and well-respected as John Stott, we should be very careful about using the 'heretical' label."

"How strong is their case?"

"They rally significant biblical support," he said. "They cite such biblical language as *destruction*, *perish*, and *death*, as well as images of trees being cut down or chaff and branches being burned.[17] The New Testament talks about God's judgment being a raging fire that will consume the enemies of God.[18] Jude refers to the destruction of Sodom and Gomorrah[19] as 'an example by undergoing the punishment of eternal fire.'[20] If these cities were incinerated, shouldn't that foreshadow the fate of the unrepentant? Second Peter 2:6 suggests this—these cities were burned to ashes and made to be an example of what is going to happen to the ungodly."

I raised an eyebrow. "You sound sympathetic to their cause."

"A number of biblical texts appear to support their position. *However*," he said, raising his index finger and drawing out that word, "we have to consider the entire range of biblical teaching. Personally, their treatment of certain passages doesn't go far enough to convince me. That's why I still endorse the traditional view. The case for conditionalism, in my opinion, falls short."

"Do you take the position that annihilation is impossible because every person's soul is immortal?"

"The doctrine of the immortality of the soul is actually a Greek concept that people like Plato espoused. For him, the body is the prison of the soul, and death is a welcomed relief for the soul. As the historian of theology Jaroslav Pelikan has pointed out, Christian theology came to assimilate this idea.[21]

"The soul—that is, the self—is the basis for personal continuity, and the soul persists even after bodily death," Copan continued. "After death, the soul can exist without the body in the intermediate state and prior to the final resurrection. But this condition isn't ideal—it's what Paul calls a state of nakedness.[22] Immortality in Scripture is connected to resurrection—more specifically, to all redeemed people receiving their indestructible resurrection bodies."[23]

He went on. "Some conditionalists claim that the immortality of the soul fed the idea that all humans—whether saved or unredeemed—would endure forever. I would argue that all humans will be raised with bodies—the redeemed having immortal resurrection bodies like Christ's, and the unredeemed receiving bodies that enable them to physically exist in their state of restlessness—a 'resurrection to judgment.'[24] Their bodies are sustained in existence by God, but they don't enjoy the quality of life that believers have in the new earth. Their ongoing existence does not qualify as 'immortal.'"

Jesus the Annihilationist?

Was Jesus an annihilationist? Agnostic New Testament professor Bart Ehrman thinks so. "A close reading of Jesus's words shows that in fact he had no idea of torment for sinners after death," writes the controversial scholar. "Their punishment is that they will be annihilated, never allowed to exist again."[25] As an example, Jesus talks of two gates through which a person can pass—the broad gate leading to "destruction." Said Ehrman, "Jesus does not say it leads to eternal torture."

"What's your assessment?" I asked Copan.

"Granted, Jesus doesn't say 'eternal torture,' but he does talk about the wailing and gnashing of teeth. The idea that Jesus had no idea of torment for sinners after death is problematic for several reasons."

"For instance?"

"For one thing, there was a variety of Jewish views about the afterlife, including everlasting conscious torment. The first-century Jewish historian Josephus refers to the Pharisees as holding that the wicked are 'punished with eternal torment' and experience 'eternal imprisonment.'[26] Second, there's the story Jesus tells about the rich man and Lazarus in Luke 16, which clearly presupposes torment for the wicked."

I interrupted. "Ehrman claims the author of the gospel put this known rabbinic story into Jesus' mouth."

Copan smiled. "That's disputed," he replied. "But nevertheless, Jesus uses images of weeping and gnashing of teeth to describe the state of separation from God, which doesn't sound like immediate extinction to me.[27] What's more, Jesus was clearly familiar with such texts as Daniel 12:2, which speak of those who would be resurrected to everlasting contempt."

That verse reads, "Multitudes who sleep in the dust of the earth will awake: some to everlasting life, others to shame and everlasting contempt." As one author observed, "There is no way to escape the obvious grammatical contrast between the unending well-being of the righteous and the unending shame and contempt of the wicked. To limit the suffering of the wicked without limiting the bliss of the righteous is grammatically impossible."[28]

"So you don't think Jesus was an annihilationist," I said, more as a statement than a question.

"No, I don't. Consider his teaching about sheep and goats in Matthew 25, where Jesus says in verse 46 that the unredeemed 'will go away to eternal punishment.' Jesus not only says in verse 41 that the *fire* for the unredeemed will be eternal, but here he emphasizes that the *punishment itself* will be eternal. That's a formidable challenge for annihilationists."

"Annihilationists say that the Greek word for the adjective *eternal*—*aionios*—can sometimes mean 'pertaining to the age,'" I pointed out.[29]

"Sometimes, yes," said Copan. "But listen to verse 46 in context: 'Then they will go away to eternal punishment, but the righteous to eternal life.' You can't escape the obvious parallelism. If life in heaven will be eternal, then you need to conclude that life in hell would be eternal too."

Indeed, Augustine made the same observation sixteen hundred years ago. He said in *The City of God*, "As the eternal life of the saints shall be endless, so too the eternal punishment of those who are doomed to it shall have no end."[30]

Copan also noted that Jesus says in verse 41 that the cursed will be thrown "into the eternal fire prepared for the devil and his angels." Asked Copan, "What happens to the devil and his minions? Revelation 20:10 says they will be cast into the lake of fire and 'tormented day and night for ever and ever'—a fate, it appears, that will be shared by the unrepentant."

He added, "The Greek verb for *torment*—*basanismo*—indicates conscious suffering. We see this throughout the New

Testament. Revelation 14:11 says that 'the smoke of their [unbelievers'] torment will rise for ever and ever.' As New Testament scholar G. K. Beale said, the word for torment is used nowhere in Revelation or biblical literature in the sense of annihilation of personal existence. Revelation, without exception, uses it of conscious suffering on the part of people."[31]

I looked up from the notes I was furiously scribbling. "These are serious challenges to the annihilation theory," I said.

"They are—and there are others too."

Biblical Obstacles to Annihilationism

I asked Copan about the verses that talk about the destruction of the unredeemed. "As Bart Ehrman pointed out, Jesus said the broad gate leads to 'destruction.'[32] On the surface, that sounds an awful lot like annihilation."

"Hold on a moment," Copan replied. "Destruction doesn't always mean cease to exist."

That seemed counterintuitive. "Really?" I asked. "Can you give an example?"

"Yes, 2 Peter 3:6 says that the world in Noah's day was destroyed. But we know it actually continued to endure. The same Greek word for destroy—apollymi—can be translated as 'lost,' as in the story about the lost—but existing—coin in Luke 15:9. Also, a 'second death' doesn't necessarily suggest being extinguished. After all, we were once dead in our trespasses and sins, though physically alive."[33]

"What other passages argue against annihilationism?"

"There's 2 Thessalonians 1:9, which says the unrepentant will be 'punished with everlasting destruction and shut out from the presence of the Lord.' Why mention being excluded from God's presence if 'everlasting destruction' means they have totally perished? In contrast, 1 Thessalonians 4:17 says believers 'will be with the Lord forever.' Again, we see a parallel, indicating ongoing existence for both the redeemed and the unredeemed."

Copan went on to discuss several other New Testament passages that make more sense if hell involves eternal consciousness:

- "Consider Judas. Jesus said in Mark 14:21 that it would have been better for him if he had not been born. That doesn't sound like Jesus is speaking of him moving from nonexistence to existence and then back into nonexistence again. The weightiness of Jesus' pronouncement is far more damning than that. Jesus has in mind more than simply Judas's permanent reputation of infamy.
- "Jesus said it would be better to be maimed—without an eye or a hand—than to lose an intact sinning body by being thrown into hell.[34] But if people simply cease to exist at some point after death, then this worry doesn't make sense. Interestingly, one scholar said that 'if hell is just lack of conscious existence, there would be a lot of situations in which people would find that to be more desirable than suffering as a maimed person in this life.'[35]
- "Jesus says blasphemy against the Holy Spirit will not be forgiven, 'either in this age or in the age to come.'[36] This suggests that those committing this sin would continue to exist in eternity.
- "In John 3:36, Jesus says that whoever rejects the Son will not see life, for God's wrath abides on them. How does the wrath of God abide on someone who doesn't exist?
- "Paul's use of the term 'everlasting destruction'[37] is a specific reference to the intertestamental Jewish book 4 Maccabees, which is the only place this phrase is used in the relevant literature. And this book has several places that talk about conscious awareness in judgment—not annihilationism.[38]

- "Annihilationists say the language of fire suggests the finality of existence. But it's curious that Jesus refers to the worm not dying and the fire not being quenched.[39] Why would he say that if he's just talking about a cessation of existence? Worms don't continue once something is consumed. Yes, fire is figurative language, but if a person ceases to exist, why emphasize that the fire does not go out?

  "And if the unregenerate will also be raised bodily, though not in glory, why emphasize the image of 'immortal' worms continuing to feed on their body? Worms' unending feeding on a physical body in hell—a picture of torment—is far more severe than death or extinction itself. What's the big deal about a worm feeding on your body if you no longer exist? The same kind of language is found in the intertestamental book of Judith; there it refers to God's judgment in sending 'fire and worms into their flesh; they shall weep in pain forever.'[40] It appears that this final state of torment is worse than mere death itself. All of this suggests that something more than annihilationism is going on here."

God's Triumph over Evil

In the previous chapter, Copan had already offered answers to the questions that John Stott raised about God's justice and proportionality of hell. But I also wanted to ask Copan what he thought of another statement by Stott: "The eternal existence of the impenitent in hell would be hard to reconcile with the promises of God's final victory over evil."[41]

Copan took a moment to ponder the question. "Here's my thinking," he said. "The fact that righteousness will dwell in the new heaven and the new earth, according to 2 Peter 3:13, is sufficient indication that good has triumphed over evil. That is, God has won the final victory. I don't believe that universal salvation or even the eradication of all evildoers is a requirement for divine victory."

I flipped my notebook closed. We could continue discussing this topic all day—in fact, entire books have been written to explore these issues. But I thought we had covered the salient points.

"As I said, annihilationists can present a good case for their position," Copan said in summary. "But to me it's insufficient to overcome the historic understanding of hell within the Christian tradition. This goes back to the earliest church fathers. For example, the apostle John's disciple Polycarp said just before he was burned alive for his faith, 'You threaten me with fire which burns for an hour, and is then extinguished, but you know nothing of the fire of the coming judgment and eternal punishment, reserved for the ungodly. Why are you waiting? Bring on whatever you want.'"[42]

Robert Peterson, a traditionalist who teamed up with annihilationist Edward Fudge to write *Two Views of Hell: A Biblical and Theological Dialogue*, said he fears the typical back-and-forth dialogue between the two camps might lead some to believe the arguments must necessarily come to a standoff.[43]

"That is simply not the case," he said. "Despite good intentions, the conditionalist exegesis of the key texts falls short."[44]

All of which leaves universalism—the idea that everyone is redeemed in the end—as the remaining logical alternative to an eternal hell. I wanted to quiz Copan to see whether this theological view makes any biblical sense.

Universalism: Will All Be Saved?

The idea of eternal conscious torment in hell is "morally corrupt, contrary to justice, perverse, inexcusably cruel, deeply irrational, and essentially wicked." Indeed, if everlasting hell were true, then "Christianity should be dismissed as a self-evident morally obtuse and logically incoherent faith."[45]

So says influential academic theologian David Bentley Hart of the University of Notre Dame in his often-acerbic 2019 book *That All Shall Be Saved*, a 224-page screed with 118 derogatory comments about theologians who disagree with him, their views, their God, and their understanding of hell.[46] Indeed, theologian Douglas Farrow says Hart "all but exhausts the world's stock of insults."[47]

Former pastor Rob Bell puts it in a kinder, gentler way in his bestseller *Love Wins*, where he writes approvingly of universalism. "At the heart of this perspective is the belief that, given enough time, everybody will turn to God and find themselves in the joy and peace of God's presence," he writes. "The love of God will melt every hard heart, and even the most 'depraved sinners' will eventually give up their resistance and turn to God."[48]

Christian universalism says in the end God will forgive and adopt all people through Christ—perhaps after a limited period of restorative punishment in hell for some. Thus, says Hart, "I for one do not object in the least to Hitler being purged of his sins and saved."[49]

Universalists emphasize God's overarching narrative of creation, the fall, then Christ reconciling everything—and everybody—to himself. They cite such verses as Titus 2:11 ("For the grace of God has appeared that offers salvation to all people"); John 12:32 ("And I, when I am lifted up from the earth, will draw all people to myself"); 1 Corinthians 15:22 ("For as in Adam all die, so in Christ all will be made alive"); and 2 Peter 3:9 ("The Lord is . . . not wanting anyone to perish, but everyone to come to repentance").

"Christian universalism is a minority voice within the church, but it is not some new-fangled liberal theology," said universalist Robin Parry. "It is, rather, an ancient Christian theological position that in the early church stood alongside annihilation and eternal torment as a viable Christian opinion."[50]

The best-known early advocate of universalism was Origen (ca. 185–254), whose views were declared heretical by the fifth ecumenical church council in 553.[51] "For over 1,600 years, hardly any major theologians argued that everyone will be saved," said Francis Chan and Preston Sprinkle in *Erasing Hell*. "This all began to change in the 1800s, when several thinkers resurrected Origen's beliefs and put them back on the table."[52]

In recent decades, there has been an uptick in interest, driven among academics by the writings of Swiss theologian Karl Barth and among the broader public by Rob Bell's high-profile ministry, which has attained the heights of Oprah.

The Power to Say No to God

Copan's reaction to universalism was firm. "I believe universalism is an aberrant and dangerous doctrine," he said flatly. "You certainly get no hint of it in the Old Testament, where Psalm 1:6 reads, 'For the LORD watches over the way of the righteous, but the way of the wicked leads to destruction.'"

"Can a person be both a Christian and a universalist?" I asked.

"Universalists can be authentic Christians. The nineteenth-century Scottish pastor and author George MacDonald was a universalist who profoundly influenced C. S. Lewis. Lewis praised him as being 'continually close . . . to the Spirit of Christ Himself.'[53] Still, universalism falls outside the pale of the mainstream Christian tradition, although there are pockets of it in church history."

"Certainly, there's an emotional tug to it," I commented.

"Yes, who doesn't want everyone to be saved? Even God desires it!" he declared, his eyes widening. "As 1 Timothy 2:4 and 2 Peter 3:9 say, he wants all to come to a knowledge of the truth. But Christ is the *potential* Savior of all, not the *actual* Savior of all.[54] In other words, salvation is *universal in intent*—that is, God's desired will—but it's not achieved *in fact*—that is, God's permissive will. While salvation is *potentially* offered to all, not all freely accept it.[55]

"The Scriptures," he continued, "repeatedly indicate there will always be creatures who fully and finally say *no* to God. Finite, moral agents—whether angelic or human—have the capacity to choose contrary to God's moral order. Only God is necessarily good; he cannot do what is wrong. The same isn't true for contingent moral creatures like us who can choose lesser finite goods over the Ultimate Good. They can turn a good thing into a God substitute and fall prey to idolatry."

I interrupted to say, "In Colossians 1:16, Christ is said to have been the agent through whom 'all things' were created. Four verses later, he is called the agent through whom 'all things' are to be reconciled. Doesn't that sound suspiciously like universalism?"

"You have to keep reading to get the full picture," Copan answered. "Paul goes on to say 'now he has reconciled you . . . *if* you continue in your faith, established and firm, and do not move from the hope held out in the gospel.'[56] So there's a condition there. We see something similar in Romans 5—just as 'all' in Adam fall, so 'all' in Christ—the second Adam—are reconciled to God. But these aren't identical groups. To be 'in Adam'—the old, fallen humanity—is to face condemnation; to be part of the new humanity 'in Christ' through faith is to experience redemption."

I nodded. "In other words, you're in one camp or the other."

"Right. And you can't disconnect these texts from what Paul says elsewhere—that some will end up 'shut out from the presence of the Lord,'[57] or that those who preach a false gospel are 'under God's curse.'"[58]

"What about the Bible's use of the word *all* to describe those who are ultimately redeemed, as in 1 Timothy 2:6, which says Jesus 'gave himself as a ransom for all people'?"

"Again, we need to examine that word closely. For example, when the gospel of Mark says 'all the people of Jerusalem' flocked to be baptized by John, he doesn't mean every single individual was doing that. It simply meant a lot of people.[59] In this case, Jesus did pay for all the sins of the world and made grace available to all sinners, but we have to accept that payment on our behalf if we're going to benefit from it. Not everyone will do that."

"What about Jesus' mission, which was 'to seek and to save the lost.'[60] If some were actually left behind, did he fail?"

"No, he didn't consider it to be a failure just because there would be those who refused to take the narrow road. Jesus acknowledged that the eleven disciples the Father had given to him were preserved, even though 'the son of perdition'—Judas— didn't truly belong to Jesus.[61] At the cross, Jesus completed his mission: 'It is finished.'[62] Isaiah 53 says God would see the anguished death of his Suffering Servant as an atoning work that would 'justify many'[63]—even if not all would embrace the Messiah. Jesus identified with us in life and death in order to save those who would choose the narrow path.

"Think of the parable of the prodigal son," he added. "Jesus leaves his hearers with this implicit challenge: Will we go inside to celebrate with the repentant sinner, or will we stay outside as the self-righteous older brother? God doesn't cancel the celebration just because there are some who don't want to go inside. Why should God defer to the naysayers over the willing participants? It's up to humans to say yes or no to God's initiating grace. Jesus' very teaching assumes that some will embrace him while others will not—a point that the parable of the four soils makes in Matthew 13."

The Freedom to Say No

I scanned through some notes before finding the quote I was searching for. "The commentary author William Barclay said, 'If one man remains outside the love of God at the end of time, it means that that one man has defeated the love of God—and that is impossible.'"[64]

I barely completed the sentence before Copan jumped in. "But," he said, "we can't ignore the many Scriptures that indicate some will have their own way and get their divorce from God, despite his best efforts. God doesn't force his love on people. Jude 21 reminds us, 'Keep yourselves in God's love.' That suggests that we can remove ourselves from God's loving influence. If God's 'undefeatable sovereignty' means that all will be saved, how is this accomplished since it's up to human beings whether to accept or reject God's initiating grace? Even divine love can be resisted.

"We routinely read in Scripture that God does his utmost to reach people, only to be rebuffed. God actually appears exasperated at the rebellion of his people. For example, in the parable of the vineyard in Isaiah 5, when Israel produces 'bad fruit,' God asks, 'What more could have been done for my vineyard'—that is, Israel—'than I have done for it?'

"In Matthew 23, Jesus weeps over Jerusalem, longing to gather the city as a hen gathers her chicks, but Jerusalem refused. In Acts 7:51, before he was stoned, Stephen accuses his stiff-necked persecutors of always resisting the Holy Spirit. For stubborn rebels, the more God pours out his grace, the more they want to flee. They want to find happiness on their own terms."

With that, Copan pulled out a quote from C. S. Lewis: "I would pay any price to be able to say truthfully, 'All will be saved.' But my reason retorts, 'Without their will, or with it?' If I say, 'Without their will,' I at once perceive a contradiction; how can the supreme voluntary act of self-surrender be involuntary? If I say, 'With their will,' my reason replies, 'How, if they *will not* give in?'"[65]

"It seems," said Copan, "that a number of universalists who believe in robust libertarian free will and aren't sympathetic to Calvinism still assume a kind of 'irresistible grace.'"

"Still," I said, "Philippians 2:10–11 says 'every knee should bow . . . and every tongue acknowledge that Jesus Christ is Lord.' Doesn't this suggest that everyone will eventually come to faith?"

"But will they bow *willingly*?" Copan responded. "Paul is citing Isaiah 45:23 there, and he's aware that not all bowing before God springs from humble, repentant hearts. God's defeated foes will bow before him in shameful, reluctant acknowledgment that he is Lord.[66] Just a few chapters later, Isaiah 49:23 indicates that some will bow down before God and lick the dust at his feet. His enemies exhibit a feigned obedience. In Psalm 81:15 (NASB), the psalmist says, 'Those who hate the LORD would pretend to obey Him, and their time of punishment would be forever.'"

Salvation after Death?

Logically speaking, universalism would only "work" if God were to allow people to repent *after* their death. I mentioned to Copan that some Christian thinkers, such as Martin Luther, have left open this possibility.

Wrote Luther, "It would be quite a different question whether God can impart faith to some in the hour of death or after death so that these people could be saved through faith. Who would doubt God's ability to do that? No one, however, can prove that he does do this."[67]

"Yes, in that quotation Martin Luther—who was *not* a universalist—at least opens up the idea of postmortem opportunity[68] for certain uninformed persons to hear and understand the gospel clearly so they may be saved through faith in Christ. Interestingly, in another place, Luther called the Roman statesman Cicero 'the best philosopher' and 'a valuable man,' adding, 'I hope God will forgive such men as Cicero their sins.'[69] In this spirit, some theologians argue that certain persons may have a chance after death to hear the gospel clearly presented and to decide about Jesus in a fully informed manner."

I interrupted. "Who would these 'certain persons' be?"

"Those without special revelation before Christ, the

unevangelized, those who die in infancy, those who are mentally disabled, and the pseudo-evangelized."

That was a new term for me. "What does *pseudo-evangelized* mean?"

"I didn't coin it, but the term refers to those whose understanding of the Christian faith has been distorted by misrepresentations or caricatures."

"What are some examples?"

"For instance, Jews who have been persecuted by so-called 'Christians' and have been called 'Christ killers' could well have associated the gospel with anti-Semitism. The philosopher Jerry Walls agrees—God may give the unevangelized or those who only heard a muddled gospel a chance to respond to a proper explanation after death."[70]

I pressed Copan for clarity. "How widely does God extend this offer?"

"First, according to this position, those who have knowingly rejected the clear gospel message in this life won't receive any such postmortem opportunity. It's only for those who haven't heard the gospel, didn't hear it clearly articulated, or for some reason were prevented from grasping it. Second, even for those who do receive this postmortem opportunity, it isn't available indefinitely. These persons make their choice and then live forever with the consequences."

Copan reminded me that the respected Reformed theologian J. Oliver Buswell Jr., former president of Wheaton College, said that those who die in infancy are capable of accepting Christ because of the Spirit's work of enlarging their intelligence.[71] Copan said that theologians holding to postmortem opportunity could press this comment further. "They could say it isn't a huge theological stretch that the intelligence of these infants could be enlarged *just after* death. Such a suggestion about postmortem opportunity wouldn't threaten orthodoxy in any serious way."

Exploring the "Luther Option"

When I pushed back on this idea of salvation after death—saying "it sounds pretty speculative"—Copan acknowledged that this was true to a point. "Biblical support for postmortem salvation is inferred rather than direct, and one should certainly not rely on sheer speculation."

"Absolutely, I agree," I said.

"But," he continued, "while there's no clear specific text that allows for postmortem conversions, there are no particular verses, as far as I can tell, that decisively exclude it. We also must consider other theological truths: God loves the whole world,[72] has made saving provision for the 'whole world,'[73] desires for all to be saved,[74] and commands each person to repent."[75]

One conflicting verse sprang to mind. I asked Copan about Hebrews 9:27, which affirms that "people are destined to die once, and after that to face judgment."

He responded by asking, "But does that judgment follow *instantly* on the heels of physical death? We're not told. The next verse suggests that this is merely a general sequence. After all, Jesus after having been 'sacrificed once' will then 'appear a second time . . . to bring salvation.' There are two thousand years between those two events! Perhaps Luther's own hopefulness reminds us that we should leave open certain divine options that may not be expressly revealed to us."

I asked Copan about the implications of this view. "How does this affect the Great Commission? After all, why preach the gospel if those who would respond affirmatively to it will get to do so in the afterlife?"

"Luther would insist that we should share the gospel simply because Christ commanded it—full stop. This is in the spirit of how Jesus replied to Peter when he asked about the fate of 'the disciple whom Jesus loved.' Jesus responded by saying, 'What is that to you? Preach the gospel!'[76] Also, we know that God sometimes uses unconventional methods of reaching people—for instance, through Jesus appearing in dreams to Muslims, who have then found salvation.[77] That doesn't stop us from endeavoring to make disciples of all the nations."

"Are there other reasons to leave open the 'Luther option' on postmortem salvation?" I asked.

"To critics who say God isn't obvious enough—for instance, that he's too hidden or the gospel message is too distorted—theologians like Luther would reply that God may well give full opportunity for people to encounter God and understand the gospel thoroughly, even if this means it's after their death.

"After all, Luther asserted, why assume the clear communication of God's love is restricted to this life? That isn't the case for those with mental impairments or infants who die. If God commands each person without exception to repent,[78] then wouldn't he surely give each person sufficient grace to fulfill that command—despite their incapacities, ignorance, or unwitting inaccurate views of the gospel?"

Opiate for Theologians

The idea of salvation after death was intriguing and certainly warranted further investigation. Still, much of it still seemed speculative to me. However, universalism absolutely depends on postmortem conversions being possible; if it's impossible on a broad scale to receive salvation after death, then universalism fails.

On the other hand, even if postmortem salvations were true, it wouldn't necessarily mean universalism is true. Perhaps, as the "postmortem opportunity" theologian would argue, only certain people who didn't get a fair chance to respond to the gospel in this world might have postmortem opportunities for salvation, not every human being who has ever lived in world history.

Copan had already offered a strong critique of universalism, but I asked him to conclude with any other reasons this view falls short biblically.

He replied by saying, "Both the Old and New Testaments reveal the opposite of universalism. We see the contrast between the righteous and unrighteous in Psalms, Proverbs, and Daniel 12:2, which talks about those awakening to 'everlasting life' and others to 'shame and everlasting contempt.' In the New Testament, there's the judgment of the sheep and goats,[79] or the simple contrast in John 3:16 between those who have 'eternal life' and those who 'perish.'

"In Revelation 13:8, we find a limited, unexpanding number of names written in the Lamb's 'book of life'—without which one cannot be in the presence of God.[80] In Romans 9:3, Paul wished he could be condemned so that his Israelite brothers and sisters could be saved. Matthew 12:31–32 talks about the unpardonable sin that won't be forgiven in the life to come. When asked whether only a few would be saved, Jesus replied in Luke 13:24, 'Make every effort to enter through the narrow door, because many, I tell you, will try to enter and will not be able to.' None of these fit the universalist narrative."

For a magazine article in 2019, Copan interviewed Michael McClymond, professor of modern Christianity at St. Louis University, about his masterful two-volume historical and theological analysis of universalism called *The Devil's Redemption*,[81] a 1,325-page tome with 3,500 footnotes, written partly in response to Rob Bell's popularization of the discredited doctrine.

"Universalism isn't just a theological mistake," McClymond said. "It's also a symptom of deeper problems. In a culture characterized by moralistic therapeutic deism, universalism fits the age we inhabit . . . Universalism is the opiate of the theologians. It's the way we would want the world to be. Some imagine that a more loving and less judgmental church would be better positioned to win new adherents. Yet perfect love appeared in history—and he was crucified."[82]

So where does all of this leave us? With the traditional view of hell, which should chasten us and motivate us to tell as many people as we can that there *is* indeed a judgment, but there is also a divinely ordained escape route—that is, the gift of eternal life that God freely offers to everyone who will receive it in repentance and faith.

Francis Chan says his grandmother's death was the saddest moment in his life. "When that EKG monitor flatlined, I freaked out," he said. "I absolutely lost it! According to what I knew of the Bible, she was headed for a life of never-ending suffering. I thought I would go crazy. I have never cried harder, and I don't ever want to feel like that again. Since that day, I have tried not to think about it. It has been over twenty years . . . I would love to erase hell from the pages of Scripture."[83]

But, of course, hell can't be erased; it can't be ignored. It can't be papered over with thin tissues of bad exegesis or philosophized out of existence, and so we need to study it with fear and trembling, with tears and courage—and then resolve once more to bring as many people to heaven with us as we can.

Chan said that when a friend asks him the question he dreads—"Do you think I'm going to hell?"—he wishes he could scoff and say, "No! There's no such place!"[84]

But he doesn't have that option—and neither do we. At least, not if we're going to faithfully follow the Scriptures, as difficult and heartrending as they may be at times. Yes, there's much we don't understand, and God can work in people's hearts in unconventional ways. But theological speculations can't obliterate the reality of hell.

Fortunately, while hell is a hard truth, it's not the *only* truth in Scripture. I'm grateful that Jesus is *the* truth,[85] and that through him, the gates to heaven can be opened.

CHAPTER 9

The Reincarnation Sensation[1]

What If Life Is Cyclical?

*While we cannot, of course, decide the
truthfulness of a belief by head count, the
influence of reincarnation in our 'Westernized'
society is certainly surprising.*

PHILOSOPHER GARY HABERMAS,

IMMORTALITY: THE OTHER SIDE OF DEATH

When I was young, the astonishing case of Bridey Murphy plunged America into what *Life* magazine called a "hypnotizzy," fueling a national fascination with the idea of reincarnation.[2]

Forget heaven and hell—her case and others like it are cited as proof that after death, people are repeatedly reborn into new life. In fact, this radically different view of the afterlife is embraced by an estimated 1.4 billion people around the planet.[3] But is reincarnation true?

The Bridey Murphy craze blossomed in the 1950s after a twenty-nine-year-old Chicago-born housewife named Virginia Tighe was repeatedly put into a trance by hypnotist Morey Bernstein, a proponent of reincarnation.

While under hypnosis, Virginia stunned listeners by claiming she was Bridey Murphy, born in 1798 to Duncan and Kathleen

Murphy in the Irish town of Cork. Speaking in a light Irish brogue, she described her upbringing and eventual marriage at age twenty to Sean Brian Joseph MacCarthy. He became a barrister in 1847 and also taught at Queens University in Belfast. They had no children. In her early sixties, Bridey suffered broken bones in a bad fall. She "withered away" and died at the age of sixty-six.[4]

"Bernstein as well as the others attending the [hypnotic] sessions found several of the features of Bridey's responses overwhelmingly convincing," said Paul Edwards in his book *Reincarnation*. "Her Irish brogue seemed entirely genuine. She constantly used strange Irish words and she seemed to possess a wealth of information about nineteenth-century Ireland."[5]

At one point, she even danced an Irish jig. "The episode was doubly impressive because Virginia was known to be a poor dancer," Edwards said. "She was also not given to reading books and, according to Bernstein's account, there is no evidence that she had ever engaged in the study of Irish history and customs. When the tapes were played back to Virginia and her husband, they became convinced that her recollections were authentic. Neither had believed in reincarnation prior to the hypnotic sessions, but they could not conceive of any other explanation of the material on the tapes."[6]

Her case was reported in the media and became a national sensation. Bernstein's 1956 book *The Search for Bridey Murphy* hit number one on the *New York Times* bestseller list, was subsequently translated into thirty languages, and was condensed in more than forty newspapers. The *New York Times* called it "a parapsychological classic."[7] Bridey Murphy costume parties, where people were invited to "come as you *were*," broke out around the country. The Time-Life book *Psychic Voyages* called Bridey Murphy the "all-time superstar" among cases of previous lives recovered through hypnosis.[8]

"The Bridey Murphy mania reached a tragic climax," said Edwards, "when a nineteen-year-old newsboy in Shawnee, Oklahoma, shot himself with a rifle leaving a note that said 'I am curious about the Bridey Murphy story—so I am going to investigate the theory in person.'"[9]

Ever since the Bridey Murphy phenomenon, enthusiasm for reincarnation has only grown in popular culture, thanks partly to notable entertainers who profess past lives.

"I know that I must have been many different people in many different times," said actress Shirley MacLaine.[10] She claimed, for example, that she had been a court jester who was beheaded by Louis XV "for telling impertinent jokes."[11] Actor Sylvester Stallone said he shared a similar fate in a prior existence, having been decapitated during the French Revolution. Oh, and he added that he may very well have been a monkey in Guatemala.[12]

Country singer Loretta Lynn believes she has been reincarnated at least half a dozen times, including as a Cherokee princess and a maid for a king of England.[13] But the Golden Globe–winning actress Anne Francis topped it all. She declared, "I was Mary Magdalene's mother!"[14]

Salvation, Damnation, or Reincarnation

Belief in reincarnation has had a profound impact worldwide. Said William Alger, known for his work in comparative religions, "No other doctrine has exerted so extensive, controlling, and permanent an influence upon mankind as that of the metempsychosis [or reincarnation]—the notion that when the soul leaves the body it is born anew in another body, its rank, character, circumstances, and experience in each successive existence depending on its qualities, deeds, and attainments in its preceding lives."[15]

The roots of reincarnation run deep in history. In the sixth century BC, Greek philosopher Pythagoras believed in some form of transmigration of the human soul.[16] Writing in the fourth century BC, Plato described the soul's "continued rebirth"[17] and said that "by making the right use of the things remembered from the former life, by constantly perfecting himself in the perfect mysteries, a man becomes truly perfect."[18]

In the Bhagavad Gita ("The Song of God"), the Hindu scriptures that date back 2,200 to 2,400 years, the god Krishna assures his disciple Arjuna that it's unnecessary to feel sorrow over someone's death. Said Krishna, "Death is inevitable for the living; birth is inevitable for the dead . . . The Self of all beings, living within the body, is eternal and cannot be harmed. Therefore, do not grieve."[19]

Merriam-Webster offers a succinct definition of reincarnation: "rebirth in new bodies or forms of life, *especially*: a rebirth of a soul in a new human body."[20] Most forms of reincarnation include animals as well. In Latin the word *reincarnation* literally means "to come again in the flesh."[21]

One writer boiled it down this way: "Nearly a billion Hindus have for thousands of years held a cyclical view of life. You are born. You live. You die. And because nobody's perfect, your soul is born again and will continue to be born again until the negative karmic imprints on your soul from bad thoughts, words or deeds have been expunged."[22] In many versions, the ultimate destination isn't paradise; rather, it's being absorbed into The Absolute or The Void.

But brief definitions only hint at the complexity of the subject. One book sets forth no less than ten distinct models of reincarnation.[23] Hinduism, Buddhism, Jainism, and Sikhism each offer their own variations on the reincarnation theme—not to mention permutations of the doctrine in contemporary Western beliefs and even in African tribal traditions.

Even so, some common threads can be identified in both

Eastern and Western views. For instance, theologian Norman Geisler said they all share a belief that the human race will ultimately be perfected; that progress toward perfection is made through multiple rebirths; that one's past lives influence the kind of life one will have in future incarnations (called the law of *karma*); that the self survives through successive afterlives; that the bodies into which the reincarnations occur are perishable; and that there are multiple worlds in which reincarnations can take place.[24]

Some proponents of reincarnation contend their beliefs are backed by evidence. For example, they point to cases like Bridey Murphy, where people under hypnosis mysteriously remember prior lives. These hypnotic regressions are actually "quite common" and can be "very impressive," said Edwards.[25]

There are also instances in which people—typically, youngsters—spontaneously recall details of an earlier existence. The most vigorous researcher in this area has been Ian Stevenson, professor of psychiatry and director of the division of parapsychology at the University of Virginia, who has collected well over a thousand examples.[26]

Other reincarnationists point to child prodigies, claiming that children who display extraordinary talent at a tender age could be the result of their having learned skills in a prior life. How else, they ask, can we explain Mozart composing music at age four?

In a similar way, it's common for people to experience déjà vu, the uncanny sense that they've heard something or been somewhere before. Three-quarters of respondents in one survey reported that they've had an episode of this nature.[27] Might this actually be an echo from our preexistence?

Further, there are examples of *xenoglossy* (literally, "foreign tongue"), which is when people are able to read or speak in a foreign language that they didn't learn in their current life.

Lutheran theologian Hans Schwarz says that when people converse in the other language, this constitutes the most impressive evidence for a prior life.[28]

"Jesus Taught Reincarnation"

However, if Christianity is true, as scholar Chad Meister argued in an earlier chapter, doesn't that automatically rule out reincarnation as a viable possibility? After all, Hebrews 9:27 says "people are destined to die once, and after that to face judgment." No do-overs. No working toward perfection through a succession of lifetimes.

Well, hold on a moment. There are writers who maintain that reincarnation is actually consistent with the Bible's teachings and was even originally part of Christian doctrine. Surprisingly, a survey revealed that an astounding 24 percent of Christians in America already believe in reincarnation.[29]

"Jesus taught reincarnation," declares Herbert Bruce Puryear, a psychologist and minister at an interfaith church in Arizona. "The teachings of Jesus and the concept of reincarnation are so deeply interwoven as to be part of the same tapestry."[30]

Quincy Howe Jr., who earned his doctorate at Princeton University, said the New Testament (pointing to John 9:1–3) offers "incontrovertible support for a doctrine of human preexistence" and that "a plausible case can be made that Jesus and John the Baptist accepted reincarnation."[31]

Geddes MacGregor, distinguished professor of philosophy emeritus at the University of Southern California, said "there is remarkable support for [the doctrine of reincarnation] in Scripture, in the Fathers, and in later Christian literature" and that reincarnation ideas "appear unexpectedly and persistently in the history of Christian thought." Why isn't this better known? He speculates these beliefs have been stifled by "ignorance, prejudice, intellectual confusion, or fear."[32] MacGregor points out that while the word *reincarnation* isn't found in the Bible, neither is the word *Trinity*, and yet overall biblical teaching supports God's triune nature. "There is no reason at all why the doctrine of reincarnation *might* not be a similar case," he said.[33]

What about these claims? Does the evidence really support reincarnation beliefs? Could multiple rebirths be a better description of the afterlife than heaven and hell? Does the Bible lend credence to repeated lifetimes? In other words, can a person be an authentic Christian and still believe in reincarnation?

As I pondered these questions, one scholar's name jumped into my mind. I logged onto the internet and booked a flight to Denver for a return visit to the cramped and book-cluttered office of noted philosopher Douglas Groothuis.

Interview #7: Douglas Groothuis, PhD

When I last met with Groothuis (pronounced GRŌTE-hice) several years ago, his wife was dying of a rare brain disorder. I came to interview him for my book *The Case for Miracles*—specifically, for a chapter on why some miracles don't occur despite our pleas to God.[34] It was one of the most profound conversations I have ever experienced. Groothuis later penned the book *Walking through Twilight*, which is a masterpiece on the topic of lament.[35] His wife, Becky, died shortly after his book came out.

Those were somber days for Groothuis. I even commented during the interview that he looked exhausted. "I *am* exhausted," he replied. "This is a daily struggle."[36]

That era left an indelible mark on Groothuis, but fortunately life has progressed for him. He fell in love with a woman he had known since high school, and they got married. He shed sixty-five pounds. He shaved off his scraggly beard. Though he naturally tends toward a melancholy personality, he is more upbeat now. He smiles—frequently. "I'm learning to be happy again," he said.

I sought out Groothuis, first, because he is a highly regarded philosopher. He earned his doctorate at the University of Oregon and is the longtime professor of philosophy at Denver Seminary. Among his eleven books is the 752-page *Christian Apologetics*, a comprehensive overview of arguments for the faith.[37]

His book *Philosophy in Seven Sentences* creatively unpacks pivotal observations from such notable Western thinkers as Socrates, Aristotle, and Kierkegaard.[38] His award-winning book *Truth Decay* persuasively defends Christianity against postmodernism.[39] His scholarly articles appear in numerous professional journals.

But, second, I pursued Groothuis because he was among the first Christian philosophers in the current era to critique Eastern religions and their influence on the blossoming New Age movement. His book *Unmasking the New Age* was published in 1986; it was followed two years later by *Confronting the New Age*; then *Revealing the New Age Jesus* came two years after that.[40] His expertise on key Eastern doctrines such as reincarnation and the law of karma are what ultimately drew me to his office at the seminary.

Our conversation unfolded on a sunny Friday afternoon, just prior to Groothuis taking his wife, Kathleen, to visit their native state of Alaska for the summer. I pulled up a chair to a small round table and placed a recorder between us.

"I Totally Bought into Reincarnation"

I began by asking Groothuis what prompted him as a Christian scholar to investigate Eastern philosophy and the New Age movement more than thirty years ago—and frankly, his answer stunned me.

"Because I used to believe in reincarnation myself," came his reply.

"Really?" I said. "Tell me about it."

"As a teenager, I got interested in Eastern spirituality because some of the musicians I liked were very influenced by Eastern

190

mysticism," he explained. "Then at college I learned about Hinduism and Buddhism. I read books about the occult and paranormal. I became quite entranced by these ideas. So for about a year, I totally bought into reincarnation."

"Then what happened?"

"After I became a Christian, I realized that the teachings of Jesus were incompatible with Eastern religions, so I spent years going back and relooking at these ideas that had once interested me so much. After I scrutinized them more thoroughly, I came to believe they weren't supported by the evidence."

"Can you see why ideas like reincarnation tend to capture so many Americans?"

"Oh, sure," he said. "They see reincarnation as offering a romantic sense of adventure. Think of it—you've lived before; you might live again. Who knows what escapades you could have? Back in the day, Shirley MacLaine talked about her previous lives and all the things she experienced. She said she had been a teacher on Atlantis before it sank. She gave colorful details, like when she was decapitated by Louis XV, her severed head landed face up and a big tear came out of one eye.[41] Now, that's the stuff of the silver screen!

"But, of course, it's a completely non-Hindu and non-Buddhist view of reincarnation. The classic teaching is that you want to *stop* being reincarnated and attain enlightenment. You don't want to come back. Your goal is to get off the so-called wheel of suffering."

"Which you do . . . how?"

"Through the law of karma, which is a kind of moral cause and effect. There's good karma and bad karma, but eventually you want to get off the wheel of karma entirely by becoming enlightened."

"In other words," I said, "the idea of karma is that you reap what you sow. Sounds fair."

"Well, Americans tend to look at it as an infinite way to better themselves from lifetime to lifetime. They import from Christianity the idea that life is worth living and an adventure. But the classic Hindu or Buddhist view sees life as disease, decay, disappointment, and injustice."

"Some people think that nirvana, the goal of reincarnation, is the equivalent of heaven," I observed.

"Actually, there's no heaven involved. Nirvana has been described as what's left when you blow out a candle, so it's the extinguishing of the self. There's no person. There's no individual. There's no relationship to anything. We're to be snuffed out, to have no desire.

"In contrast, heaven is a world of restored relationships, and as Jonathan Edwards pointed out, it's a place of pure love—lovely objects, lovely people, lovely relationships. We'll be with God, who is love, in open fellowship and in a restored creation. Love requires individuals caring about each other. You have nothing comparable to this in Buddhism and Hinduism. Nirvana is . . . well, it's really oblivion."

Logically Insupportable, Irrational, and False

I reached into my briefcase to extract some notes. "The British physicist Raynor Johnson made a bold statement," I said, flipping through pages until I came upon the quote. "He declared flatly, 'The idea of reincarnation presents no logical difficulties.'"[42] I tossed my papers on the table. "That's quite an unambiguous claim," I observed. "Is he right?"

The response from Groothuis was quick. "Not at all," he said. "Honestly, classic reincarnation beliefs face a whole raft of philosophical obstacles. Fatal ones, in my view."

I gestured for him to continue. "Give me some examples."

"First," he said, sitting up straight in his chair, "for reincarnation and karma to be true, there must be individual, personal selves that endure and continue as themselves from lifetime to lifetime."

"Granted."

"Well, that's a problem for Buddhism and Advaita Vedanta Hinduism.[43] They don't believe in the existence of individual, personal selves. That means they can't logically support the existence of selves that endure from lifetime to lifetime. Without souls, there is no possibility of reincarnation. So these religions are logically inconsistent and therefore necessarily false."

He paused for a few moments to let his argument sink in and then continued. "There are also problems with the standard teaching that we've been reincarnated an infinite number of times in the past," he said. "You see, it's impossible to traverse an actual past infinite. It's like philosopher William Lane Craig says in debates on the origin of the universe: going from an infinite past to now would be like jumping out of a bottomless pit; you'd never get to the *now*. And yet we're here. So the idea of an infinite number of past lives is also logically incoherent."

Groothuis turned his attention to karma, beginning with the fact that Hinduism and Buddhism describe it as being akin to a scientific law. Indeed, the Hindu G. R. Malkani, longtime director of the Indian Institute of Philosophy and editor of *Philosophical Quarterly*,[44] said karma "automatically produces the appropriate results like any other law in the natural domain." He added, "Nobody can cheat the law. It is as inexorable as any natural law."[45]

"Actually, karma isn't like the law of gravity, which is an impersonal law of nature," Groothuis explained. "Gravity is part of the way God fine-tuned the universe. It doesn't make decisions. Gravity works even though there's nobody there to operate it. But with karma, you're talking about a *moral* law—a totally different category.

"Moral laws are based on moral judgments, and if you're

talking about rewards and punishments, you need to have an evaluator and an administrator. If karma is true, then it's an incredibly complicated system that has to be implemented. How do you explain it apart from a mind or entity behind it?

"Now, some have tried to get around this. The British theosophist Annie Besant popularized the idea of 'the lords of karma,' which supposedly are beings that dole out karma. But most reincarnationists don't accept that."

In fact, I had just been reading *Life after Death* by mystic and media darling Deepak Chopra. He said there's no need to invoke the idea of the lords of karma. Why? "The specific calculations [for karma] are made by the universe itself," he said.[46]

"Let's face it," Groothuis added with a chuckle, "if you have to conjure up an ad hoc idea like the lords of karma to rescue a theory, it shows the theory's inherent weakness. Chopra is just ignoring a glaring problem.

"There's also the problem that we don't remember our past lives," he went on. "How fair is it that I'm being punished for something I can't even recollect? How can I possibly improve from lifetime to lifetime if I can't recall what I did previously? There's something dysfunctional about that. In addition, karma says there is no unjust suffering. Everyone ultimately gets what he or she deserves. That strikes me as counterintuitive."

"Why?"

"Think about innocent children who suffer. There's a girl in my church who has been blind and disabled from birth. Do you really want to look at little Greta, whom everyone loves, and say she did something evil in a previous existence and therefore she fully deserves to suffer in this lifetime?

"It would be reprehensible for a reincarnationist minister to tell a grieving mother that the death of her severely deformed child was deserved because of some evil done in a prior life. As Paul Edwards said, if he were that mother and a baseball bat were handy, he would clunk the minister over the head and say, 'You deserve your pain not because of a sin in a previous life but because you are a monster right now.'"[47]

All of which brought another objection to Groothuis's mind. "And by the way, maybe we shouldn't even try to help people who are suffering. Why alleviate pain? Why try to eliminate poverty? After all, these people are getting what they deserve. In fact, it would be wrong to help them because they need to pay off their bad karma. By stepping in to assist them, you're actually hurting them by short-circuiting the process."

Groothuis's conclusion was swift. "In my opinion," he said, "the notion of karma is logically insupportable and therefore irrational and false."

The Ghost of Bridey Murphy

If reincarnation is logically inconsistent, then what about the evidence that proponents cite in its favor? How would Groothuis respond to instances in which people remember details of past lives?

I rummaged through my briefcase, looking for my 1956 first edition of *The Search for Bridey Murphy*, a hardcover with its yellowed jacket still bearing the original $3.75 price tag. I paid a rare book dealer twelve times that amount for this historic copy from the initial print run.

Even today, the Bridey Murphy saga influences people toward reincarnation. In 2018, an online reviewer wrote, "I read this book when I was fifteen years old. It set the course of my spiritual path. I recently read it again . . . [and] it still inspired me and again influenced my life greatly." Added another reader, "It still rings true today."[48]

I closed my briefcase. It turns out I had forgotten to bring the vintage book along. Well, no matter. I knew Groothuis wouldn't need a prop to recall such an infamous tale. In fact, when I started to broach the topic of an American woman who supposedly had a previous life in Ireland, Groothuis jumped in.

"Bridey Murphy," he said.

"That's right," I replied. "Isn't that good evidence for reincarnation?"

Unfazed, Groothuis dismissed the case entirely. "It's only prima facie evidence, so you need to look deeper," he said. "That case was thoroughly investigated, and all of the evidence could be explained without reincarnation."

Bridey Murphy—*debunked?* Actually, yes, that's the conclusion of experts who have probed the matter carefully. Like a lot of examples of hypnotic regression, this case simply fell apart once it was closely examined.

"The case is utter and total rubbish," concluded Paul Edwards.[49] He said when fact-checkers sifted through Irish records to try to corroborate the Bridey Murphy story, they got "almost uniformly negative results on all points of importance."[50]

Under hypnosis, Virginia Tighe said she was born as Bridey Murphy on December 20, 1798, in Cork, Ireland, and died on a Sunday in 1864 in Belfast—but local records failed to support those claims. City directories from that era don't list Murphy's family. There's no record of any will from Murphy, though her husband was supposedly a lawyer. Belfast newspapers carried no obituary for her.

She recalled a wedding ceremony at St. Theresa's Church, but there was no such church in Belfast at that time. She said she lived with her husband on Dooley Road, but no such street ever existed. She said she attended Mrs. Strayne's Day School, yet there's no record of such a place. She said her husband taught at Queens University, though no faculty member by that name has ever been listed.

She said she bought a camisole at "Cadenns House," but while there's no record of such a store in Belfast, there was one by that name in the Chicago neighborhood where Tighe spent her childhood. Even though she was supposedly speaking as Bridey Murphy under hypnosis, Tighe's language was peppered with uniquely American words that someone from nineteenth-century Ireland would have never used.[51]

Interestingly, the parents with whom she lived during the early part of her life were revealed to have been part Irish. On top of that, the neighbor across the street was an Irish immigrant named Bridie Murphy Corkell.[52]

After analyzing the data, *Life* magazine said there was nothing in Bridey's story that couldn't be explained "either on the basis of occasional coincidence or on subconscious memory of overheard conversations from someone well familiar with Ireland circa 1910."[53] A noted medical hypnotist even said the Irish jig she danced would not be hard to reproduce for anyone who had seen one in a theater or movie.[54]

Further, researcher Melvin Harris said that as a youngster Tighe probably would have met "a veritable army of people" who were among the millions that toured an extensive reproduction of an Irish village, including a full-sized version of the Tower of Blarney Castle and a replica of the Blarney Stone, right there in Tighe's hometown at the Chicago World Exposition.[55]

"Thus, she could easily have acquired all her information about nineteenth-century Ireland without ever reading a book on the subject," Edwards said.[56] "The Bridey Murphy tapes were utterly worthless as evidence for reincarnation."[57]

In the end, Tighe herself seems to have changed her mind. Nearly twenty years after the Bridey Murphy hoopla, *Newsweek* carried a follow-up article on November 22, 1970, that said Tighe's hypnotic regression "has not even made her a firm believer" in past lives.[58]

So what can the infamous Bridey Murphy case tell us about the truth of reincarnation? Nothing, as it turns out. Of course, this fiasco doesn't by itself invalidate every other account about a past life. Nevertheless, it's a cautionary tale about why we should be wary of hypnotic regression.

The Danger of Hypnobabble

Pursuing that topic further, I asked Groothuis to elaborate on why he distrusts hypnosis to yield accurate information about previous lives.

"People think the subconscious is like a movie of things that have happened, or some sort of super memory that always accurately conveys the past," he explained. "Actually, the subconscious doesn't piece everything together perfectly. It's scrambled with bits of pieces of things we've seen and experienced. So maybe a person saw a film on ancient Egypt, and when a hypnotist probes about a prior life, the person calls up an image of Cleopatra and thinks, *I was Cleopatra*."

Scientists have long known that hypnosis subjects are highly suggestible and frequently seek to tell the hypnotist what they think they want to hear. Subtle cues from hypnotists can greatly influence a response.

Said reincarnation advocate Ian Stevenson, himself a psychiatrist, "When the hypnotist says, 'You will go back before your birth to another time and place,' the subject tries to oblige . . . These instructions tell the subject that he should remember something, and when he cannot do so accurately, he often furnishes an incorrect statement in order to please the hypnotist. Most subjects doing this do not realize that they are mixing truth and falsehood in what they tell the hypnotist."[59]

Writing in *Science* magazine, psychologists Kenneth Bowers and Jane Dywan put it this way: "During hypnosis, you are *creating* memories."[60]

In one study, Canadian psychologists made sure a group of subjects could not recall anything about a particular night. Then they asked a leading question under hypnosis: Did you hear a noise that awakened you? Half of the group responded by saying they had heard something. In fact, "some were so certain that they still claimed to have heard the sounds even after they were told that the hypnotist had suggested it."[61]

"I'm highly skeptical about supposed past lives discovered through hypnosis," Groothuis told me, "especially because of a phenomenon called *cryptomnesia*" (also called *cryptoamnesia*).

"Which is—what?"

"It's when a person takes in information but then forgets the source of it. He later recalls the information but believes it's from a previous life because he has no other recollection of where it came from. For example, under hypnosis he can write in a foreign language that he doesn't otherwise know. The implication is that this was his language in prior existence. But in reality, maybe he was exposed to some writing in that language in his past but simply forgot about it."

Actually, that's what happened with a patient of Canadian psychiatrist Harold Rosen. Under hypnosis, the subject began writing in Oscan, an extinct language that was spoken in southern Italy from about 500 BC to AD 100. Later, the patient insisted he knew nothing about Oscan. It would have been easy to presume that he learned this language in an earlier lifetime, perhaps as a Roman centurion in Jesus' day.

However, further hypnosis elicited the fact that he was once sitting in a library when someone beside him opened a book to the Oscan "Curse of Vibia." You guessed it—that was the curse that the patient had reproduced.[62]

Many believe that the Bridey Murphy case was the result of cryptomnesia, though some question that.[63] "Regardless," said Groothuis, "this phenomenon can account for many instances where reincarnation is unnecessarily presumed to have occurred."

Weighing Other Alternatives

The pattern, said Groothuis, is quite clear: claims of evidence for reincarnation typically have other—and far more credible—explanations.

"As for children who recall past lives—well, kids have creative imaginations," he said. "Many of these cases come from India or other societies that embrace reincarnation, and so parents might be encouraging their children to tell stories of prior lives. Even Ian Stevenson is quite modest about what he thinks the evidence shows."

In fact, Stevenson introduces his book *Children Who Remember Previous Lives* by saying that the case studies he presents shouldn't convince any skeptic that reincarnation is true. "I shall be content," he said, "if I have succeeded in making the idea of reincarnation *plausible* to persons who have not thought it was."[64]

He concedes that even his strongest cases have some weaknesses, prompting reincarnation critic Edwards to retort, "This is a gross understatement. They *all* have big holes, and they do not even begin to add up to a significant counterweight to the initial presumption against reincarnation."[65]

"What about child prodigies?" I asked Groothuis.

"People come into the world with different abilities. Some are geniuses who are way ahead of the rest of us. Why invoke this elaborate doctrine of reincarnation to explain something that seems to have more natural explanations that can account for the phenomenon? Typically, we go for the simpler explanation. You would really need powerful, multiply attested pieces of evidence in order to put reincarnation on the table as a legitimate reality."

"And that robust evidence doesn't exist," I said.

"Precisely. Just because a person has some knowledge about something from the past doesn't mean he or she actually lived back then. There are lots of ways that knowledge could have been attained. Invoking reincarnation would be a huge leap."

I asked, "How do you respond to cases of déjà vu? Reincarnation supporters say these experiences point toward a prior existence."

"Déjà vu can be explained," he replied. "A person enters a village where he has never visited and feels like he has been there before. Is that because he lived there in a prior life? Well, that's a big stretch. What if he had an earlier dream about a similar location? Or saw a similar scene in a film or television program he had otherwise forgotten?"[66]

"But what about the hard cases?" I asked Groothuis. "The ones where someone remembers a previous life, and in fact, several details are borne out by fact-checking and there's no obvious way to account for it. Or cases of xenoglossy, where people speak in languages they apparently haven't studied. These aren't so easy to dismiss."

"There are explanations for things like xenoglossy," he replied. "Perhaps the person was exposed to another language through television or conversations they overheard from foreign relatives when they were a child and subconsciously picked up on it."

Stevenson once hypnotized a woman who claimed she had previously lived in nineteenth-century Amsterdam. She even began speaking in Dutch, which she had never studied. On the surface, this would seem to be a classic case of xenoglossy. However, xenoglossy was later disproven when Stevenson figured out she was speaking German—a language she had apparently picked up as a tourist.[67]

"Still," I persisted, "there are cases that are more difficult to explain. You'd concede that, wouldn't you?"

"Of course. And sometimes we may need to consider other possibilities."

"Such as?"

"Demonic influence or possession of some sort," he said. "Certainly the Bible affirms that this sort of thing can happen.[68]

And since reincarnation pulls people away from the Christian gospel, there would be a motivation for dark forces to fan those flames."

Philosopher Gary Habermas reports the case of a novelist who said she had been reincarnated more than a dozen times. Only later was it revealed that she had been provided historical details through her personal link to a spirit. Said Habermas, "This suggests . . . that the so-called evidences for reincarnation could be coming from deceptive nonhuman spirit beings."[69]

Groothuis went on. "There have also been instances of outright fraud," he said. "That doesn't account for many cases, but we always have to be looking at whether someone is profiting from propagating reincarnation claims."

Groothuis gathered his thoughts before resuming. "Let's keep something else in mind: We have powerful and persuasive evidence that Christianity is true. If Jesus really is the Son of God who died for our sins, then his account of the afterlife is the most credible of all. And the Bible talks in terms of resurrection, not reincarnation. You would need a lot more concrete evidence about reincarnation to overturn all of that. Frankly, it's just not there."

I rubbed my hands together. "Ah, but what if Christianity actually *did* teach reincarnation?" I teased. "Surely that would change everything."

A smile. "Yes," Groothuis said. "*If.*"

Passages That Puzzle

Incredulity, frustration, indignation—those were the vibes I was picking up from Groothuis as I recited to him some of the claims that Jesus taught reincarnation. Finally, I put down the yellow legal pad I was reading from and quipped, "I sense you're not buying this."

He sighed. "It's totally unfounded," came his reply. "These esoteric interpretations, where Eastern philosophy is read into

the words of Jesus, are completely misleading. The goal in understanding the Bible is to discern the intent of the authors. When
we do that, we find very quickly that none of them are teaching
reincarnation."

In short order, Groothuis proceeded to correct key errors
made by reincarnation proponents. For example, in Matthew
11:14, Jesus says of John the Baptist, "And if you are willing to
accept it, he is the Elijah who was to come." This is the quote
that prompted Shirley MacLaine to declare that Jesus believed
in reincarnation.[70]

"On the surface, that may seem reasonable, but we have to
put it into context," Groothuis said. "First, the Old Testament
says Elijah never died but was taken bodily into heaven.[71] So if
Elijah never died, he couldn't have been reincarnated.

"Second, Jesus took some disciples to a mountain where he
was transfigured—his face shining like the sun—and then Moses
and Elijah appeared and spoke with him.[72] By this time, John
the Baptist was already dead. If John had been the reincarnated
Elijah, then Elijah couldn't have appeared on the Mount of
Transfiguration."

I put up my hand to stop him. "But the King James Version
calls this a vision, which suggests Elijah wasn't literally there."[73]

"The Greek word that's used, *horama*, is best defined as
something seen with the eyes, not a hallucination.[74] Modern
translations reflect that,"[75] Groothuis said. "Then there's a third
reason why John the Baptist isn't the reincarnated Elijah. Earlier,
he was asked point-blank, 'Are you Elijah?' His response is crystal
clear: 'I am not.'"[76]

"So then what did Jesus mean?" I asked.

"He was speaking of John's function or office as a prophet,
not his identity as a person. You see, an angel had earlier proph-
esied that John would come 'in the spirit and power of Elijah.'[77]
This meant he would have the same office and function as

Elijah—and so in that sense, he *was* Elijah. He certainly had an Elijah-like ministry." His face soured. "But reincarnation? Definitely not."

Next I turned to the passage that Quincy Howe said is the most persuasive for reincarnationists.[78] In John 9:1-3, Jesus and some disciples encountered a man blind from birth. The disciples asked, "Rabbi, who sinned, this man or his parents, that he was born blind?" Reincarnation advocates say the only way he could have sinned would have been in a previous life, since he was born blind.

I said to Groothuis, "Howe called this incident 'incontrovertible support for a doctrine of human preexistence.'"[79]

"Well, let me controvert what he thinks is incontrovertible," said Groothuis. "First, the disciples were Jewish; they didn't believe in reincarnation. But let's pretend for a moment they did. Notice that Jesus never affirms what they said. He replies, 'Neither this man nor his parents sinned, but this happened so that the works of God might be displayed in him.'[80] Then he healed him. In other words, Jesus was saying, 'Guys, you're asking the wrong question.' He certainly wasn't endorsing what they said.

"Furthermore, in that day, Jewish theologians believed someone could sin in their mother's womb. This would be prenatal sin—that is, before birth, not before conception or in a previous life."[81]

"Really?" I asked. "I've never heard of that."

"Yes. We can disagree with that kind of thinking today, but my point is that this was the Jewish mindset back then. So the disciples were drawing on this understanding, not on some notion of preexistence. Again, what initially looks like support for reincarnation crumbles under the weight of reasoned analysis."

The Constantinople Conspiracy

In going through reincarnation literature, I found that conspiracy theories are often espoused. A popular one is the allegation that reincarnation was actually stricken from the Bible at the Second Council of Constantinople in AD 553.

For example, Kenneth Ring in *Heading toward Omega* says, "Although variants of this doctrine were acceptable to and promulgated by the early Church Fathers, reincarnation was declared heretical and expunged from Christian dogma in the sixth century."[82]

"What about that claim?" I asked. "Were the early church fathers really supportive of reincarnation?"

"Absolutely not," he answered. "There's so much misinformation out there."

"What, specifically?"

"Nothing was stricken from the Bible at Constantinople," he replied. "If they did expunge teachings about reincarnation, don't you think they would have removed the teachings that reincarnationists often jump on, like the man blind from birth and John the Baptist being Elijah? Yet they're still in the Bible."

He let that question hang for a moment. Then he added, "What actually did happen at the council was that fifteen anathemas, or condemnations, were adopted against a prominent church scholar named Origen."[83]

"Because he taught reincarnation?"

"No, because he taught the preexistence of souls. He believed that human spirits predated their existence in human bodies, which is not biblical. He never endorsed reincarnation; in fact, he explicitly rejected reincarnation. At one point, he said reincarnation 'is foreign to the church of God and not handed down by the Apostles, nor anywhere set forth in Scriptures.'[84]

"Let's get this straight," Groothuis continued. "Not one of the New Testament or Old Testament documents teaches reincarnation. The doctrine lacks any roots in Judaism or Christianity. Rather, resurrection is uniformly taught. Such early church leaders as Irenaeus, Justin Martyr, Jerome, Tertullian, Gregory of

Nyssa, and Augustine—they all expressed opposition to the idea of reincarnation."[85]

For a moment, he didn't speak. Then something else came to mind. "Remember one other thing: the law of karma is the absolute antithesis of Jesus' teaching about grace," he said. "Karma is a works-based theology taken to the extreme. One lifetime isn't even enough to pay for all our sins. We have to keep coming back to somehow shed our bad karma.

"But the Bible teaches that we can't earn our salvation; rather, it's a pure gift of God's grace. So karma and grace are like oil and water—they can't be mixed. The Bible can't contain any teaching—like reincarnation—that fundamentally contradicts its central message that Jesus died in our place to pay for our sins and offers total forgiveness as a free gift.[86]

"That's why, logically speaking, a person can't be a true Christian and believe in reincarnation at the same time. It's incoherent. It's hard to imagine someone who really trusts in Christ as their Savior still seeing a need for reincarnation. If you've been forgiven, what's your need for another life to work everything out? It's like saying, 'I believe in Jesus as my Lord and Savior, and I'm going to work as hard as I can to try to get into heaven.' No, it doesn't work that way."

His eyes met mine. "Case closed?" he asked.

Well, not quite yet.

The Future for Becky

I hesitated to ask my last question. Maybe it was too personal. Maybe it was too soon. I took a breath and then decided to go ahead and pose it to Groothuis.

"The last time I was in your office, your wife, Becky, was suffering from a terrible illness, and of course, she died pretty quickly after that," I said. "So if you had your choice—if you were able to choose between reincarnation or resurrection as being true—which would you select? Would it give you more comfort to know she is going to live on in successive lives, or that she had gone directly to be with the Lord?"

Groothuis was somber at first. "Well, there's no contest," he said, a small smile breaking out at the thought. "I would choose the promise of Scripture—that Becky was fully forgiven of all her sins based on Christ's work on the cross, that she is with the Lord, and that she would eventually be resurrected, living in a disease-free body in the new heaven and the new earth—forever and ever.

"How could I find any comfort if she were reincarnated to live in a fallen world and face death again and again and again? Maybe she'd get another disease like the one she had and have to suffer through that once more. And then in the end, what would she face? She'd be extinguished, snuffed out, cease to exist. No, I wouldn't find any encouragement in that.

"Becky and I found hope in the self-giving love at the heart of reality. God is love. God loves the world so much that he sent his Son to conquer disability, disease, and death, and he offers eternal life as a gift of his amazing grace. That's the heart of the gospel. That was the source of our encouragement.

"You know, when Becky was on her deathbed, I would read her passages from the Bible to soothe her spirit. Sometimes I'd open the Bible to Revelation 21."

He glanced at the leather-clad black Bible on the round wooden desk where we sat. He picked it up and flipped to the opening words of that chapter, reading aloud:

> Then I saw "a new heaven and a new earth," for the first heaven and the first earth had passed away, and there was no longer any sea. I saw the Holy City, the new Jerusalem, coming down out of heaven from God, prepared as a bride beautifully dressed for her husband. And I heard a loud voice

from the throne saying, "Look! God's dwelling place is now among the people, and he will dwell with them. They will be his people, and God himself will be with them and be their God. He will wipe every tear from their eyes. There will be no more death or mourning or crying or pain, for the old order of things has passed away."[87]

My eyes misted. Groothuis closed the book. "Becky and I found comfort in those words, not just because of what they promise, but because their promises are true," he said. "This is not wishful thinking, make-believe, legend, or mythology. This is the glorious future that awaits all who put their trust in Christ."

He paused a beat.

"Reincarnation? No, as I said, there's no contest. Resurrection, Lee—*that's* the beautiful and loving future that awaits us."

CHAPTER 10

On the Edge of Eternity

Facing Death with an Eye on Heaven

At death we put the signature on our life's portrait. The paint dries. The portrait's done. Ready or not.

RANDY ALCORN, *THE LAW OF REWARDS*

There was a knock at Matilde's front door. The wife of a successful building contractor in Argentina, she was pregnant with her first child at the time. She opened the door and was greeted by a British man who was holding a beautifully bound book.

"*Buenos dias, senora,*" he said. "Would you like a copy of the Word of God?"

Though she faithfully attended Mass and confessed regularly to her priest, Matilde had never been able to find the peace that her soul craved. She gratefully accepted the Spanish-language Scriptures—and so great was her reverence for this Holy Book that she insisted on reading it on her knees.

As she devoured its message—especially the words of Jesus—she opened her heart wide to his offer of forgiveness, cleansing, and grace. Before long she was flooded with the peace and joy she had so fervently sought.

Brimming with gratitude, Matilde prayed fervently for the

son growing in her womb. "Lord," she pleaded, "I want him to be a preacher of the gospel!"[1]

God answered beyond her wildest dreams. Now, eighty-five years later, I was sitting with Matilde's son, Luis Palau Jr., born shortly after she received the Bible. Over more than six decades, he and his ministry have shared the gospel with a billion people worldwide.[2] Yes, you read that right—a *billion* people. The *New York Times* called him "one of the world's leading evangelical Christian figures."[3]

And here he was in the twilight of his life, dying of cancer and on the cusp of reuniting with his beloved mother and father in heaven. "I can't wait," he said softly, his eyes damp.

Palau was suffering from incurable stage 4 lung cancer. Doctors had given him a maximum of a year to live, though after intensive chemotherapy he managed to exceed that. It wasn't until a few months after our conversation that he finally went home to heaven. Understandably, his dire prognosis had stirred deep thoughts about life after death.

What goes through someone's mind when they're getting ready to step into eternity? What insights might this longtime hero of mine offer? How might his experience help me and you when we come to the end of our time on this earth? How does heaven look different when it's just around the corner?

Those questions prompted me to fly to Oregon to spend the day with Palau and his wife, Patricia, at their unpretentious house in Portland. His sons Kevin and Andrew, both leaders in his ministry, dropped by. We talked in the dining room, enjoyed sandwiches in the kitchen, told stories, reminisced, laughed, prayed—and I shed some tears, as did Luis.

"I feel like I'm on heaven's doorstep," he said at one point. "I'm knocking, but it's not time to go in yet. Soon though. Maybe quite soon."

Interview #8: Luis Palau

The numbers and facts about Luis Palau are well known. Palau was only a youngster when his father died, plunging his family into poverty. He rose to become "the Billy Graham of Latin America," an indefatigable evangelist whose ministry brought at least a million people into God's kingdom through the years.

He influenced presidents and popes; he spoke in seventy-five nations; his elaborate festivals preached Jesus in major cities; his radio program was heard in Spanish and English on 4,200 stations in nearly fifty countries; and he wrote a string of books, including *A Friendly Dialogue between an Atheist and a Christian*, which he coauthored with a former Chinese Communist official. His recent spiritual memoir, *Palau: A Life on Fire*, focuses on key people who influenced his life, and the 2019 feature film *Palau: The Movie* portrays the inspiring story of his early life and ministry.

Palau met his wife, an aspiring missionary, while they attended Multnomah School of the Bible (today Multnomah University) in Portland, Oregon. Now they were approaching their sixtieth wedding anniversary, although they calculated they had been apart a total of fifteen years while he had been away on speaking engagements.

All of this is common knowledge within evangelicalism, where Palau is a revered figure. What is less known were his personal, one-on-one efforts to tell people about Jesus, whether it was the Hispanic busboy at a Mexican café or the young clerk at a grocery store—or especially among his large and growing family.

I saw this up close in the early 1990s when my ministry associate Mark Mittelberg and I had dinner with Palau at a rustic restaurant in suburban Chicago. Somewhere between the rainbow trout and the apple crisp, as if he were suddenly gripped by an urgent impulse, Luis reached out and clasped our forearms.

"Friends, I have a favor to ask," he said in his Argentinian accent. "Would you pray for my son Andrew? He's far from the Lord, and we're very concerned about him."

We weren't sure if Palau meant for us to drop our forks and pray right then and there—but when Luis Palau asked you to pray, you did it immediately! By God's grace, Andrew, the third of his four sons, did end up coming to faith several years later.[4]

In fact, when Andrew was born in 1966, his grandmother made a spontaneous prediction to her son-in-law Luis: "This one is going to be an evangelist!" Sure enough, today Andrew is Luis's preaching successor at the Luis Palau Association.

I had always admired Luis's passion for Jesus, his fidelity to the Bible, his fearless proclamation of the gospel, and his winsome emphasis on the love of God. But I have to say that the unabashed fatherly concern he showed that day in a crowded restaurant was what really endeared him to me.

On this day, Palau's black hair had fully surrendered to gray; his face was drawn. His legendary energy was flagging, and walking up a short flight of stairs left him winded. After our interview, he sent me a text: "Apologies if I came across as very tired. Ever since the first treatments, tiredness is one of the unshakable side effects. Thanks for your patience."

Still, if you wanted to see Palau's enthusiasm flare, all you had to do was tell him the story of someone whose life had been radically transformed by Jesus. Invariably, he would call out with excitement to Pat in the next room: "Honey, have you heard this? Come listen to what the Lord has done!"

"Which Is Better by Far"

Palau and I started the day sitting across from each other at his dining room table. He was casually dressed in a dark blue pullover sweater with a checkered shirt and khaki slacks. When I confessed that I felt awkward—even ghoulish—for coming to talk with him about death, Palau waved off my concerns.

"I tell people I'm dying, and they say, 'Hey, some weather we're having,'" he told me. "People don't like to talk about death, but I want to. So don't feel bad about bringing it up." He flashed a reassuring smile. "I think it helps me."

"How did you get the diagnosis?"

"I came back from a trip with a cold that I couldn't shake. My doctor told me I'd be all right—but then, at the end, he said, 'Hey, just for kicks, let's take an X-ray.' He looked at the X-ray and said, 'Oh, man, I don't like this. It looks bad.' I thought it must be a mistake, but he sent me to an oncologist."

"What did the specialist say?"

"Well, he was blunt. He said, 'I'm sorry, but it's stage 4. It's incurable. Surgery won't work. I'll give you treatment to make your life as pleasant as possible, but in nine to twelve months, you're gone. If you don't take the treatment, you'll be dead in four months.'"

"You must have been shocked!"

"I was. I'd never been in the hospital a single day. Hardly ever taken any aspirin and then, suddenly—*boom!* You're on your way out. It grips you."

"What were your first thoughts?"

"They were almost childish, really. I thought, *I won't be able to pick up the phone and talk to Pat or the boys.* That saddened me. Then I thought, *Do I have all my documents and financial stuff in order for Pat?*"

"Practical stuff."

"Right," he said. "And since then I've turned into a bit of a crybaby. Not that I'm especially sad or weeping all the time, but poignant things bring tears to my eyes. Grandchildren. Nostalgic memories. Things I'll miss. Tears well up. It can be embarrassing."

"Did you pray for healing?"

"Actually, I didn't. You have to die from something, and I was already approaching my mid-eighties."

"Did you ask God why he was allowing this?"

"Yes, you wonder why. But think about this. We worked for fifteen years to transfer the ministry to Kevin and Andrew, yet I still kept my foot in the door. Now it became urgent—I had to totally get out of the way and let them lead. And that's a good and necessary step."

Shortly after his diagnosis, about seventy key participants in his ministry flew to Portland for a meeting that became quite emotional. "This was my chance to say things I needed to say. I apologized to anybody I may have hurt. I wanted to clear the decks. A couple of people I had personal conversations with. I didn't want to leave without saying I was sorry if I had inadvertently offended someone over the years."

Palau told me that his life, which had been consumed by frenetic travel and ministry, had now slowed so he could be more introspective, more attentive to Pat, and more at peace.

"I've been obeying God and serving him for such a long time that I had forgotten how to simply delight in him," he said. "Now I'm taking time to revel in his grace. That's so refreshing! My prayers are deeper and richer and full of gratitude and wonder and awe."

"Do you fear death?" I asked.

"No," he said quickly, then he paused briefly. "No," he repeated, more emphatically this time. "I don't really. I'm so convinced from Scripture that after I close my eyes for the last time, I go to be with God. The apostle Paul says that to be absent from the body is to be present with the Lord.[5] I'll be honest with you—I'm a little disappointed he hasn't taken me sooner. I got myself all ready. My conscience is clear. I have everything in order. But—not yet."

Instead, he continued with regular chemotherapy sessions, which sapped his energy, and he endured tests and radiology treatments to stem the cancer's spread to his spine.

"You know," he said, "after they do the bone scans, the technicians put a warm blanket over me. It feels so good. And I said, 'Lord, that's how I want to go. Put a nice warm blanket on me, and I'm gone.'"

"Were you present when your father passed?" I asked.

Palau glanced off to the side as he collected his thoughts. "I arrived home right after he went to be with the Lord. I was just a boy, but they told me what happened. Not long before he died, he sat up in bed and sang a hymn about heaven: 'Bright crowns up there, bright crowns for you and me.' His head fell back on the pillow, and he pointed upward."

"Did he say anything?"

"He said, 'I'm going to be with Jesus,' then quoting Paul's words in Philippians, 'which is better by far.'"[6]

"Those were his last words?"

"Yes—in *this* world," he replied. "He taught me how to die— with a hymn in my heart and Scripture on my lips."

Seeing the Face of God

I asked Palau, "How has your view of heaven changed since you were diagnosed?"

"Not changed—enhanced," he said. "Now I read the Bible with very open eyes. Every mention of heaven is underlined in green, with a little dot. Things that didn't seem so important before now have taken on a whole new meaning. They've become personal. I've started visualizing *me* seeing the great throne of God, *me* walking the glorious streets, *me* reuniting with those who have gone before."

"What do you especially want to see in heaven?"

His eyes lit up. "Of course, the very face of Jesus, my Savior," came his reply. "The first thing I'll do is fall before him with a heart overflowing with gratitude and praise. And I want to encounter the Father and the Holy Spirit in a personal way."

"In the middle of the 1700s," I observed, "Jonathan Edwards said that seeing the face of God in heaven will be a 'truly happifying' experience."[7]

That prompted a grin. "*Happifying,*" he said, drawing out the word as he considered it. "Yes, yes. I like that very much."

"Do you want to hear Jesus say, 'Well done, good and faithful servant?'" I asked.[8]

"Don't we all desire that? I don't dare presume to say how Jesus will greet me. That's not for me to know right now. Just seeing him—that will be incredible. Of course, we all have mental images of him that we've picked up through the years. But soon, I'll look into his face."

"Who else do you want to see?"

He swallowed hard. "I want to see my dad," he said, eyes glistening. "I haven't seen him since I was a ten-year-old boy. I wonder, *Has he been able to watch what transpired since he left this world? Is he aware of the legacy he left?* The Bible says to honor your father and mother. I want to ask him, 'Dad, do you feel I've honored you with my life?' I hope that I have. He left such a great example for me.

"And I want to spend time with my mother and with all the great heroes of the faith," he continued. "I want to meet Augustine, Wesley, Whitefield, Moody. And, of course, I want to see Billy Graham again. He was an incredible encouragement to me. And Spurgeon. I was recently reading a sermon he wrote on heaven in which he said, 'Think of this: we'll never sin again.' I had never pondered that before. We'll never have to say, 'O God, forgive me.' I mean, that's an awesome thought, you know?"

"It is," I said. "What else do you want to see?"

"The throne of God," he replied. "Just read Revelation 4—it's magnificent, it's breathtaking, it will blow your mind. The One sitting on it has the appearance of jasper and ruby. There's a rainbow shining like an emerald; there are flashes of lightning and peals of thunder; there's a sea of glass, clear as crystal. There are the twenty-four elders and fantastic creatures, with everyone praising the Lord—'Holy, holy, holy is the Lord God Almighty'! How much of that is literal? How much is a word picture to point us toward something we can't even comprehend at this point? Well, I can't wait to find out."

With that, a chuckle. "Lee," he added, "I wish I could send you a text from heaven and tell you all about it! I know that the journalist in you would want every detail."

Doubts versus Questions

To me, Palau's faith in Christ always seemed rock-solid. He exuded deep confidence in Scripture, radical reliance on God, and certainty in the central doctrines of the church. When he talked about Jesus, you felt like he was chatting about a close friend. But had the specter of death shaken him at all? Did he feel any cracks in the foundation of his beliefs?

"Do I have doubts?" Palau asked, echoing my question. "No, not doubts, but I do have questions."

"What's the difference?" I asked.

"Questions are about the *what*—what happened and why. A doubt can be more about the *who*, and sometimes that can get to the core of God's character. As for me, I've never doubted the reality or the goodness of God, but I do have questions."

"Such as?"

"Why did my father die so young? He had served God so faithfully and generously. Why did we have to go through such poverty after his death? It's not that I'm being critical. I'm just interested. And I'd be interested in knowing why God allows so much evil in the world. I'd love for him to say, 'Well, Luis, let me tell you.' I know he has reasons—his ways are perfect—but it would be great to hear him explain it."

"Has your diagnosis rocked your faith in any way?" I asked.

"I did go through a turbulent time during the first several weeks," he replied. "And people need to know this can happen when their end is approaching. The Puritans wrote about it. You find that Satan accuses, attacks, and seeks to destroy the work of God in us."

"You experienced that?"

"Yes, the struggle was very real. It was as if Satan were saying, 'Palau, you preached to multitudes, but what if you're one of those to whom the Lord said, "I never knew you. Away from me, you evildoers!"[9] I felt like Satan was saying, 'You're a hypocrite; you have a dirty mind; you have a dark heart. You showed many people the way to heaven, but you're not going.'"

"That must have been disconcerting," I said.

"It was. Rationally, I knew I was forgiven by Christ, but emotionally—well, Satan is good at what he does. He had the audacity to try to tempt the Son of God, so little weasels like us should expect nothing less for ourselves."

"How did you overcome that?"

"Through prayer and studying the Bible, especially chapters 7–10 of Hebrews, which affirm that Jesus appeared once for all to do away with sin. His sacrifice covers each of our sins and shortcomings, and he intercedes for us before the Father. He's defending us. So that means we can say, as Jesus told his disciples, 'The prince of this world is coming. He has no hold over me.'[10] Because ultimately, he doesn't," Palau said firmly. "If you put your trust in the Lord, your salvation is secure."

In fact, Palau said he sensed God urging him to "make much of the cross" in his final days in this world. "This theme of 'once for all' is stressed repeatedly in Hebrews," Palau said to me. "Through Christ's sacrifice on the cross, *all* of our sins are atoned

218

for—paid in full—finally, completely, for all time. For example, Hebrews 7:27 says with crystal clarity, 'He sacrificed for their sins once for all when he offered himself.' This can help people if they feel insecure about God's forgiveness. They can be confident that they're forgiven if they receive God's grace through repentance and faith."

When I asked Palau about the legacy he hoped to leave for others, I got an answer I hadn't expected. He didn't talk about his worldwide impact as an evangelist or the vast crowds that cheered his teaching.

"If I've ever impressed anybody," he said, "I hope it's because they realized I'm not very special. There are other speakers who are more articulate. I hope they say, 'If God can use an ordinary person like Luis, why can't he use me?' Isn't that the greater testimony—that God uses the weak? Then all the credit goes to him! All of us can be faithful. You don't have to be a genius. You can just be a boy from a small town in southern Argentina. And if we're faithful, the sky's the limit—because the power comes from God."

Messages from Heaven

Upstairs from where we were sitting was a souvenir that encapsulated the message Palau had spread for so many decades. It was a large painted sign that used to hang above the pulpit in the sheet metal chapel where his family worshiped when Luis was a boy in the Argentine town of Ingeniero Maschwitz.

Dios es Amor. "God is Love."

"In my early years of preaching, I tended to be harsh," he told me. "And that wasn't always a bad thing. Fear is the beginning of wisdom, and sometimes you have to put the fear of God into people, so my main theme was 'turn or burn.'

"But," he continued, "there's a difference between wanting to avoid hell and genuinely wanting to spend eternity with God in heaven. So more and more over the years I've emphasized God's kindness, his generosity, his forbearance, his love, his goodness. He sets us free! What's better than that? Our relationship with God can be full of joy and laughter and happiness. After all, the Bible says it's God's *kindness* that leads to repentance."[11]

"Is that the message you want to be remembered for?" I asked.

"I hope I've been balanced. I haven't shied away from the bad news that our sin has separated us from God and so we're headed for hell. But the good news is that Christ offers forgiveness and eternal life in heaven if we repent and follow him. People need to hear that positive and uplifting message."

I sat back in my chair and scanned my notes to see what I was missing. I looked up at Palau and said, "A few minutes ago, you joked that you'd like to send me a text from heaven. But in a serious vein, if you could send back a message from heaven to your fellow Christians, what would it say?"

"To go for it," Palau said with vigor. "Take a risk—tell others about the good news of Christ. Remember that it's the job of the Holy Spirit to convict them of their sin. He's your partner—let him do his work in them. *You* bring them the best news on the planet—that there's redemption, there's a relationship with God, there's heaven, there's an eternal party that's waiting for them."

Palau recalled that when he was a new Christian, his mother would urge him to take the gospel to nearby towns that didn't have a church. "She kept encouraging me and pushing me," he said. "She'd say, 'Go, go, go. Get out and reach people with the good news!'"

"What did you say?" I asked.

"I was slow to step out in faith. I'd say to her, 'Mom, I'm waiting for the call.'"

"I'm guessing she didn't respond well to that."

"No. She was getting upset. She said to me, 'The call? The *call*? The call went out two thousand years ago, Luis! The Lord's waiting for *your* answer! You're not waiting for *his* call!' And she was right. The Bible makes our task clear—go out and reach people with the gospel, whether they're friends, family members, neighbors, colleagues, or just people we meet along the path of life. That should be the default assignment for all of us. The absence of a specific call should never be an excuse for inaction."

"Did that get you moving?"

"It was one of the defining moments of my life," he answered. "I realized I didn't need to wait around; instead, I needed to *do*. And that's how I'd encourage my fellow believers—step out in faith, take action, strike up a conversation with someone far from God. Whether they accept the gospel is up to them. You can't control that. But I can tell you from personal experience that at the end of your life, when all is said and done, you'll never regret being courageous for Christ."

His comment made me think of the words of evangelist Becky Manley Pippert: "We are living after Jesus came from heaven to earth and before Jesus returns again to bring heaven to earth. What is the significance of God placing us here at this particular juncture in history? It is so that we can join God in his quest to love, seek, and invite people to come home to God!"[12]

"And what about people who aren't Christians?" I asked Palau. "What message would you send them from heaven?"

Palau didn't mince words. "I'd tell them, *'Don't be stupid!'*"

We both burst out laughing. "Seriously?" I said. "That's *it*?"

"Sure—don't be stupid! Don't pass up what God is offering out of his love and grace. Why embrace evil when goodness beckons? Why turn your back on heaven and choose hell? Why expose yourself to the harmful side effects of a sinful life when you can follow God's path of righteousness and healing? Don't miss the party that God has waiting for you in heaven!"

Somehow, when I had gotten on the plane to fly to Oregon to meet with one of the world's most renowned evangelists, I didn't expect our interview to end with him simply saying, "Don't be stupid." Then again, that stark exhortation does sum up this book pretty well.

The evidence points to heaven being a reality. Jesus has flung open the gates for everyone who wants to enter through repentance and faith. Hope is waiting. Grace is calling. The party is starting. The admission is paid. Eternity is in the balance.

Seek God. Trust him. Follow him. Heed the words of my friend and hero Luis Palau.

"Don't be stupid!"

Conclusion
Walking God's Path to Heaven

*If you read history you will find that the
Christians who did most for the present world
were just those who thought most of the next.*

C. S. LEWIS, *MERE CHRISTIANITY*

My friend Nabeel was afflicted with stomach cancer. There I was, sitting at his hospital bedside in Houston just days before he died. His face was gaunt; his legs were thin and bony. He was wasting away at the age of thirty-four.

Nabeel Qureshi was a devout Muslim whose investigation of the evidence for Christianity brought him to faith in Jesus. Already a medical doctor, he went on to earn two more advanced degrees and become a bestselling author and worldwide speaker. His death was a blow to all of us who called him friend.

He died in 2017. But just today, as I was preparing to mention him in this book, I saw him again—this time, through a video someone tweeted on the third anniversary of his passing. In a speech given at some unspecified time in his ministry, here's what Nabeel was saying:

> In our post-Enlightenment world, especially in university settings, it's a popular belief that there is no such thing as the

supernatural. What the resurrection means, then, is that this is wrong. There's something *more* to this world—something that can bring people back from the dead. And if that is true, then that means if it comes to a point in your life where it seems there is no hope—where it seems like even death is inevitable and there's no way to escape it—well, death is not the end. There's more. There's hope—no matter what.[1]

Yes, heaven means hope—not a vapid kind of wishful thinking or a cross-your-fingers sort of blind optimism, but a confident hope. I *trust* I will be reunited with my friend Nabeel someday—and the persuasive evidence for the resurrection and the reality of heaven tells me that my trust is indeed well placed.

The truth is that the resurrection is nothing less than the pivot point of history. Said N. T. Wright, "Jesus' resurrection is the beginning of God's new project not to snatch people away from earth to heaven but to colonize earth with the life of heaven."[2]

Here's the story of Jesus that Scot McKnight told so succinctly in my interview with him: "He was the Messiah; he died unjustly at the hands of sinners; God overturned his death and raised him; he ascended; and he's coming back to rule." No wonder the Bible calls *this* the gospel—it truly is "good news"!

And it means that for followers of Jesus, who gratefully embrace him as their forgiver and leader, death is merely a doorway to a world of grandeur and wonder, of satisfaction and joy, of flourishing friendships and stimulating experiences, of gazing with gratitude at the face of our Savior and Lord—and yes, as Charles Spurgeon said, receiving his kisses.[3]

Have you ever tried to imagine what *forever* will be like? "At our most creative moment, at our deepest thought, at our highest level, we still cannot fathom eternity," said Max Lucado.[4] I mentioned that to philosopher Chad Meister when I was interviewing him for this book, and he responded with a story.

"Tammy and I love going to the Caribbean," he said. "Imagine walking down the beach, picking up a handful of sand, and then picking out one grain. That single grain would seem insignificant compared to all the sand in your hand. Now compare it to all the sand on that beach. Then compare it to all the sand on every beach and in every desert on the whole planet.

"Imagine that one grain of sand represents your entire lifetime in this world. All the mountains upon mountains of sand on the planet—all the lifetimes that those grains represent—would just be the beginning of eternity.

"But now imagine you lived the worst possible life in this world—a lifetime of hardship and difficulties. I don't want to diminish the suffering some people go through, but if that one grain of sand represents an entire lifetime of struggle, it would pale in comparison to the mind-boggling bounty of sand in the entire world."

I processed that for a minute. Then I said, "That reminds me of a quote attributed to Saint Teresa of Ávila: 'In light of heaven, the worst suffering on earth will be seen to be no more serious than one night in an inconvenient hotel.'"[5]

He smiled. "I don't know about you," said this academic superstar who was once on the verge of suicide as a spiritual skeptic, "but I find that *so* encouraging."

Power as Power Is Needed

If the Jesus story is encouraging to us, think about what it did for the people whose lives were intertwined with his. "Jesus was radically reconfigured and redefined by resurrection," said Eugene Peterson. "And now they [the disciples] were being just as radically reconfigured and redefined by resurrection."[6]

Now they knew for sure that God was fulfilling his promise of heaven—and that certain knowledge revolutionized their lives in *this* world. Their mission, their attitudes, their relationships, and their priorities were all turned upside down and inside out.

What about you and me? How can our lives change *today* in light of heaven? Well, if the Jesus story is what leads us to our heavenly home, shouldn't we delve deeper into his teachings—and commit to applying his wisdom to our everyday lives?

Knowing that we will someday inherit the riches of heaven, shouldn't we stop clinging to the earthly possessions that take our attention away from what's really important? Anticipating a paradise of eternal pleasures, shouldn't we stop our mindless pursuit of substitute indulgences that only bring fleeting enjoyment and leave lasting regret?

In the new heaven and the new earth, everything will be made right, so shouldn't we start setting things right in our own relationships now? The Jesus story culminates in our clemency, so can't we offer forgiveness to those who have offended us—and shouldn't we seek forgiveness from those we've hurt?

I know how difficult it can be to set things right. A while ago, I knew I should reconcile with someone I had mistreated, but I felt too intimidated and embarrassed to do it. It was going to be hard for me to admit fault, and I was concerned he might lash out at me. I knew I would be acting in accordance with God's will if I reached out to that friend, because the Bible says, "If it is possible, as far as it depends on you, live at peace with everyone."[7] So I prayed, asking God to give me the courage to follow through.

Did I immediately feel electrified by God's power? No, I still felt apprehensive and inadequate. Nevertheless, as I walked toward the phone in obedience and forced myself to punch in the man's number, God gave me strength as strength was needed. And sure enough, as the conversation unfolded, God emboldened and guided me through a very difficult talk—and today I'm fully reconciled with that friend.[8]

Can you take steps toward righting a wrong in your life, with

God's help? Since Jesus' story is all about reconciliation with God, let's not wait until heaven to make amends for past transgressions and to repair fractured friendships. I've learned that as we walk down the path of Jesus, he will unfailingly give us power along the way.

Brother Andrew, known for smuggling Bibles into closed countries, found this to be true over and over. When he sensed that God was leading him to bring Christian materials into a nation, he took concrete action in obedience, even when the door of entry seemed securely shut at first. Somehow as Brother Andrew approached the border with his books, God would always empower him to fulfill his mission.

"The door may seem closed, but it's only closed the way a supermarket door is closed," he said. "It stays shut when you remain at a distance, but as you deliberately move toward it, a magic eye above it sees you coming, and the door opens. God is waiting for us to walk forward in obedience so he can open the door for us to serve him."[9]

Can We Trust God to Do What's Right?

Perhaps for you, there's still a hitch in the story about Jesus. You're wondering if God is really fair. If Jesus holds the keys to heaven, what's the fate of those who never get a chance to hear his message of redemption and eternal life? This issue troubled me so deeply as a new Christian that I drove hundreds of miles to meet with a well-known scholar to get answers.

What I learned was that God hasn't told us explicitly how he is going to deal with them. "The secret things belong to the LORD our God, but the things revealed belong to us and to our children forever," says the Bible.[10] But we do know a few things to help us sort through this issue.

First, we know from Scripture that everyone has a moral

standard written on their heart by God and that everyone is guilty of violating that standard.[11] That's why our conscience bothers us when we do something wrong. Second, we know that everyone has enough information from observing the created world to know that God exists, yet people have suppressed that truth and rejected God anyway.[12]

But both the Old and New Testaments tell us that those who wholeheartedly seek God will find him.[13] In fact, the Bible says that the Holy Spirit is seeking us first, making it possible for us to seek him. This suggests to me that people who respond to the understanding that they have and who earnestly seek after the one true God will find an opportunity, in some way, to receive the eternal life that God graciously provides through Jesus.

Sometimes we get a glimpse into how God accomplishes this. I remember meeting a man who had been raised by gurus in an area of India where there were no Christians. As a teenager, he concluded there were too many contradictions in Hinduism and its teachings couldn't satisfy his soul. He called out to God for answers—and in an absolutely remarkable series of events, God brought people into his life who shared the story of Jesus with him. As a result, he became a follower of Christ.

In my book *The Case for Miracles*, I document example after example of how Jesus is appearing in spectacular dreams to Muslims in countries that are closed to the gospel, pointing people down the path to eternal life with him.[14] There has been a virtual tsunami of these cases around the Middle East and beyond, including in my late friend Nabeel Qureshi's journey toward Christ.[15] We can be confident that whenever people—of any race, in any culture, at any time—cry out to God, he will respond, often in stunning and unexpected ways.

After all, we see in Scripture that God is scrupulously fair. The very first book of the Bible asks, "Will not the Judge of all the earth do right?"[16] Observed one author, "When God is finished dealing with all of us, none will be able to complain that they were treated unfairly."[17] In other words, when history is consummated, we will each personally marvel at how absolutely perfect God's judgment is.

Finally, we know that apart from the payment that Jesus made on the cross, nobody has a chance of getting off death row. Exactly how much knowledge a person has to have about Jesus, or precisely where the lines of faith are drawn, only God knows. He and he alone can expose the motives of a person's heart.[18]

In the end, all we really needed to know about the matter is this: God is good, God is loving, and God is fair. When we're confident of those foundational truths, we can thoroughly trust him for the outcome.[19]

The Formula of Faith

As for you and me, the issue isn't ignorance. Even if you had never heard it before, you've read the story of Jesus in this book. Over these many pages, you've sifted the evidence and considered the reasoning that supports the truth of Christianity. I hope you've also felt a bit of the urgency that gripped me when I was at death's doorstep several years ago. In a sense, you've been a juror in the case for heaven during the time you've been reading this book—and at some point, a good juror reaches a verdict.

Maybe the time for that is now. Now you know the pathway Home.

I remember the day when all of this hit me full force. It was November 8, 1981. After two years of investigating the evidence as an atheist, I concluded that the Jesus story is true. Not sure how to respond, I found the answer in John 1:12: "Yet to all who did *receive* him, to those who *believed* in his name, he gave the right to *become* children of God" (italics added).

That verse embodies the formula of faith: Believe + Receive

= Become. I *believed* the Jesus story, so I *received* his forgiveness through a heartfelt prayer in which I confessed my sinful behavior and turned to walk his path, and with that I *became* a child of God—for eternity. And as a result, over time God transformed my character, morality, values, worldview, attitudes, relationships, and priorities—for the better.

How about you? God doesn't want you living in a state of anxiety or uncertainty about where you stand with him. The very first verse I memorized as a new follower of Jesus was 1 John 5:13: "I write these things to you who believe in the name of the Son of God so that you may *know* that you have eternal life" (italics added).

Yes, you can *know*—right now, with certainty—that you will revel in the goodness of God in heaven forever. If you *believe* the Jesus story as best you can, then *receive* his gift of forgiveness and eternal life in a sincere prayer of repentance and faith, and you will *become* his child for eternity. You will dwell with God, and he will dwell with you—in the new heaven and the new earth.

And when we're both in heaven, I suspect you'll often find me sitting on my veranda. Why don't you come over sometime, and we can celebrate all the ways God has lavished goodness and grace on us? Together, we'll lift our voices in praising the One who made all of this possible.

And, oh, while you're there, let me introduce you to my dear friend, Nabeel Qureshi. You'll love him as much as I do!

For Further Evidence

Chapter 1: The Quest for Immortality

Becker, Ernest. *The Denial of Death*. New York: Free Press, 1973.

Billings, J. Todd. *The End of the Christian Life: How Embracing Our Mortality Frees Us to Truly Live*. Grand Rapids: Brazos, 2020.

Jones, Clay. *Immortal: How the Fear of Death Drives Us and What We Can Do about It*. Eugene, OR: Harvest House, 2020.

Stowell, Joseph. *Eternity: Reclaiming a Passion for What Endures*. Chicago: Moody, 1995.

Chapter 2: Searching for the Soul

Baker, Mark C., and Stewart Goetz. *The Soul Hypothesis: Investigations into the Existence of the Soul*. New York: Bloomsbury, 2013.

Cottingham, John. *In Search of the Soul: A Philosophical Essay*. Princeton, NJ: Princeton University Press, 2020.

Dirckx, Sharon. *Am I Just My Brain?* London: Good Book, 2019.

Goetz, Stewart, and Charles Taliaferro. *A Brief History of the Soul*. Malden, MA: Wiley-Blackwell, 2011.

Moreland, J. P. *The Soul: How We Know It's Real and Why It Matters*. Chicago: Moody, 2014.

Moreland, J. P., and Scott B. Rae. *Body & Soul: Human Nature & the Crisis in Ethics*. Downers Grove, IL: IVP Academic, 2000.

Swinburne, Richard. *Are We Bodies or Souls?* Oxford: Oxford University Press, 2019.

Chapter 3: Near-Death Experiences

Burke, John. *Imagine Heaven: Near-Death Experiences, God's Promises, and the Exhilarating Future That Awaits You*. Grand Rapids: Baker, 2015.

Carter, Chris. *Science and the Near-Death Experience: How Consciousness Survives Death*. Rochester, VT: Inner Traditions, 2010.

Habermas, Gary R., and J. P. Moreland. *Immortality: The Other Side of Death*. Nashville: Nelson, 1992.

Holden, Janice Miner, Bruce Greyson, and Debbie James. *The Handbook of Near-Death Experiences: Thirty Years of Investigation*. Santa Barbara, CA: Praeger, 2009.

Long, Jeffrey. *Evidence of the Afterlife: The Science of Near-Death Experiences*. New York: HarperCollins, 2010.

Marsh, Michael N. *Out-of-Body and Near-Death Experiences: Brain-State Phenomena or Glimpses of Immortality?* Oxford: Oxford University Press, 2010.

Sabom, Michael B. *Recollections of Death: A Medical Investigation*. New York: Harper & Row, 1982.

van Lommel, Pim. *Consciousness beyond Life: The Science of the Near-Death Experience*. New York: HarperCollins, 2010.

Chapter 4: The Pyramid to Heaven

Meister, Chad V. *Building Belief: Constructing Faith from the Ground Up*. Grand Rapids: Baker, 2006.

On Truth

Beckwith, Francis, and Gregory Koukl. *Relativism: Feet Firmly Planted in Mid-Air*. Grand Rapids: Baker, 1998.

Groothuis, Douglas. *Truth Decay: Defending Christianity against the Challenges of Postmodernism*. Downers Grove, IL: InterVarsity, 2000.

On Worldviews

Nash, Ronald. *Worldviews in Conflict: Choosing Christianity in a World of Ideas*. Grand Rapids: Zondervan, 1992.

Sire, James. *Naming the Elephant: Worldview as a Concept*. Downers Grove, IL: InterVarsity, 2004.

On Theism

Craig, William Lane. *Reasonable Faith: Christian Truth and Apologetics*, 3rd ed. Wheaton, IL: Crossway, 2008.

Strobel, Lee. *The Case for a Creator: A Journalist Investigates Scientific Evidence That Points toward God*. Grand Rapids: Zondervan, 2004.

On Revelation

Blomberg, Craig. *Can We Still Believe the Bible? An Evangelical Engagement with Contemporary Questions*. Grand Rapids: Brazos, 2014.

Cowan, Steven B., and Terry L. Wilder. *In Defense of the Bible: A Comprehensive Apologetic for the Authority of Scripture*. Nashville: Broadman & Holman, 2013.

Köstenberger, Andreas J., Darrell L. Bock, and Josh Chatraw. *Truth in a Culture of Doubt: Engaging Skeptical Challenges to the Bible*. Nashville: B&H Academic, 2014.

Morrow, Jonathan. *Questioning the Bible: 11 Major Challenges to the Bible's Authority*. Chicago: Moody, 2014.

On the Resurrection

Habermas, Gary R., and Michael R. Licona. *The Case for the Resurrection of Jesus*. Grand Rapids: Kregel, 2004.

Licona, Michael R. *The Resurrection of Jesus: A New Historiographical Approach*. Downers Grove, IL: InterVarsity, 2010.

Strobel, Lee. *In Defense of Jesus: Investigating Attacks on the Identity of Christ*. Previous titled *The Case for the Real Jesus*. Grand Rapids: Zondervan, 2007.

Wright, N. T. *The Resurrection of the Son of God*. Minneapolis: Fortress, 2003.

On the Gospel

McKnight, Scot. *The King Jesus Gospel: The Original Good News Revisited*, rev. ed. Grand Rapids: Zondervan, 2016.

Mittelberg, Mark. *The Reason Why: Faith Makes Sense*. Carol Stream, IL: Tyndale, 2011.

Strobel, Lee. *The Case for Grace: A Journalist Explores the Evidence of Transformed Lives*. Grand Rapids: Zondervan, 2015.

Wright, N. T. *Simply Good News: Why the Gospel Is News and What Makes It Good*. San Francisco: HarperOne, 2015.

Chapter 5: Heaven: A Guide

Alcorn, Randy. *Heaven*. Carol Stream, IL: Tyndale, 2004.

Boersma, Hans. *Seeing God: The Beatific Vision in Christian Tradition*. Grand Rapids: Eerdmans, 2018.

Eareckson Tada, Joni. *Heaven: Your Real Home . . . From a Higher Perspective*, rev. ed. Grand Rapids: Zondervan, 2018.

Eldredge, John. *All Things New: Heaven, Earth, and the Restoration of Everything You Love*, rev. ed. Nashville: Nelson, 2018.

Frazee, Randy. *What Happens After You Die? A Biblical Guide to Paradise, Hell, and Life After Death*. Nashville: Nelson, 2017.

McKnight, Scot. *The Heaven Promise: Engaging the Bible's Truth about Life to Come*. Colorado Springs: WaterBrook, 2015.

Wright, N. T. *Surprised by Hope: Rethinking Heaven, the Resurrection, and the Mission of the Church*. San Francisco: HarperOne, 2008.

Chapter 6: Seven on Heaven

Gomes, Alan W. *40 Questions about Heaven and Hell*. Grand Rapids: Kregel Academic, 2018.

Hanegraaff, Hank. *Afterlife: What You Need to Know about Heaven, the Hereafter & Near-Death Experiences*. Brentwood, TN: Worthy, 2013.

Hitchcock, Mark. *55 Answers to Questions about Life after Death*. Sisters, OR: Multnomah, 2005.

Kreeft, Peter. *Everything You Ever Wanted to Know about Heaven . . . but Never Dreamed of Asking!* San Francisco: Ignatius, 1990.

Walls, Jerry. *Heaven, Hell, and Purgatory: Rethinking the Things That Matter Most.* Grand Rapids: Brazos, 2015.

———. *Heaven: The Logic of Eternal Joy.* New York: Oxford University Press, 2002.

Chapter 7: The Logic of Hell

DeStefano, Anthony. *Hell: A Guide.* Nashville: Nelson, 2020.

Gomes, Alan W. *40 Questions about Heaven and Hell.* Grand Rapids: Kregel Academic, 2018.

Gregg, Steve. *All You Want to Know about Hell: Three Christian Views of God's Final Solution to the Problem of Sin.* Nashville: Nelson, 2013.

Peterson, Robert A. *Hell on Trial: The Case for Eternal Punishment.* Phillipsburg, NJ: P&R, 1995.

Sprinkle, Preston, gen. ed. *Four Views on Hell,* 2nd ed. Grand Rapids: Zondervan, 2016.

Walls, Jerry. *Hell: The Logic of Damnation.* South Bend, IN: University of Notre Dame Press, 1992.

Chapter 8: Escape from Hell

Beilby, James K. *Postmortem Opportunity: A Biblical and Theological Assessment of Salvation after Death.* Downers Grove, IL: IVP Academic, 2021.

Chan, Francis, and Preston Sprinkle. *Erasing Hell: What God Said about Eternity, and the Things We've Made Up.* Colorado Springs: Cook, 2011.

Copan, Paul. *Loving Wisdom: A Guide to Philosophy and Christian Faith,* 2nd ed. Grand Rapids: Eerdmans, 2020.

Fudge, Edward William, and Robert A. Peterson. *Two Views of Hell: A Biblical and Theological Dialogue.* Downers Grove, IL: InterVarsity, 2000.

McClymond, Michael. *The Devil's Redemption: A New History and Interpretation of Christian Universalism.* 2 vols. Grand Rapids: Baker Academic, 2018.

Morgan, Christopher W. and Robert A. Peterson. *Hell Under Fire: Modern Scholarship Reinvents Eternal Punishment.* Grand Rapids: Zondervan, 2004.

Chapter 9: *The Reincarnation Sensation*

Edwards, Paul. *Reincarnation: A Critical Examination.* Amherst, NY: Prometheus, 1996.

Geisler, Norman, and J. Yutaka Amano. *The Reincarnation Sensation.* Eugene, OR: Wipf & Stock, 2004.

Groothuis, Douglas. *Christian Apologetics: A Comprehensive Case for Biblical Faith.* Downers Grove, IL: IVP Academic, 2011.

———. *Confronting the New Age: How to Resist a Growing Religious Movement.* Eugene, OR: Wipf & Stock, 2010.

Habermas, Gary R., and J. P. Moreland. *Immortality: The Other Side of Death.* Nashville: Nelson, 1992.

Chapter 10: **On the Edge of Eternity**

Alcorn, Randy. *In Light of Eternity: Perspectives on Heaven.* Colorado Springs: WaterBrook, 1999.

Billings, J. Todd. *The End of the Christian Life: How Embracing Our Mortality Frees Us to Truly Live.* Grand Rapids: Brazos, 2020.

Graham, Billy. *Where I Am: Heaven, Eternity, and Our Life Beyond.* Nashville: W Publishing, 2015.

Keller, Timothy. *On Death.* New York: Penguin, 2020.

Palau, Luis. *Palau: A Life on Fire.* Grand Rapids: Zondervan, 2019.

What Happens
After We Die?

After the emergency room physician told me several years
ago that I was on the verge of dying, I lapsed back into
unconsciousness. When I was revived a while later, I was a little
surprised I was still alive. One of my first thoughts was, *If I don't
make it through this ordeal, what happens to me next?*

Like most Christians, I knew I would continue to live, even
after my physical body expired. But I was a little hazy on the exact
sequence of events. I had never been particularly concerned
about it until suddenly it became so very relevant.

Surprisingly, the Bible offers few concrete details about what
happens immediately after death. What seems apparent is that
our soul separates from our body and enters the intermediate
state, where our spirit is conscious and aware of our situation.[1]
Jesus' parable of the rich man and Lazarus in Luke 16:19–31
indicates there will be two separate locations in this disembodied
existence.

One locale can be called paradise, where followers of Christ
will enjoy God's presence. As Jesus told the thief on the cross in
Luke 23:43, "Today you will be with me in paradise." We can
be confident that this will be a sublime and blissful experience,
although we will have a sense of incompleteness because our
souls will be separated from our bodies.[2]

The other location in the intermediate state is commonly
referred to as Hades, a place of isolation and torment for non-
believers where they will be separated from God.[3] "It will be like

waking up every day on death row, with no chance of a stay of execution," said pastor and author Randy Frazee. "In essence, Hades is banishment from the very presence of God and the life we were made to live while we await our final judgment."[4]

That final judgment marks the onset of the last stage of our existence—our forever life. Upon Jesus' triumphant return to earth, followers of Christ in the intermediate state will receive their imperishable resurrected body and graduate into the new heaven and the new earth for eternity. The unrepentant will receive their resurrected body but will have their sentence to hell confirmed. These are irrevocable destinations where forever will be lived out.

What will the final judgment be like? "The FJ [final judgment] is the great time of reckoning, at the end of history and before the eternal state, when God will judge all of his moral creatures, whether men or angels, demanding of them an account of everything they have thought, said, or done," said theologian Alan Gomes.[5]

Gomes said that at the judgment, God "will display his mercy in pardoning those who have repented of their sins and have received the forgiveness grounded in Christ's atoning work, which satisfied divine justice through his death on the cross. Moreover, in punishing the finally unrepentant, he will reveal his righteousness, and 'by no means clear the guilty' (Nah. 1:3)."[6]

Gomes is among the scholars who believe that at the final judgment Christians also will receive rewards based on "the quality and extent of service" for God.[7]

Said Gomes, "Our Lord himself . . . exhorts his disciples to stand firm in persecution, in the knowledge that their reward in heaven will be great.[8] He tells them not to invest their lives in the cares and pursuits of this world but to lay up for themselves imperishable treasure in heaven.[9] The most seemingly minor and trivial acts of service will not escape his notice, and even for these he shall compensate his children richly."[10]

Other scholars, however, believe the incredible joys of heaven will be the great reward for all followers of Christ equally.[11] "In the kingdom of God the principles of merit and ability may be set aside so that grace can prevail," said New Testament scholar Simon Kistemaker.[12]

Regardless, the simple answer to what happens after death is this: "We continue to live." The nature of our final abode will be based on who is paying for our sins. Have we received the gift of forgiveness that Jesus purchased for us on the cross?[13] If so, we will spend forever in his presence in heaven. If not, we must pay for our sins ourselves as we spend eternity separated from him.

What happens to us after death, then, depends entirely on how we respond to Christ before we die.[14]

Scripture Speaks

Some of My Favorite Verses Dealing with Heaven

Psalm 16:9–10

Therefore my heart is glad and my tongue rejoices;
        my body also will rest secure,
because you will not abandon me to the realm of the dead,
        nor will you let your faithful one see decay.

Psalm 23:4, 6

Even though I walk
        through the darkest valley,
I will fear no evil,
        for you are with me;
your rod and your staff,
        they comfort me . . .
Surely your goodness and love will follow me
        all the days of my life,
and I will dwell in the house of the LORD
        forever.

Psalm 84:10

Better is one day in your courts
        than a thousand elsewhere;
I would rather be a doorkeeper in the house of my God
        than dwell in the tents of the wicked.

Psalm 116:3–4

The cords of death entangled me,
> the anguish of the grave came over me;
> I was overcome by distress and sorrow.
Then I called on the name of the Lord:
> "Lord, save me!"

Isaiah 11:6

The wolf will live with the lamb,
> the leopard will lie down with the goat,
the calf and the lion and the yearling together;
> and a little child will lead them.

Isaiah 65:17

"See, I will create
> new heavens and a new earth.
The former things will not be remembered,
> nor will they come to mind."

Daniel 6:26–27

"For he is the living God
> and he endures forever;
his kingdom will not be destroyed,
> his dominion will never end.
He rescues and he saves;
> he performs signs and wonders
> in the heavens and on the earth."

Matthew 6:19–21

"Do not store up for yourselves treasures on earth,
where moths and vermin destroy, and where thieves break
in and steal. But store up for yourselves treasures in heaven,
where moths and vermin do not destroy, and where thieves
do not break in and steal. For where your treasure is, there
your heart will be also."

Matthew 25:21

"His master replied, 'Well done, good and faithful servant! You have been faithful with a few things; I will put you in charge of many things. Come and share your master's happiness!'"

Luke 23:42–43

Then he said, "Jesus, remember me when you come into your kingdom."

Jesus answered him, "Truly I tell you, today you will be with me in paradise."

John 14:2–4

"My Father's house has many rooms; if that were not so, would I have told you that I am going there to prepare a place for you? And if I go and prepare a place for you, I will come back and take you to be with me that you also may be where I am. You know the way to the place where I am going."

Romans 6:23

For the wages of sin is death, but the gift of God is eternal life in Christ Jesus our Lord.

Romans 8:18

I consider that our present sufferings are not worth comparing with the glory that will be revealed in us.

1 Corinthians 2:9

However, as it is written:

"What no eye has seen,
       what no ear has heard,
and what no human mind has conceived"—
       the things God has prepared for those who love
   him . . .

1 Corinthians 15:42–44

So will it be with the resurrection of the dead. The body that is sown is perishable, it is raised imperishable; it is sown in dishonor, it is raised in glory; it is sown in weakness, it is raised in power; it is sown a natural body, it is raised a spiritual body. If there is a natural body, there is also a spiritual body.

1 Corinthians 15:54–57

When the perishable has been clothed with the imperishable, and the mortal with immortality, then the saying that is written will come true: "Death has been swallowed up in victory."

"Where, O death, is your victory?
Where, O death, is your sting?"

The sting of death is sin, and the power of sin is the law. But thanks be to God! He gives us the victory through our Lord Jesus Christ.

2 Corinthians 5:1

For we know that if the earthly tent we live in is destroyed, we have a building from God, an eternal house in heaven, not built by human hands.

1 Thessalonians 4:13–14

Brothers and sisters, we do not want you to be uninformed about those who sleep in death, so that you do not grieve like the rest of mankind, who have no hope. For we believe that Jesus died and rose again, and so we believe that God will bring with Jesus those who have fallen asleep in him.

2 Timothy 4:7–8

I have fought the good fight, I have finished the race, I have kept the faith. Now there is in store for me the crown of righteousness, which the Lord, the righteous Judge, will award to me on that day—and not only to me, but also to all who have longed for his appearing.

1 John 5:11

And this is the testimony: God has given us eternal life, and this life is in his Son.

Revelation 3:5

"The one who is victorious will, like them, be dressed in white. I will never blot out the name of that person from the book of life, but will acknowledge that name before my Father and his angels."

Revelation 7:16–17

"'Never again will they hunger;
    never again will they thirst.
The sun will not beat down on them,'
    nor any scorching heat.
For the Lamb at the center of the throne
    will be their shepherd;
'he will lead them to springs of living water.'
    'And God will wipe away every tear from their
eyes.'"

Revelation 21:1–5

Then I saw "a new heaven and a new earth," for the first heaven and the first earth had passed away, and there was no longer any sea. I saw the Holy City, the new Jerusalem, coming down out of heaven from God, prepared as a bride beautifully dressed for her husband. And I heard a loud voice from the throne saying, "Look! God's dwelling place is now among the people, and he will dwell with them. They will be his people, and God himself will be with them and be their God. 'He will wipe every tear from their eyes. There will be no more death' or mourning or crying or pain, for the old order of things has passed away."

He who was seated on the throne said, "I am making everything new!" Then he said, "Write this down, for these words are trustworthy and true."

Revelation 21:23–26

The city does not need the sun or the moon to shine on it, for the glory of God gives it light, and the Lamb is its lamp. The nations will walk by its light, and the kings of the earth will bring their splendor into it. On no day will its gates ever be shut, for there will be no night there. The glory and honor of the nations will be brought into it.

Revelation 22:4–5

They will see his face, and his name will be on their foreheads. There will be no more night. They will not need the light of a lamp or the light of the sun, for the Lord God will give them light. And they will reign for ever and ever.

Discussion Guide

Questions for Group Interaction or Personal Reflection

Whenever I read about a subject that intrigues, inspires, or challenges me, the first thing I like to do is discuss it with someone. I've found that I'm more likely to apply the lessons of a topic if I'm in a circle of friends who each offer insights. In community, truth often goes deeper.

I've written this guide to stimulate your thoughts on the topic of an afterlife. Yes, the questions can aid you in privately reflecting on what you've read, but my hope is that you'll join with a few friends to grow together in your understanding and application of the insights from the experts I've interviewed for this book.

This is not a Bible study. Instead, it's designed to encourage your thinking about what happens to us after we leave this world. There may be more questions for each chapter than you're inclined to wrestle with. That's all right; sift through them and select the ones that best fit you or your group. Notice that I refer to myself in the third person. That's because it makes the questions more understandable if they are read aloud during a discussion.

Regardless of where you find yourself on your spiritual journey, I hope this guide will lead you into a more robust appreciation of the topic of heaven and how it applies to your own circumstances. In the safety of authentic community, let's engage in honest dialogue so we can emerge ever more invigorated and transformed by God's teachings about life after death.

Introduction

1. As you begin this book, where are you on your spiritual journey? Imagine a scale of one to ten, with one representing staunch atheism, five representing the point of coming to faith in Christ, and ten representing full devotion to him. What number would best reflect your current spiritual status? Why did you choose that number? What would it take for you to move up on the scale?

2. Philip Yancey wrote, "Grace means there is nothing we can do to make God love us more . . . And grace means there is nothing we can do to make God love us less."[1] If this is true, what does this say about God's love? Do you *really* believe there is nothing you could do to make God love you less? Please explain.

3. The introduction describes Lee's brush with death. Have you ever come close to dying? What were the circumstances? What emotions did you experience? In what ways did this incident alter your view of life and death?

4. If you could ask God any one question about the afterlife and you knew he would give you an answer right now, what would you ask him—and why?

5. Do you believe it's possible to *know* with reasonable certainty what happens to us after we die? What would you need in order to have that kind of confidence?

6. The introduction previews many of the topics this book will cover: our fear of death, the existence of the soul, near-death experiences, evidence for Christianity, heaven, hell, and reincarnation. Which of these issues are the most intriguing to you and why?

7. When you were a child, what was your image of heaven? How has that vision changed as you've grown into adulthood?

8. Joni Eareckson Tada has said her first impulse in heaven won't be to jump out of her wheelchair to run and dance, but rather to fall on her knees in worship of her Savior. Can you relate to that? Why or why not?

Chapter 1: The Quest for Immortality

1. Describe what frightens you. Snakes? Confined spaces? Heights? Failure? Finances? Drowning? Public speaking? Are your fears purely irrational, or do they stem from a trauma that you went through, possibly as a child?

2. Specifically, do you fear death? What is it about dying that particularly concerns you? Is it the process of dying? The uncertainty of what comes after this life? Losing all that you have in this world? Can you relate to the physician, Alex Lickerman, who said, "I've tried to resolve my fear of death intellectually and come to the conclusion that it can't be done, at least by me." Elaborate as best you can.

3. Do you think very often about dying, or do you generally avoid contemplating your death? Is it difficult for you to ponder the subject? Do you ever discuss this topic with family members or others? What's at the root of our general reluctance to broach this issue?

4. What do you want written on your tombstone? Can you put it in a sentence or two?

5. Staks Rosch said in a *Huffington Post* article that "depression is a serious problem within the greater atheist community and far too often, that depression has led to suicide." In your view, what are some reasons for this? Does spiritual skepticism always have to lead to hopelessness, or can people find courage and optimism without a belief in God? Try imagining that there is no God. What are some ways you would seek to inject hope into your life?

6. Clay Jones in his book *Immortal* described various approaches that people take to outlive themselves through symbolic immortality and other means. Can you relate to any of those? Do you think some people are motivated to have children in order to leave a legacy?

7. Do you have a desire for your name to be remembered after your death? What was your reaction to the fact that very few people can give the first names of their great-great-grandparents—and they don't really care about their ancestors? How would it feel to you to have your name lost from memory?

8. Science fiction writer Isaac Asimov is quoted as saying, "Whatever the tortures of hell, I think the boredom of heaven would be even worse." What's your reaction to that observation? Because it lasts for eternity, is it inevitable that heaven will be boring? Why or why not?

Chapter 2: Searching for the Soul

1. Psychiatrist Ralph Lewis said, "There is simply no room for belief in a spiritual realm, in a scientific view of reality. Period." After reading this chapter, do you agree or disagree with him? What are some reasons for your conclusion?

2. Some experts believe all our actions and emotions are simply the product of brain activity. In fact, philosopher Patricia Churchland said, "Gosh, the love that I feel for my child is really just neural chemistry? Well, actually it is. But that doesn't bother me." Would that bother you? Do you believe everything we feel and do is just the product of interacting molecules? If so, what are some of the implications this would have?

3. Philosopher J. P. Moreland gives biblical reasons for believing that our soul separates from our body at the point of death as we enter into a temporary intermediate state of disembodiment until the general resurrection of the body. Are the verses he provides sufficient to convince you that this is the biblical teaching? How so?

4. As a bright and curious youngster, Sharon Dirckx suddenly became aware of her own consciousness, asking the questions, *Why can I think? Why do I exist? Why am I a living, breathing, conscious person who experiences life?* Have you personally wrestled with thoughts like this? Describe when your consciousness became apparent to you.

5. Dirckx went away to college thinking it's incompatible for a scientist to believe in God. Have you ever held that opinion—or do you now? Does this make sense to you? Why do you think many people hold this belief?

6. How would you describe the smell of coffee? Do you agree with Dirckx that to understand what coffee smells like, you need to *experience* it? How would you describe the difference between a first-person and third-person point of view? Why do you think this is relevant to the question of whether we have a soul?

7. Dirckx uses a framework of three questions to investigate whether we are just our brains and nothing more: (1) Is this idea internally consistent? (2) Does it make sense of the world? and (3) Can it truly be lived? What's your opinion of her analysis? Do you agree with her that the brain-only hypothesis fails these tests? How so?

8. Some philosophers say that because God is conscious, this explains why we are conscious. Is that persuasive to you? Why or why not?

Chapter 3: Near-Death Experiences

1. According to one survey, as many as one out of ten people over thirty-five countries have had a near-death experience (NDE). Have you or anyone you know undergone one? If so, what was it like? Has it altered your thinking about the afterlife?

2. Before you read this chapter, what was your reaction when someone described an NDE? Were you receptive? Were you intrigued? Were you mostly agnostic on the validity of the experience, or were you skeptical? Describe any way in which your attitude about NDEs has shifted after reading Lee's interview with researcher John Burke.

3. A few people have been caught making up stories about a near-death experience for publicity purposes or to make a profit. How much does that fact influence your skepticism as you evaluate the legitimacy of NDEs? Do you believe other people can have a sincere motive in describing their NDE? How would you evaluate whether someone is sincere or lying?

4. Some Christians won't even consider the possibility that NDEs are legitimate, because they consider them to be the product of the occult or New Age thinking. Yet, other Christians, notably theologian R. C. Sproul, urge people to keep an open mind and conduct more research. Based on the expert testimony of John Burke, what do you think is the wisest approach toward NDEs?

5. Which story of an NDE in the chapter intrigued you the most? What was it about that case that sparked your interest?

6. How did you react to the story of Howard Storm's violent and frightening near-death experience? What emotions did it evoke? Do you believe it has the ring of truth? Explain.

7. Echoing the sentiments of neuroscientist Sharon Dirckx, Lee said that just one well-documented case of an NDE would be sufficient to constitute strong evidence that our consciousness continues after clinical death. Do you believe this threshold has been met? What kind of research should be pursued in the future as NDEs are further investigated?

8. Lee took a rather conservative approach to NDEs by zeroing in on instances in which there is some sort of external corroboration—for example, the story about the woman who saw a tennis shoe on the upper ledge of the hospital while she was out of her body, as well as other such cases. Lee concluded that, at a minimum, NDEs show that our consciousness can survive our clinical death, at least for a while. Do you believe that's a reasonable way to look at the evidence? Why or why not?

Chapter 4: The Pyramid to Heaven

1. As you began reading this chapter, how would you have classified yourself—as a hardcore skeptic, a moderate skeptic, spiritually neutral, a spiritual seeker, a believer in Christ, or a strong and confident Christian? Did this chapter change where you fit along that continuum? In what way?

2. Chad Meister went through a period of doubting Christianity after he encountered credible people with conflicting beliefs. Have you ever doubted your faith? What happened? How did you process that experience? Did you come to any resolution?

3. Does the "heaven pyramid" make sense to you? Do you believe it covers the essential issues that need to be investigated? Which level of the pyramid was the most important for you and why?

4. In John 18:38, Pontius Pilate famously asked, "What is truth?" How would you answer him?

5. Meister gave three reasons for believing in God: the origin of the universe, the fine-tuning of the universe, and the existence of objective morality. In what ways do you find these arguments persuasive?

6. The Qur'an and the Bible make conflicting claims. How important is the eyewitness nature of the Christian claims? Is corroboration of Christianity from outside sources important to you? On a scale of one to ten, with one being absolute skepticism and ten being a belief that the Bible is trustworthy, where would you place yourself and why?

7. Why do you think the resurrection of Jesus is the key to Christianity? If he did, indeed, return from the dead, what are some of the implications for the world? For your life and future?

8. If Jesus was resurrected, it would be a miracle—but miracles are possible if God exists. Philosopher Richard Purtill described a miracle as an event brought about by the power of God that is a temporary exception to the ordinary course of nature for the purpose of showing that God has acted in history.[2] Have you ever had an experience in your life that you can only describe as a miracle? If so, describe what happened and how it affected you.

9. The top level of the heaven pyramid is the gospel. If someone asked you why Jesus died "for our sins," what would you say to him? Does God's kingdom, as Meister described it, sound attractive to you? Are you confident at this point that you will spend eternity with God? Please explain.

Chapter 5: Heaven: A Guide

1. In a sense, astrophysicist Sarah Salviander describes climbing the heaven pyramid in her spiritual journey, coming to the conclusion that Christianity is true. But it was the death of her stillborn baby that ended up cementing her faith. What did you think of her story? Can you relate to any of it? In what ways?

2. What do you think of John Eldredge's observation that "nearly every Christian I have spoken with has some idea that eternity is an unending church service. We have settled on an image of the never-ending sing-along in the sky, one great hymn after another, forever and ever, amen. And our heart sinks. *Forever and ever? That's it? That's the good news?* And then we sigh and feel guilty that we are not more 'spiritual.' We lose heart, and we turn once more to the present to find what life we can." Have you ever wrestled with feelings like that? How has this chapter helped change that?

3. Theologian Scot McKnight gave nine reasons he believes in heaven. Which of those resonated with you the most? Did you find some of the reasons more persuasive than others? If so, which ones?

4. McKnight said the Bible teaches that heaven isn't some ethereal place populated by disembodied souls, but it's the "new heaven and new earth"—the renewal and renovation of creation, where we will have resurrected bodies like Jesus did. Was that a new concept for you? What is your reaction to it?

5. McKnight said some people see heaven purely as "theocentric," or exclusively focused on individuals worshiping God, while others see it as more "kingdom-centric,"

stressing the community aspect of the afterlife. Which camp do you most naturally fall into and why? Do you think it's possible to have a balanced view between these two perspectives?

6. McKnight describes the first hour in heaven being filled with people reconciling with those they have been in conflict with. He said this could be instantaneous or take place over a period of time. How do you feel about that? Is there someone you would wince at seeing in heaven because you are currently estranged from them? What would it feel like to live in harmony even with those you disagree with? Would you look forward to this period of reconciliation or would it concern you?

7. McKnight uses the veranda as a way of describing the social aspects of heaven. Which would you tend to use most: the veranda or a garden in the backyard? Why?

8. How do you feel emotionally about the prospect of see-ing God face-to-face? What do you think that will be like? Does McKnight's illustration of the "magic eye" help you at all? The famous preacher Charles Spurgeon said, "The very glory of heaven is that we shall see him, that same Christ who once died upon Calvary's cross, that we shall fall down, and worship at his feet—nay, more, that he shall kiss us with the kisses of his mouth, and welcome us to dwell with him forever." How do you feel about that quote?

9. As you finished reading McKnight's chapter, what aspect of heaven are you the most curious about?

Chapter 6: Seven on Heaven

1. Do you believe that God welcomes our questions or do you think he is offended by them? Have you had an expe-rience in which a question about God has hindered your

faith but you eventually received a satisfactory explanation that removed this obstacle? If so, describe what happened.

2. The question of whether pets will be in heaven sounds trivial, but actually it's a significant concern for a lot of people. What was your favorite pet as a child or adult? What did you appreciate the most about your pet? Do you expect to see this pet in heaven? If you did, what would that say about God?

3. Scholars are split on whether there will be marriage in heaven. As for McKnight, he believes there won't be any *new* marriages there. Everything seems to hinge on the one verse that McKnight discusses. Whose position do you favor and why?

4. New Testament scholar Craig Blomberg says the motivation of Christians ought to be to please God, not to strive for rewards in heaven. He believes the gospel should "liberate believers from all such performance-centered conceptions of the Christian life."[3] On the other hand, McKnight said he does find some motivation in verses that speak in terms of heavenly rewards. Where do you come down on this issue? Will everyone be treated the same in heaven, or do you believe some Christians will be rewarded more than others?

5. Heaven will be a perfect place populated by holy people, yet most, if not all, Christians haven't achieved that status prior to death. Does the idea of purgatory make sense to you? Or do you believe that God will instantly perfect believers at death by an act of glorification? Which position makes the most biblical sense to you and why?

6. Casket or urn? Do you want to be buried or cremated when you die? After reading the section on this issue, has your attitude changed? If you want to be cremated, how would you describe your motivation?

7. Have you or someone you know gone through a miscarriage or the death of a young child? It's a heartrending experience. Are you encouraged by McKnight's comments about whether children will be in heaven? If God is loving, good, and just, how do you think he may deal with them?

8. Jesus said in John 14:6 that he is the only route to heaven. Does this claim rankle you? Or does it make sense? How would you recount the story of Jesus that McKnight tells? Why is it "good news"?

Chapter 7: The Logic of Hell

1. Jesus warned in Matthew 7:13 that "broad is the road that leads to destruction, and many enter through it," and yet only 2 percent of Americans believe they'll end up in hell. How would you reconcile these two statements?

2. Many people react vehemently against the teaching that hell involves eternal conscious suffering. One Bible teacher called it the "crazy uncle" that the church has kept locked in the back bedroom for centuries because of "justifiable embarrassment." What's your visceral reaction to the idea that the unrepentant will undergo torment forever? Do you believe Christians should nevertheless continue to teach that doctrine if the Bible supports it?

3. Have you ever heard a sermon on hell? If so, did it make sense to you? What emotions did it evoke? If not, do you believe churches are negligent in failing to proclaim the whole counsel of God? Are congregations well served if pastors ignore this topic? If you were to write a sermon on hell, what are some of the points you would want to emphasize?

4. How would you describe the difference between *torture* and *torment*?

5. Philosopher Paul Copan said that God doesn't *send* people to hell, but that people "who reject the rule of God *send themselves* to hell." As musician Michael Card says, God "simply speaks the sentence that they have passed upon themselves." Does this distinction make sense to you? Why or why not?

6. Lee admitted he once struggled with reconciling the doctrine of hell with the justice of God, but he was helped when he realized there are different degrees of punishment in hell. How does it affect your attitude toward this topic to know that in hell, one size doesn't fit all?

7. What's your reaction to *The Twilight Zone* episode that Copan described? Alternatively, how do you feel about the afterlife as it's depicted in the popular Netflix show *The Good Place*?

8. Read the parable of Lazarus and the rich man in Luke 16:19–31. Granted, this is a parable and it's about the intermediate state. But are there some lessons you can take away from this story? If so, what are some of them?

9. Pastor Richard Wurmbrand was tortured for his faith under Romanian dictator Nicolae Ceauşescu. Wurmbrand later wrote, "The cruelty of atheism is hard to believe. When a man has no faith in the reward of good or the punishment of evil, there is no reason to be human. There is no restraint from the depths of evil that is in man. The Communist torturers often said, 'There is no God, no hereafter, no punishment for evil. We can do what we wish.'" Do you believe teachings about hell provide a deterrent to evil behavior in our world? How much of the world's current cruelty can be attributed to people losing their belief in any kind of an afterlife?

Chapter 8: Escape from Hell

1. What's your reaction to evangelical icon John Stott "tentatively" embracing annihilationism? He denied he was motivated by emotion, but is it really possible to divorce our feelings from this issue? In your opinion, how much does his stature as a Christian leader give credibility to the idea of annihilationism?

2. Stott offered several reasons for why God might snuff the unrepentant out of existence rather than subject them to an eternity of torment. Which of his reasons, if any, did you find the most persuasive and why?

3. Paul Copan defended the traditional teachings on hell by using a variety of Bible references, philosophy, and logic. Did he succeed, in your view? Which, if any, of his counterarguments against annihilationism carried the most weight with you?

4. Agnostic New Testament scholar Bart Ehrman claims that Jesus was an annihilationist. If he made that statement to you, how would you respond? What evidence would you use to defend your position?

5. Christian universalism says that in the end God will forgive and adopt all people through Christ, perhaps after a limited period of restorative punishment in hell for some. Copan called this "an aberrant and dangerous doctrine." In your view, what's the strongest argument in favor of universalism and the most persuasive case against it?

6. How does Copan respond to the assertion that even God wants everyone to be saved (1 Timothy 2:4; 2 Peter 3:9)? How would you describe the difference between Christ being the *potential* Savior of all but not the *actual* Savior of all? If everyone doesn't end up in heaven, do you

believe Jesus failed in his mission "to seek and to save the lost" (Luke 19:10)? Why or why not?

7. Martin Luther, though not a universalist, nevertheless speculated that some people might have an opportunity after their death to come to faith in Christ. What's your reaction to this "Luther option"? Are there good biblical reasons for endorsing it? What would its implications be?

8. If someone who was not a Christian asked you directly, "Am I going to hell?" how would you respond to them?

Chapter 9: The Reincarnation Sensation

1. Why do you think that the ancient idea of reincarnation has become such a popular belief in modern Western societies?

2. What's your reaction when celebrities like Shirley MacLaine, Loretta Lynn, and Sylvester Stallone say they had previous lives? Are you intrigued? Skeptical? Amused?

3. What did you think of the Bridey Murphy phenomenon when you read about it at the beginning of the chapter? What captured your imagination? Can you see why it became a national phenomenon? What was your reaction when you read the rest of the story later in the chapter? What evidence against her do you think was the most damaging?

4. Douglas Groothuis offered several reasons why reincarnation doesn't make logical sense. Which of those explanations resonated most with you? What are some of the shortcomings of the law of karma?

5. How would you describe the difference between heaven and nirvana?

6. If someone made the claim to you that Jesus taught reincarnation, how would you answer?

7. Have you ever experienced déjà vu? Can you give an example? What natural explanations do you have for it?

8. Douglas Groothuis said if he had a choice, he would rather that his deceased wife, Becky, face resurrection than reincarnation. What would you prefer for yourself? What are your reasons?

Chapter 10: On the Edge of Eternity

1. Before reading this chapter, were you familiar with evangelist Luis Palau's ministry? How so?

2. Palau described how his oncologist was blunt in telling him he only had a short time to live. Can you imagine getting that kind of news for yourself? What would be your first thought? What emotions would you feel? What are the first three things you would want to do?

3. Palau described the last words of his father before he died. Palau said, "He taught me how to die—with a hymn in my heart and Scripture on my lips." If you could orchestrate your final moments in this world, what would they be?

4. During Lee's interview with Palau, he described some questions he would like to ask God. If you could ask God any question in heaven, what would it be and why?

5. Besides God, who are the top three people you'd like to meet in heaven? Why did you choose these individuals? What's the first question you'd like to ask them?

6. Over the years, Palau said his approach to preaching has changed, so that today he tries to focus on the love and grace of God. Do you feel you spend enough time meditating on those attributes of the Father? Or do you tend to linger on your own unworthiness of his affection? Which do you feel more—the smile of God or his critical judgment? Why is this so? What would it take for you to bask in God's love?

7. Palau said he would tell believers "to go for it" by taking risks to tell others the good news of the salvation available through Jesus. Can you recall a time when you got into a spiritual conversation with someone who was far from God? What were the circumstances? What did you feel before and after the encounter? What keeps you from taking more risks to share Christ with others?

8. Palau said he would tell non-Christians, "Don't be stupid!" What do you think he meant by that? Do you feel he was speaking out of harshness or genuine love? If you're a Christian, how did you react to his advice? If you're not a Christian, were you offended? Challenged? Encouraged? What were your emotions?

Conclusion

1. Have you ever visited someone shortly before they died? What do you remember most about the encounter? Did they say or do something that you remember to this day?

2. Author Max Lucado said we cannot fathom eternity, and that's true. Did Chad Meister's illustration of sand on a beach give you a peek into what "forever" is like? How would you try to help someone "feel" the extent of eternity? In light of heaven's infinite nature, the suffering from this lifetime will fade into distant memories. Are there particular aspects of your life that you'd like to see swallowed up by eternity?

3. Jesus' resurrection and the promise of heaven revolutionized his disciples in *this* world, changing their values, mission, and priorities. In what ways might living in the light of heaven change your attitudes today?

4. Why wait until heaven to reconcile with someone you're at odds with? Are you in conflict with another person? Bring

their face to your mind. What are three steps you can take to become reconciled with them? What are the depths you would go to forgive? Or is there a line that could be crossed that would be "too far" for you to forgive someone? Explain.

5. If someone asked you about the fate of people who have never heard the Jesus story, what would you tell them?

6. The first verse Lee memorized as a new Christian was 1 John 5:13: "I write these things to you who believe in the name of the Son of God so that you may know that you have eternal life." How confident do you feel that you have been safely adopted into God's family forever? Do you know in your heart and mind that you will spend eternity with God in heaven? On a scale of one to ten, with one being totally doubtful and ten being totally confident, what number would best represent you? Why did you choose that number?

7. Lee became a Christian when he applied the "formula of faith" to his life: *Believe + Receive = Become*. Maybe you've believed the Jesus story for a long time, but your life and values have never really changed. Could it be because you have never received Jesus' freely offered gift of forgiveness and eternal life? If you lack confidence that you're safely adopted as a child of God, is there anything keeping you from praying the kind of prayer that changed Lee's life and eternity?

8. If you're not a follower of Christ, what additional evidence would you need to believe the Jesus story? What are some concrete steps you can take to investigate Christianity further? Are you willing to commit to taking those steps with urgency? Remember, you don't have to know *everything* to know *something*. If the evidence discussed in this book is sufficient, is there any reason why you wouldn't receive Jesus right now as your forgiver and leader through a prayer of repentance and faith?

Acknowledgments

I'm glad you've paused here. It's important for you to know that even though the author's name is on the cover, the creation of a book like this is very much a team project that draws on the talent, expertise, and hard work of many dedicated people.

I'm always grateful for the advice and input of my ministry associate Mark Mittelberg. We like to joke that we're "joined at the brain," but that's actually more than just a quip. We share the same vision for ministry and are committed to sharpening each other as iron sharpens iron (Proverbs 27:17).

My literary agent Don Gates offered sage wisdom during the process. My editor Andy Rogers provided astute feedback that significantly improved the flow and focus of the book. Dirk Buursma and the team of designers, marketers, and salespeople at Zondervan were invaluable in getting this resource into your hands.

My wife, Leslie, as always, was a steady source of encouragement. Finally, I am beholden to the various scholars and experts who allowed me to interview them.

As we Texans like to say, "Ah 'preciate all y'all."

One more thing. Let me be the first to announce a reunion party someday in heaven, when we'll gather to celebrate what God alone was able to accomplish through his willing servants. He deserves the glory for whatever ministry this project fulfills.

Meet Lee Strobel

A theist-turned-Christian Lee Strobel, the former award-winning legal editor at the *Chicago Tribune*, is a *New York Times* bestselling author of more than forty books and curricula that have sold millions of copies. He is founding director of the Lee Strobel Center for Evangelism and Applied Apologetics at Colorado Christian University.

The *Washington Post* described Lee as "one of the evangelical community's most popular apologists." He received his journalism degree from the University of Missouri and his Master of Studies in Law from Yale Law School. Lee was a journalist for fourteen years at the *Chicago Tribune* and other newspapers, winning Illinois's highest honors for both investigative reporting and public service journalism from United Press International.

After probing the evidence for Jesus for nearly two years, Lee became a Christian in 1981. He was later a teaching pastor at three of America's largest churches and hosted the national TV program *Faith under Fire*. He also taught First Amendment law at Roosevelt University.

In 2017, Lee's story was depicted in an award-winning motion picture, *The Case for Christ*. He has won numerous national awards for his books, which include *The Case for Christ*, *The Case for Faith*, *The Case for a Creator*, *The Case for Grace*, *In Defense of Jesus*, and *The Case for Miracles*.

Lee and Leslie have been married for forty-nine years. Their daughter, Alison, is a novelist, and their son, Kyle, is a professor of theology. They have four grandchildren.

Notes

Introduction

1. Quoted in Nicholas Kristof, "Reverend, You Say the Virgin Birth Is 'a Bizarre Claim'?" *New York Times*, April 20, 2019, www.nytimes.com /2019/04/20/opinion/sunday/christian-easter-serene-jones.html.
2. See Tracy Munsil, "*AWVI 2020* Survey: 1 in 3 US Adults Embrace Salvation through Jesus; More Believe It Can Be 'Earned,'" Arizona Christian University: Cultural Research Center, August 4, 2020, www.arizonachristian.edu/blog/2020/08/04/1-in-3-us-adults-embrace -salvation-through-jesus-more-believe-it-can-be-earned.
3. Andrew Sullivan, "What Do Atheists Think of Death?" *The Atlantic*, May 16, 2010, www.theatlantic.com/daily-dish/archive/2010/05/what-do -atheists-think-of-death/187003.
4. Bart D. Ehrman, *God's Problem: How the Bible Fails to Answer Our Most Important Question—Why We Suffer* (San Francisco: HarperOne, 2008), 127.
5. Andrew Sullivan, *Love Undetectable* (New York: Vintage, 1999), 217.

Chapter 1: The Quest for Immortality

1. Philippians 1:21.
2. Irvin D. Yalom, *Staring at the Sun: Overcoming the Terror of Death* (San Francisco: Jossey-Bass, 2008), 5–6.
3. Clay Jones, *Immortal: How the Fear of Death Drives Us and What We Can Do about It* (Eugene, OR: Harvest House, 2020).
4. J. P. Moreland, "Endorsement," in Clay Jones, *Why Does God Allow Evil? Compelling Answers for Life's Toughest Questions* (Eugene, OR: Harvest House, 2017), 1.
5. Frank Turek, "Endorsement," in Jones, *Immortal*, 1.
6. Luc Ferry, *A Brief History of Thought: A Philosophical Guide to Living*, trans. Theo Cuffe (New York: HarperCollins, 2011), 12.
7. Plato, *Phaedo*, 67.4–6, trans. David Gallop (Oxford: Oxford University Press, 2009), 14.
8. Michel de Montaigne, "To Philosophize Is to Learn How to Die," in

Michel de Montaigne, *The Complete Essays*, trans. M. A. Screech (New York: Penguin, 2003), 89.

9. Arthur Schopenhauer, *The World as Will and Representation*, vol. 1, trans. E. F. J. Payne (Indian Hills, CO: Falcon's Wing, 1958), 249.

10. See Ernest Becker, *The Denial of Death* (New York: Free Press, 1973).

11. Becker, *Denial of Death*, xvii.

12. Zygmunt Bauman, *Mortality, Immortality, and Other Life Strategies* (Stanford, CA: Stanford University Press, 1992), 31.

13. Staks Rosch, "Atheism Has a Suicide Problem," *Huffington Post*, December 8, 2017, www.huffpost.com/entry/atheism-has-a-suicide -problem_b_5a2a902ee4b022ec613b812b.

14. Miguel de Unamuno, *Tragic Sense of Life*, trans. J. E. Crawford Flitch (New York: Dover, 1954), 150.

15. Kanita Dervic et al., "Religious Affiliation and Suicide Attempt," *American Journal of Psychiatry* 161, no. 12 (December 2004), https://ajp .psychiatryonline.org/doi/full/10.1176/appi.ajp.161.12.2303.

16. Researchers tracked more than 100,000 nurses and health-care professionals for seventeen years for the study. See Ying Chen et al., "Religious Service Attendance and Deaths Related to Drugs, Alcohol, and Suicide among US Health Care Professionals," *JAMA Psychiatry* 77, no. 7 (May 6, 2020), https://jamanetwork.com/journals /jamapsychiatry/fullarticle/2765488.

17. David Smith, "2050—And Immortality Is within Our Grasp," *Observer/ Guardian*, May 21, 2005, www.theguardian.com/science/2005/may/22 /theobserver.technology.

18. See Ashlee Vance, "Elon Musk Unveils Brain Computer Implanted in Pigs," *Bloomberg News*, August 28, 2020, www.bloomberg.com/news /articles/2020-08-28/elon-musk-to-unveil-neuralink-brain-computer -implanted-in-pigs.

19. Quoted in Ben Makuch, "Frozen Faith: Cryonics and the Quest to Cheat Death," *Motherboard*, May 5, 2016, www.youtube.com /watch?v=m5KuNAeOtJ0&feature=youtu.be.

20. Quoted in David McCormack, "We Did It Out of Love," *Daily Mail*, May 19, 2014, http://dailymail.co.uk/news/article-2632809/We-did-love -baseball-legend-ted-williams-daughter-finally-speaks-brother-spent -100-000-fathers-body-cyrogenically-frozen.html-#ixzz5HCs7Ap5I.

21. Quoted in Larry King interview with Conan O'Brien, "Larry King Demands Conan Freeze His Corpse," YouTube, February 13, 2014, www.youtube.com/watch?v=PF7NpKG_S8g.

22. Sam Keen, "Foreword," in Becker, *Denial of Death*, xiii.

23. Edwin Shneidman, A *Commonsense Book of Death: Reflections at*

Ninety of a Lifelong Thanatologist (New York: Rowman & Littlefield, 2008), 34.

24. Nathan A. Heflick, "Children and the Quest for Immortality," *Psychology Today,* February 21, 2012, www.psychologytoday.com/us /blog/the-big-questions/201202/children-and-the-quest-immortality.

25. Quoted in Jones, *Immortal,* 62.

26. Richard Wade, "Ask Richard: Atheist Haunted by the Fear of Death," *Patheos,* August 23, 2010, https://friendlyatheist.patheos.com /2010/08/23/ask-richard-atheist-haunted-by-the-fear-of-death/.

27. Quoted in Jones, *Immortal,* 67. This quote is widely attributed to Michelangelo.

28. Quoted in Gill Perry and Colin Cunningham, eds., *Academies, Museums, and Canons of Art* (New Haven, CT: Yale University Press, 1999), 88.

29. See Michael Kinsley, *Old Age: A Beginner's Guide* (New York: Crown, 2016), 130.

30. Quoted in Caroline Shively and the Associated Press, "Wichita Police: 'BTK Is Arrested,'" Fox News, February 26, 2005, www.foxnews.com /story/wichita-police-btk-is-arrested.

31. Quoted in "Mark David Chapman Killed Lennon for Fame," UPI, October 15, 2004, www.upi.com/Archives/2004/10/15/Mark-David -Chapman-killed-Lennon-for-fame/2571097812800.

32. Quoted in Associated Press and Ashley Collman and Alex Greg, "It Took Incredible Planning and Incredible Stalking," *Daily Mail,* August 28, 2014, www.dailymail.co.uk/news/article-2737101/Mark-David -Chapman-brags-incredible-planning-stalking-notorious-murder-John -Lennon.html.

33. See Saul M. Kassin and Lawrence S. Wrightsman, *The American Jury on Trial: Psychological Perspectives* (New York: Routledge, 2012), 89.

34. Rafael Olmeda, "Parkland Shooter Nikolas Cruz Brags on Cellphone Videos, 'I'm Going to Be the Next School Shooter,'" *Sun Sentinel,* May 30, 2018, at http://sun-sentinel.com/local/broward/parkland /florida-school-shooting/fl-reg-florida-school-shooting-phone-video -release-20180530-story.html.

35. Marcus Aurelius, Meditations, 8:44, quoted in David R. Loy, *A Buddhist History of the West: Studies in Lack* (Albany, NY: SUNY, 2002), 67.

36. Quoted in Jones, *Immortal,* 97. This is an often-quoted comment, but its origins are obscure.

37. Stephen Fry, "'What Should We Think about Death?' Narrated by

Stephen Fry — That's Humanism!" March 17, 2014, www.youtube
.com/watch?v=pR7e0fmfXGw.

38. See Revelation 21:5.

39. 1 Corinthians 2:9 NLT.

40. Steve Jobs, "Commencement Address," Stanford University, June 12,
2005; cited in John Brownlee, "Steve Jobs: 'Death Is Very Likely the
Best Single Invention of Life,'" Cult of Mac, October 5, 2011, https://
www.cultofmac.com/121101/steve-jobs-death-is-very-likely-the-best
-single-invention-of-life-it-is-lifes-change-agent.

41. Cited in Jones, *Immortal*, 110.

42. Sam Harris, "Sam Harris on Death," *Big Think*, June 2, 2011,
www.youtube.com/watch?v=d_Uahu9XNzU.

43. See Thomas Nagel, *Mortal Questions* (Cambridge, UK: Cambridge
University Press, 2012), 3, 11.

44. Alex Lickerman, "Overcoming the Fear of Death," *Psychology Today*,
October 8, 2009, https://psychologytoday.com/blog/happiness-in-world
/200910/overcoming-the-fear-death.

45. Jones, *Immortal*, 139, italics in original.

46. Ferry, *Brief History of Thought*, 261.

47. Quoted in Mary Bowerman, "Heaven 'Is a Fairy Story': This Is What
Stephen Hawking Says Happens When People Die," *USA Today*,
March 14, 2018, www.usatoday.com/story/tech/nation-now/2018/03/14
/heaven-fairy-story-what-stephen-hawking-says-happens-when-people
-die/423344002/.

48. Quoted in Heather Tomlinson, "Ten Quick Responses to Atheist
Claims," *Christian Today*, October 8, 2014, www.christiantoday.com
/article/ten.quick.responses.to.atheist.claims/41439.htm.

Chapter 2: Searching for the Soul

1. Quotes excerpted from Ralph Lewis, "Is There Life after Death?
The Mind-Body Problem," *Psychology Today*, July 18, 2019,
www.psychologytoday.com/us/blog/finding-purpose/201907/is-there
-life-after-death-the-mind-body-problem. He tells his story in *Finding
Purpose in a Godless World* (Amherst, NY: Prometheus, 2019).

2. Daniel Dennett, *Consciousness Explained* (Boston: Little, Brown and
Company, 1991), 33.

3. Colin Blakemore, *The Mind Machine* (London: BBC Books, 1990), 270.

4. Graham Lawton, "The Benefits of Realising You're Just a Brain," *New
Scientist*, November 27, 2013, www.newscientist.com/article
/mg22029450-200-the-benefits-of-realising-youre-just-a-brain.

5. Physicalism, also known as monism (literally, *one-ness*), and dualism are broad terms that have been broken down by philosophers into a dizzying number of subcategories, including substance dualism, naturalistic dualism, holistic dualism, emergent dualism, two-aspect monism, reflexive monism, constitutional materialism, nonreductive physicalism, eliminative materialism, and so forth. For the purposes of my discussion, I will basically deal with the overarching claims of physicalism and dualism.

6. Colin McGinn, *The Mysterious Flame: Conscious Minds in a Material World* (New York: Basic, 1999), 13–14.

7. Mark C. Baker and Stewart Goetz, eds., *The Soul Hypothesis: Investigations into the Existence of the Soul* (New York: Bloomsbury, 2013), 1–2.

8. Dualists today include Oxford philosophers Richard Swinburne and Keith Ward; J. P. Moreland, who holds degrees in science, theology, and philosophy; physicist and philosopher Robin Collins; Templeton Prize–winning analytic philosopher Alvin Plantinga; Jeffrey Schwartz, a researcher in neuroplasticity at UCLA; and Mario Beauregard, a cognitive neuroscientist at the University of Arizona.

9. See Jesse Bering and David Bjorklund, "The Natural Emergence of Reasoning about the Afterlife as a Developmental Regularity," *Developmental Psychology* 40 (2004): 217–33.

10. Baker and Goetz, eds., *Soul Hypothesis*, 3.

11. Nancey Murphy, "Human Nature: Historical, Scientific, and Religious Issues," in *Whatever Happened to the Soul?* ed. Warren S. Brown, Nancey Murphy, and H. Newton Malony (Minneapolis: Fortress, 1998), 13.

12. Daniel Dennett, *Freedom Evolves* (New York: Viking, 2003), 1.

13. Baker and Goetz, eds., *Soul Hypothesis*, 20.

14. Paul Copan, *"How Do You Know You're Not Wrong?" Responding to Objections That Leave Christians Speechless* (Grand Rapids: Baker, 2005), 95, italics in original.

15. Most Christian philosophers believe animals also have souls. Writes philosopher J. P. Moreland, "But the animal soul is not as richly structured as the human soul, it does not bear the image of God, and it is far more dependent on the animal's body and its sense organs than is the human soul" (*The Soul: How We Know It's Real and Why It Matters* [Chicago: Moody, 2014], 145).

16. Arthur C. Custance, *The Mysterious Matter of Mind* (Grand Rapids: Zondervan, 1980), 90, http://209.240.156.133/Library/MIND/epilogue .html.

17. Quoted in Lee Strobel, *The Case for a Creator: A Journalist Investigates Scientific Evidence That Points toward God* (Grand Rapids: Zondervan, 2004), 261.

18. Moreland, *The Soul*, 44.

19. See Moreland, *The Soul*, 70–71.

20. See Luke 23:43: "Today you will be with me in paradise."

21. See 1 Peter 3:18–20.

22. See 2 Corinthians 5:8.

23. See Matthew 22:23–33; Acts 23:6–8.

24. See Revelation 21:1.

25. Patricia S. Churchland, *Touching a Nerve: The Self as Brain* (New York: Norton, 2013), 63.

26. Sharon Dirckx, *Why? Looking at God, Evil and Personal Suffering* (London: Inter-Varsity, 2013).

27. Psalm 8:3–4.

28. See Sharon Dirckx, *Am I Just My Brain?* (London: Good Book, 2019), 47–48. She attributes this thought experiment to Frank Jackson.

29. See Gottfried Wilhelm Leibniz, *Philosophical Papers and Letters*, 2nd ed. (Boston: Reidel, 1976).

30. Adrian Owen, "How Science Found a Way to Help Coma Patients Communicate," *The Guardian*, September 5, 2017, www.theguardian .com/news/2017/sep/05/how-science-found-a-way-to-help-coma-patient -communicate.

31. Wilder Penfield, *The Mystery of the Mind: A Critical Study of Consciousness and the Human Brain* (Princeton, NJ: Princeton University Press, 1975), 77–78.

32. See Dirckx, *Am I Just My Brain?* 69, 84.

33. Cited in Dirckx, *Am I Just My Brain?* 64.

34. Sam Harris, *Free Will* (New York: Free Press, 2012), 5.

35. See Nick Pollard, *Evangelism Made Slightly Less Difficult: How to Interest People Who Aren't Interested* (Downers Grove, IL: InterVarsity, 1997), 47–68.

36. Dirckx also deals with other theories, such as *compatibilism* or *soft determinism* and *libertarianism*; see *Am I Just My Brain?* 75–90.

37. For a videotaped discussion between Sharon Dirckx and Philip Goff, a philosopher and consciousness researcher at Durham University, see "Does Consciousness Point to God? Philip Goff & Sharon Dirckx," November 1, 2019, www.youtube.com/watch?v=Ef2vvT5GfoE.

38. See "Does Consciousness Point to God?"

39. See Stewart Goetz and Charles Taliaferro, *A Brief History of the Soul* (Malden, MA: Wiley-Blackwell, 2011), 6–29.

40. Goetz and Taliaferro, *A Brief History of the Soul*, 6.
41. Dirckx, *Am I Just My Brain?* 32–33.
42. For evidence and arguments pointing toward the truth of biblical Christianity, see my interview with philosophy professor Chad Meister (PhD, Marquette) in chapter 4.
43. Genesis 1:27: "So God created mankind in his own image, in the image of God he created them; male and female he created them."
44. There are some Christians who are physicalists. According to J. P. Moreland, some Christian physicalists take the *extinction/re-creation view*: "When the body dies the person ceases to exist since the person is in some sense the same as his or her body. At the future, final resurrection, persons are re-created [by God] after a period of non-existence." Others take the *immediate resurrection view*: "At death, in some way or another, each individual continues to exist in a physical way" (*The Soul*, 71).
45. Dirckx, *Am I Just My Brain?* 131.
46. Copan, "*How Do You Know You're Not Wrong?*" 113.

Chapter 3: Near-Death Experiences

1. Eben Alexander, *Proof of Heaven: A Neurosurgeon's Journey into the Afterlife* (New York: Simon & Schuster, 2012), 8–9.
2. Alexander, *Proof of Heaven*, 9, italics in original.
3. Alexander, *Proof of Heaven*, 38.
4. See Alexander, *Proof of Heaven*, 38–42.
5. Alexander, *Proof of Heaven*, 9.
6. See Raymond Moody, *Life after Life*, anniv. ed. (San Francisco: HarperOne, 2015).
7. Quoted in Janice Miner Holden, Bruce Greyson, and Debbie James, eds., *The Handbook of Near-Death Experiences: Thirty Years of Investigation* (Santa Barbara, CA: Praeger, 2009), vii.
8. Quoted in Holden, Greyson, and James, eds., *Handbook of Near-Death Experiences*, vii, italics in original. Philippians 4:7 reads in the NIV, "And the peace of God, which transcends all understanding, will guard your hearts and your minds in Christ Jesus."
9. Quoted in Holden, Greyson, and James, eds., *Handbook of Near-Death Experiences*, vii.
10. John Martin Fischer, "Are 'Near-Death Experiences' Real?" *New York Times*, February 13, 2020, www.nytimes.com/2020/02/13/opinion/near-death-experience.html.

11. Scot McKnight, *The Heaven Promise: Engaging the Bible's Truth about Life to Come* (Colorado Springs: WaterBrook, 2015), 144.

12. Cited in Sarah Knapton, "Near Death Experiences Are Felt by One in 10 People, Study Finds," *Telegraph*, June 28, 2019.

13. See Kyle Swenson, "'The Boy Who Came Back from Heaven' Now Wants His Day in Court," *Washington Post*, April 13, 2018, www.washingtonpost.com/news/morning-mix/wp/2018/04/11/the-boy -who-came-back-from-heaven-now-wants-his-day-in-court.

14. See Luke Dittrich, "The Prophet," *Esquire*, August 2013, https://classic .esquire.com/article/2013/8/1/the-prophet. Alexander responded to critics in a *Newsweek* article titled "The Science of Heaven," *Newsweek*, November 18, 2012, www.newsweek.com/science-heaven-63823.

15. John Burke, *What's after Life?* (Grand Rapids: Baker, 2019), 5–7; see also "Mary NDE," Near-Death Experience Research Foundation, www.nderf.org/experiences/1mary_nde.html.

16. See Emily Kent Smith and Tania Steere, "Have Scientists Proved There Is Life after Death? Research into Near-Death Experiences Reveals Awareness May Continue Even After the Brain Has Shut Down," *Daily Mail*, October 7, 2014, www.dailymail.co.uk/health/article-2783030 /Research-near-death-experiences-reveals-awareness-continue-brain -shut-down.html.

17. John Burke, *Imagine Heaven: Near-Death Experiences, God's Promises, and the Exhilarating Future That Awaits You* (Grand Rapids: Baker, 2015), back cover.

18. See R. C. Sproul, *Now, That's a Good Question!* (Wheaton, IL: Tyndale, 1996), 300.

19. See J. P. Moreland and Gary R. Habermas, *Immortality: The Other Side of Death* (Nashville: Nelson, 1992).

20. See Burke, *Imagine Heaven*, 51.

21. See Bonnie Malkin, "Girl Survives Sting by World's Deadliest Jellyfish," *Telegraph*, April 26, 2010, www.telegraph.co.uk/news/7638189 /Girl-survives-sting-by-worlds-deadliest-jellyfish.html.

22. For a full report on Ian McCormack's experience, see Burke, *Imagine Heaven*, 139–41.

23. Cited in Jeffrey Long, *Evidence of the Afterlife: The Science of Near-Death Experiences* (New York: HarperCollins, 2010), 169.

24. Burke, *Imagine Heaven*, 239.

25. J. Steve Miller, *Near-Death Experiences as Evidence for the Existence of God and Heaven: A Brief Introduction in Plain Language* (Acworth, GA: Wisdom Creek, 2012), 83.

26. Matthew 10:26.
27. Matthew 12:37.
28. This could be two separate judgments or two aspects of the final judgment. Theologian Alan W. Gomes supports the latter view: "Paul makes considerable reference to the rewards Christians will receive at the FJ [final judgment]" (*40 Questions about Heaven and Hell* [Grand Rapids: Kregel Academic, 2018], 158); see 1 Corinthians 3:8–15; 2 Corinthians 5:10.
29. See Revelation 11:15–18.
30. Cited in Holden, Greyson, and James, eds., *Handbook of Near-Death Experiences*, 70.
31. Cited in Christy Somos, "One in 10 People Have Had a 'Near-Death Experience,' European Study Says," CTV News, June 28, 2019, www .ctvnews.ca/mobile/health/one-in-10-people-have-had-a-near-death -experience-european-study-says-1.4487736.
32. His story is told in Burke, *Imagine Heaven*, 215–21.
33. Kevin and Alex Malarkey, *The Boy Who Came Back from Heaven: A Remarkable Account of Miracles, Angels, and Life beyond This World* (Carol Stream, IL: Tyndale, 2010).
34. "'The Boy Who Came Back from Heaven' Recants Story, Rebukes Christian Retailers," *Pulpit & Pen*, January 13, 2015, http://pulpitandpen.org/2015/01/13/the-boy-who-came-back-from -heaven-recants-story-rebukes-christian-retailers.
35. Burke, *Imagine Heaven*, 326.
36. See Penny Sartori, *The Near-Death Experiences of Hospitalized Intensive Care Patients: A Five Year Clinical Study* (Lewiston, NY: Mellen, 2008), 212–15.
37. Cited in Long, *Evidence of the Afterlife*, 72–73.
38. Cited in Janice Miner Holden, "Veridical Perception in Near-Death Experiences," in Holden, Greyson, and James, eds., *Handbook of Near-Death Experiences*, 185–211.
39. Quoted in Kenneth Ring and Sharon Cooper, *Mindsight: Near-Death and Out-of-Body Experiences in the Blind* (Palo Alto, CA: William James Center for Consciousness Studies, 1999), 136.
40. For these and other cases, see Moreland and Habermas, *Immortality*, 74–80.
41. See Burke, *Imagine Heaven*, 47–48.
42. Long, *Evidence of the Afterlife*, 44.
43. Burke, *Imagine Heaven*, 102–3.

Chapter 4: The Pyramid to Heaven

1. Chad V. Meister, *Building Belief: Constructing Faith from the Ground Up* (Grand Rapids: Baker, 2006).
2. John 18:38.
3. See Edith Hamilton and Huntington Cairns, eds., *The Collected Dialogues of Plato* (Princeton, NJ: Princeton University Press, 1989), 262E-263D.
4. See Jonathan Barnes, ed., *The Complete Works of Aristotle* (Princeton, NJ: Princeton University Press, 1984), 4.1011b25–27. Meister said, "Richard Kirkham notes that Plato, in the *Sophist*, is presenting a correspondence theory of truth—possibly correspondence as congruence—and that Aristotle is here presenting the earliest correspondence as correlation theory" (*Building Belief*, 201; see Richard Kirkham, *Theories of Truth: A Critical Introduction* [Cambridge, MA: MIT, 1992], chapter 4).
5. "The Law of non-contradiction is one of the basic laws in classical logic. It states that something cannot be both true and not true at the same time when dealing with the same context. For example, the chair in my living room, right now, cannot be made of wood and not made of wood at the same time" ("Law of Non-Contradiction," Christian Apologetics & Research Ministry, https://carm.org/dictionary/law-of-non-contradiction).
6. John G. Stackhouse Jr., *Humble Apologetics: Defending the Faith Today* (New York: Oxford University Press, 2002), 95.
7. Carl Sagan, *Cosmos* (1980; repr., New York: Ballantine, 2013), 1.
8. See William Lane Craig and Walter Sinnott-Armstrong, *God? A Debate between a Christian and an Atheist* (New York: Oxford University Press, 2004), 32–36.
9. Richard Dawkins, *The Selfish Gene*, 2nd ed. (New York: Oxford University Press, 1989), xxi.
10. Mary Baker Eddy, *Science and Health with Key to the Scriptures* (Boston: First Church of Christ, Scientist, 1934), 480.
11. Michael Ruse and Edward O. Wilson, "The Evolution of Ethics," in *Religion and the Natural Sciences: The Range of Engagement*, ed. James E. Huchingson (Eugene, OR: Wipf & Stock, 1993), 310.
12. Jean-Paul Sartre (1905–1980) made this comment in a lecture ("Existentialism Is a Humanism") given in 1946; see Walter Kaufman, *Existentialism from Dostoyevsky to Sartre* (New York: Plume, 1975), 353.
13. See Stephen G. Michaud and Hugh Aynesworth, *Ted Bundy: Conversations with a Killer* (London, UK: Mirror Books, 2019).

14. Romans 5:3–4: "We also glory in our sufferings, because we know that suffering produces perseverance; perseverance, character; and character, hope."
15. Augustine, *On the Free Choice of the Will*, trans. Thomas Williams (Indianapolis: Hackett, 1993). Meister notes that Augustine (AD 354–430) derived his argument from the *Enneads*, written by the Neoplatonic philosopher Plotinus (ca. 205–270 BC).
16. C. S. Lewis, *The Problem of Pain* (New York: Macmillan, 1962), 93.
17. Quoted in Lee Strobel, *The Case for Miracles: A Journalist Investigates Evidence for the Supernatural* (Grand Rapids: Zondervan, 2018), 176.
18. For more detail about the many-universe theory, see my interview with Robin Collins in Lee Strobel, *The Case for a Creator* (Grand Rapids: Zondervan, 2004), 142–44.
19. See William Lane Craig, *The Kalām Cosmological Argument* (Eugene, OR: Wipf & Stock, 2000), 63.
20. Some physicists have speculated that the universe has expanded and contracted eternally, in an ongoing cycle, and thus lacks a beginning. But Alexander Vilenkin, director of the Institute of Cosmology at Tufts University, rules out this and other efforts to posit a universe: "All the evidence we have says that the universe had a beginning" (*Many Worlds in One: The Search for Other Universes* [New York: Hill and Wang, 2006], 176); see also Lisa Grossman, "Why Physicists Can't Avoid a Creation Event," *New Scientist*, January 11, 2012, www .newscientist.com/article/mg21328474-400-why-physicists-cant -avoid-a-creation-event.
21. As Meister added parenthetically, this assumes that the concept of a "prior cause" makes sense since physical time didn't even exist until the big bang.
22. See Romans 3:23: "All have sinned and fall short of the glory of God."
23. For references in the Qur'an that deny the Trinity, see sura 4:171; 5:72–75, 116–18. For the Islamic teaching that Jesus didn't die on the cross and therefore could not have been resurrected, see suras 4:157. For references in the Qur'an denying that God has a Son, see suras 19:88–93; 23:91; 112:1–4.
24. See Lee Strobel, *In Defense of Jesus: Investigating Attacks on the Identity of Christ* (previously published as *The Case for the Real Jesus*, 2007; repr., Grand Rapids: Zondervan, 2016), 68–105.
25. See Luke 1:1–4.
26. See 2 Peter 1:16.
27. See 1 Corinthians 15:3–8.

28. Jesus said in John 10:30, "I and the Father are one." The Greek word for "one" (*heis*) is not masculine but neuter, which means Jesus was not saying, "I and the Father are the *same person*," but, "I and the Father are the *same thing*"—that is, one in nature or essence. His opponents understood he was making a divine claim. John 10:33 says they picked up rocks to stone him "for blasphemy, because you, a mere man, claim to be God."

29. See Gary R. Habermas and Michael R. Licona, *The Case for the Resurrection of Jesus* (Grand Rapids: Kregel, 2004), 48–79; see also my interview with Licona in Strobel, *In Defense of Jesus*, 106–64.

30. While not as firmly held by skeptical scholars as the other historical truths mentioned, Habermas notes that roughly 75 percent of scholars who have written on the subject in English, French, and German since 1975 hold to the view that the tomb was empty based on the evidence. See Habermas and Licona, *Case for the Resurrection of Jesus*, 69–70.

31. Michael Grant, *Jesus: An Historian's Review of the Gospels* (New York: Scribner, 1977), 176.

32. William Lane Craig, *The Son Rises: The Historical Evidence for the Resurrection of Jesus* (Eugene, OR: Wipf & Stock, 1981), 107 (for an overview of this point, see 100–107 in his book).

33. See Acts 2:32.

34. See Acts 26:1–32.

35. See 1 Corinthians 15:3–8.

36. James D. G. Dunn of the University of Durham and a fellow of the British Academy said, "This tradition, we can be entirely confident, *was formulated as tradition within months of Jesus' death*" (*Jesus Remembered*, vol. 1 of *Christianity in the Making* [Grand Rapids: Eerdmans, 2003], 825, italics in original).

37. See my interview with resurrection scholar Michael Licona in Strobel, *In Defense of Jesus*, 106–64.

38. See Acts 2:32.

39. See 1 Corinthians 15:11.

40. Strobel, *In Defense of Jesus*, 124.

41. Gary R. Collins, personal communication with Gary R. Habermas, quoted in Gary R. Habermas and J. P. Moreland, *Beyond Death: Exploring the Evidence for Immortality* (Wheaton, IL: Crossway, 1998), 119–20.

42. John 14:6.

43. John 11:25.

44. John 10:27–28.

45. R. C. Sproul, "What Is the Kingdom of God?" Ligonier Ministries, June 7, 2019, www.ligonier.org/blog/what-is-kingdom-god.

46. See Romans 6:23.
47. See Galatians 5:22–23.
48. See John 14:2.
49. Revelation 21:4.
50. See Revelation 21:3.

Chapter 5: Heaven: A Guide

1. Psalm 19:1.
2. Cited in James Bishop, "Former Atheist Astrophysicist, Sarah Salviander, Explains Her Journey to Christianity," *Bishop's Encyclopedia of Religion, Society and Philosophy,* May 23, 2015, https://jamesbishopblog.com/2015/05/23/former-atheist-astrophysicist-sarah-salviander-explains-her-journey-to-christianity; see also Gerald L. Schroeder, *The Science of God: The Convergence of Scientific and Biblical Wisdom* (New York: Free Press, 2009).
3. Quoted in Walter Isaacson, "Einstein & Faith," *Time,* April 5, 2007, http://ymlibrary.com/download/Topics/God/Faith-Hope-Trust/Faith-Hope-Trust-Stories-Inspiration/Einstein%20and%20Faith.pdf.
4. Quotes taken from personal email correspondence dated September 18, 2020; see also Sarah's testimony: "My Testimony," SixDay Science, May 11, 2015, https://sixdayscience.com/2015/05/11/my-testimony.
5. 1 Corinthians 2:9 NLT.
6. Martin Luther, *D. Martin Luthers Werke: Kritische Gesamtausgabe,* 3:276.26–27 (no. 3339); quoted in J. Todd Billings, *The End of the Christian Life: How Embracing Our Mortality Frees Us to Truly Live* (Grand Rapids: Brazos, 2020), 182.
7. Billings, *End of the Christian Life,* 182, italics in original.
8. John Eldredge, *The Journey of Desire: Searching for the Life You've Always Dreamed Of,* rev. ed. (Nashville: Nelson, 2016), 115, italics in original.
9. John 6:40.
10. 2 Peter 1:11.
11. 1 John 2:25.
12. 2 Corinthians 5:1.
13. N. T. Wright, *Simply Good News: Why the Gospel Is News and What Makes It Good* (San Francisco: HarperOne, 2015), 99, italics in original.
14. See Bart D. Ehrman, *Heaven and Hell: A History of the Afterlife* (New York: Simon & Schuster, 2020), xxi.
15. See Isaiah 25:6–10; 26:19; Hosea 6:1–2; Ezekiel 37; Daniel 12:2–3. Scot McKnight said to me, "In God's providence and in the unfolding of

revelation and redemption, we only learn about a new life beyond death in the final sections of the Old Testament, the Prophets."

16. See Rodney Stark, *What Americans Really Believe: New Findings from the Baylor Study of Religion* (Waco, TX: Baylor University Press, 2008), 69–74.

17. Billings, *End of the Christian Life*, 151; see Maggie Fox, "Fewer Americans Believe in God—Yet They Still Believe in Afterlife," *Today*, March 21, 2016, www.nbcnews.com/better/wellness/Fewer-americans -believe-god-yet-they-still-believe-afterlife-n542966.

18. See Fox, "Fewer Americans Believe in God."

19. Ecclesiastes 3:11.

20. C. S. Lewis, *The Weight of Glory* (1949; repr., San Francisco: HarperSanFrancisco, 2001), 29, 32.

21. C. S. Lewis, *Mere Christianity* (1943; repr., New York: Macmillan, 1960), 120.

22. Jerry Walls, *Heaven: The Logic of Eternal Joy* (New York: Oxford University Press, 2002), 31.

23. Luke 23:43.

24. See Acts 7:55.

25. John 11:11.

26. Revelation 21:1–2.

27. Revelation 21:22.

28. See John 14:2–3.

29. 1 Corinthians 15:28.

30. See 1 Corinthians 15:20–28.

31. See 1 Corinthians 15:35–55.

32. 1 Corinthians 15:44.

33. See John 20:26; Matthew 17:1–2.

34. Arthur O. Roberts, *Exploring Heaven: What Great Christian Thinkers Tell Us about Our Afterlife with God* (San Francisco: HarperSanFrancisco, 2003), 114.

35. For a discussion of this issue, see C. S. Lewis, *The Great Divorce* (New York: Macmillan, 1946), 115–25.

36. See John 14:2–3.

37. See Nigel Dixon, *Villages without Walls: An Exploration of the Necessity of Building Christian Community in a Post-Christian World* (Palmerston North, NZ: Vox Humana, 2010), 54–62.

38. See Revelation 21–22.

39. Hans Boersma, *Seeing God: The Beatific Vision in Christian Tradition* (Grand Rapids: Eerdmans, 2018), 11.

40. Quoted in Boersma, *Seeing God*, xiii.

41. Psalm 27:4.
42. 1 Corinthians 13:12.
43. Matthew 5:8.
44. Exodus 33:20.
45. Revelation 22:4.
46. John 14:9.
47. Matthew 17:2.
48. Kieran Kavanaugh, ed., *John of the Cross: Selected Writings* (New York: Paulist, 1987), 285.
49. Jonathan Edwards, "Sermon on Revelation 21:18," *WJE Online* 42, Jonathan Edwards Center, http://is.gd/WSuP77.
50. Quoted in Ed Romine, "Spurgeon on the Hope of Heaven," Spurgeon Center for Biblical Preaching at Midwestern Seminary, May 3, 2018, www.spurgeon.org/resource-library/blog-entries/charles-spurgeon -on-heavens-hope.
51. Michael Reeves, *Delighting in the Trinity: An Introduction to the Christian Faith* (Downers Grove, IL: IVP Academic, 2012), 75.
52. John Eldredge, *All Things New: Heaven, Earth, and the Restoration of Everything You Love* (Nashville: Nelson, 2017), 25.
53. N. T. Wright, *Surprised by Hope: Rethinking Heaven, the Resurrection, and the Mission of the Church* (San Francisco: HarperOne, 2008), 93.

Chapter 6: Seven on Heaven

1. Revelation 21:4.
2. Isaiah 11:6.
3. See Stanley Brandes, "The Meaning of American Pet Cemetery Gravestones," *Ethnology* 48, no. 2 (Spring 2009): 99–118, https:// anthropology.berkeley.edu/sites/default/files/brandes_-_american_pet _cemetery_gravestones.pdf.
4. Richard J. Mouw, *When the Kings Come Marching In: Isaiah and the New Jerusalem*, rev. ed. (Grand Rapids: Eerdmans, 2002), 20.
5. Peter Kreeft, *Everything You Ever Wanted to Know about Heaven . . . but Never Dreamed of Asking* (San Francisco: Ignatius, 1990), 45.
6. Psalm 36:6 NRSV. The NIV translates it, "You, LORD, preserve both people and animals."
7. Kreeft, *Everything You Ever Wanted to Know about Heaven*, 45–46.
8. Joni Eareckson Tada, *Holiness in Hidden Places* (Nashville: Countryman, 1999), 133.
9. Hank Hanegraaff, *Afterlife: What You Need to Know about Heaven, the Hereafter and Near-Death Experiences* (Brentwood, TN: Worthy, 2013), 45.

10. Alan W. Gomes, *40 Questions about Heaven and Hell* (Grand Rapids: Kregel Academic, 2018), 271.
11. Gomes, *40 Questions about Heaven and Hell*, 257.
12. Cited in Lee Strobel, *The Case for a Creator* (Grand Rapids: Zondervan, 2004), 262–63; see Genesis 1:30; Leviticus 24:18; Ecclesiastes 3:19; Revelation 8:9.
13. Quoted in Strobel, *Case for a Creator*, 263.
14. Colleen McDannell and Bernhard Lang, *Heaven: A History*, 2nd ed. (New Haven, CT: Yale University Press, 2001), 64.
15. Randy Alcorn, "Will There Be Marriage in Heaven?" Eternal Perspective Ministries, February 3, 2010, www.epm.org/resources/2010 /Feb/3/will-there-be-marriage-heaven.
16. Gomes, *40 Questions about Heaven and Hell*, 238.
17. Mark Hitchcock, *55 Answers to Questions about Life after Death* (Colorado Springs: Multnomah, 2005), 188.
18. See Mark 12:18–27; Matthew 22:23–33; Luke 20:27–40. McKnight also dismisses two other passages—Mark 3:31–35 and John 2:1–11—that are sometimes raised against the idea of marriage in heaven. Clearly, they make no such claim (see Scot McKnight, *The Heaven Promise* [Colorado Springs: WaterBrook, 2015], 165–66).
19. Mark 12:25.
20. Luke 20:36, italics added.
21. Hitchcock, *55 Answers to Questions about Life after Death*, 189.
22. Gomes, *40 Questions about Heaven and Hell*, 243, italics in original.
23. Gomes, *40 Questions about Heaven and Hell*, 162 (for context, see 157–65).
24. Matthew 20:1–16.
25. See Craig L. Blomberg, "Degrees of Reward in the Kingdom of Heaven?" *Journal of the Evangelical Theological Society* 35, no. 2 (June 1992): 160, www.etsjets.org/files/JETS-PDFs/35/35-2/JETS _35-2_159-172_Blomberg.pdf.
26. Simon J. Kistemaker, *The Parables: Understanding the Stories Jesus Told* (1980; repr., Grand Rapids: Baker, 2002), 75.
27. These are commonly referred to as the victor's crown (1 Corinthians 9:25–27), the crown of rejoicing (1 Thessalonians 2:19), the crown of righteousness (2 Timothy 4:8), the crown of life (James 1:12; Revelation 2:10), and the crown of glory (1 Peter 5:4). Said Justin Taylor, managing editor of the *ESV Study Bible*, "Though it is popular to see these as different types of reward . . . a majority of commentators believe these are different ways of referring to the one reward of eternal life" (quoted in John Starke, "You Asked: What Are the Rewards in Heaven Jesus

Talks About?" Gospel Coalition, July 16, 2011, www.thegospelcoalition
.org/article/you-asked-what-are-the-rewards-in-heaven-jesus-talks-about).

28. Revelation 4:10.

29. Blomberg, "Degrees of Reward in the Kingdom of Heaven?" 160.

30. Blomberg, "Degrees of Reward in the Kingdom of Heaven?" 163

31. Blomberg, "Degrees of Reward in the Kingdom of Heaven?" 167.

32. Luke 19:11–27.

33. Millard J. Erickson, *Christian Theology*, 3rd ed. (Grand Rapids: Baker Academic, 2013), 1132.

34. Erickson, *Christian Theology*, 1133.

35. Jerry Walls, *Heaven, Hell, and Purgatory: Rethinking the Things That Matter Most* (Grand Rapids: Brazos, 2015), 91.

36. Walls, who earned his doctorate at the University of Notre Dame, is a philosophy professor and scholar in residence at Houston Baptist University. After he published a book about the doctrine of purgatory, he said he came under "considerable fire" from the online journal *Credo*, which devoted an entire issue to the topic (see Walls, *Heaven, Hell, and Purgatory*, 93; see also *Credo* 3, no. 1 [January 2013], https://credomag.com/wp-content/uploads/2018/05/Credo-January -2013-Purgatory-Final.pdf).

37. John Calvin, *Institutes of the Christian Religion*, ed. John T. McNeill; trans. Ford Lewis Battles (Philadelphia: Westminster, 1960), 3.5.6.

38. C. S. Lewis, *Letters to Malcolm: Chiefly on Prayer* (1963; repr., San Francisco: HarperOne, 2017), 145.

39. Walls, *Heaven, Hell, and Purgatory*, 93.

40. Walls, *Heaven, Hell, and Purgatory*, 94.

41. Walls, *Heaven, Hell, and Purgatory*, 96.

42. Lewis, *Letters to Malcolm*, 140, italics in original.

43. Gomes, 40 *Questions about Heaven and Hell*, 124.

44. See 2 Maccabees 12:32–45.

45. Theologian Alan Gomes points out that the 2 Maccabees passage "actually contradicts the Roman Catholic doctrine of purgatory in particular and the Catholic doctrine of the sacraments in general." He points out that the sin for which the prayers were offered, idolatry, is a mortal sin, not a venial one, and dying in a state of mortal sin would result in the person being sent to hell, from which there is no release. Also, those offering the prayers "were not intending to deliver them from purgatory into paradise anyway. These prayers were for them to attain the resurrection of their bodies (2 Macc. 12:43–44), which would occur at the last judgment. Deliverance from purgatory into paradise,

in contrast, happens during the intermediate state and before the final judgment" (*40 Questions about Heaven and Hell*, 123–24).

46. Although those who die immediately have their souls go to the intermediate state, this should not be confused with purgatory. As Scot McKnight said, there is no biblical support for seeing the intermediate state as a place for paying for sins or purifying people so they are fit for heaven.

47. See "Cremation Today: Trends and Statistics for Cremation in the U.S.," Green Cremation Texas, www.greencremationtexas.com/cremation -today.

48. N. T. Wright, *Surprised by Hope: Rethinking Heaven, the Resurrection, and the Mission of the Church* (San Francisco: HarperOne, 2008), 24.

49. Hanegraaff, *Afterlife*, 161–62.

50. Billy Graham, *The Heaven Answer Book* (Nashville: Nelson, 2012), 86.

51. Genesis 3:19.

52. McKnight, *The Heaven Promise*, 171–72.

53. 2 Samuel 12:23.

54. Matthew 19:14; see also Mark 10:13–16; Luke 18:15–17.

55. Graham Twelftree, *Life after Death* (Grand Rapids: Monarch, 2002), 153.

56. Molinism, named for the sixteenth-century Spanish Jesuit Luis de Molina, is a theological system that seeks to reconcile God's sovereignty with man's free will.

57. See John 14:2–3.

58. 1 Corinthians 15:3–5; *Cephas* is Aramaic for Peter.

59. 2 Timothy 2:8, italics added.

60. See Acts 2:14–39.

61. See Acts 10:27–48.

62. Kreeft, *Everything You Ever Wanted to Know about Heaven*, 248, italics in original.

63. Kreeft, *Everything You Ever Wanted to Know about Heaven*, 249, italics in original; the ending quote from Jesus is from John 14:6.

Chapter 7: The Logic of Hell

1. Dante Alighieri, *The Inferno*, trans. John Ciardi (New York: Signet, 2009), Canto III, lines 1–3, 9, https://archive.org/stream/inferno00dant _2/inferno00dant_2_djvu.txt.

2. Alighieri, *Inferno*, Canto XXXI, line 81.

3. Alighieri, *Inferno*, Canto XXXIV, line 61.

4. Alighieri, *Inferno*, Canto XXXIII, introduction.

5. Alighieri, *Inferno*, Canto V, lines 137–40.
6. Preston Sprinkle, ed., *Four Views on Hell*, 2nd ed. (1996; repr., Grand Rapids: Zondervan, 2016), 12.
7. For example, "I will show you whom you should fear: Fear the one who, after he kills, has authority to throw you into hell [*geenna*]. Yes, I tell you, fear this one!" (Luke 12:5 Mounce Reverse Interlinear New Testament).
8. Mark Jones, *Living for God: A Short Introduction to the Christian Faith* (Wheaton, IL: Crossway, 2020), 223.
9. Steve Gregg, *All You Want to Know about Hell: Three Christian Views of God's Final Solution to the Problem of Sin* (Nashville: Nelson, 2013), 17.
10. Cited in Mark Strauss, "The Campaign to Eliminate Hell," *National Geographic*, May 13, 2016, www.nationalgeographic.com/news/2016/05/160513-theology-hell-history-christianity.
11. Cited in Tracy Munsil, "*AWVI 2020* Survey: 1 in 3 US Adults Embrace Salvation through Jesus; More Believe It Can Be 'Earned,'" Arizona Christian University: Cultural Research Center, August 4, 2020, www.arizonachristian.edu/blog/2020/08/04/1-in-3-us-adults-embrace-salvation-through-jesus-more-believe-it-can-be-earned.
12. Matthew 7:13.
13. John Gerstner, *Repent or Perish* (Morgan, PA: Soli Deo Gloria, 1990), 31.
14. N. T. Wright, *Surprised by Hope* (San Francisco: HarperOne, 2008), 175, italics in original.
15. Quoted in Gregg, *All You Want to Know about Hell*, 20.
16. Clark Pinnock, "The Destruction of the Finally Impenitent," *Criswell Theological Review* 4, no. 2 (Spring 1990): 243–59, https://davidlarkin.files.wordpress.com/2012/05/pinnock-the-destruction-of-the-finally-impenitent-original-paper.pdf (p. 15).
17. Bertrand Russell, *Why I Am Not a Christian* (New York: Simon & Schuster, 1957), 17.
18. Paul Copan, *Is God a Moral Monster? Making Sense of the Old Testament God* (Grand Rapids: Baker, 2011); Paul Copan and Matthew Flannagan, *Did God Really Command Genocide? Coming to Terms with the Justice of God* (Grand Rapids: Baker, 2014).
19. Paul Copan, *Loving Wisdom: A Guide to Philosophy and Christian Faith*, 2nd ed. (2007; repr., Grand Rapids: Eerdmans, 2020), 246–57.
20. C. S. Lewis, *The Problem of Pain* (1940; repr., New York: Macmillan, 1962), 118.
21. See Genesis 18:25.

22. See Robert Bellah et al., *Habits of the Heart: Individualism and Commitment in American Life* (Berkeley: University of California Press, 2007); Allan Bloom, *The Closing of the American Mind*, rev. ed. (New York: Simon & Schuster, 2012).

23. Greg Lukianoff and Jonathan Haidt, *The Coddling of the American Mind: How Good Intentions and Bad Ideas Are Setting Up a Generation for Failure* (New York: Penguin, 2018).

24. Richard Wurmbrand, *Tortured for Christ*, 50th anniv. ed. (Colorado Springs: Cook, 2018), 52.

25. Jesus in Luke 13:3: "But unless you repent, you too will all perish."

26. John F. Walvoord, "The Literal View," in *Four Views on Hell*, ed. William Crockett (Grand Rapids: Zondervan, 1996), 28.

27. Other well-known figures and respected scholars who interpret the flames nonliterally include Billy Graham, C. S. Lewis, D. A. Carson, J. I. Packer, Sinclair Ferguson, Charles Hodges, Carl Henry, F. F. Bruce, Roger Nicole, Leon Morris, Robert Peterson, and J. P. Moreland. "These scholars note that fire imagery is used in many other places in the Bible—not just in passages relating to hell—in obviously nonliteral ways," said Francis Chan and Preston Sprinkle (*Erasing Hell* [Colorado Springs: Cook, 2011], 154).

28. See 2 Thessalonians 1:9. Writes Copan, "God, of course, will be *aware* of those separated from him; they will still be 'tormented . . . in the presence of the holy angels and *in the presence of the Lamb*' (Rev. 14:10). The point here is that Christ/God is obviously aware of those who experience this separation ('in the presence of the Lamb'). Nevertheless, the emphasis in 2 Thess. 1:9 is that unbelievers are cut off from his blessing as the source of hope and joy ('away from the presence of the Lord')" (*Loving Wisdom*, 247–48, italics in original).

29. See Acts 7:54.

30. Dallas Willard, *The Allure of Gentleness: Defending the Faith in the Manner of Jesus* (San Francisco: HarperOne, 2016), 67.

31. Michael Card, "Who Can Abide?" from the album *The Word: Recapturing the Imagination*, https://genius.com/Michael-card-who -can-abide-lyrics.

32. Willard, *Allure of Gentleness*, 67, 69.

33. This illustration is attributed to James K. Beilby, *Postmortem Opportunity: A Biblical and Theological Assessment of Salvation after Death* (Downers Grove, IL: IVP Academic, 2021).

34. John G. Stackhouse Jr., "Terminal Punishment," in *Four Views on Hell*, ed. Sprinkle, 79.

35. Rob Bell, *Love Wins: A Book about Heaven, Hell, and the Fate of Every Person Who Ever Lived* (San Francisco: HarperOne, 2011), 102; cf. 175.

36. See Denny Burk, "Postscript on Hell," July 13, 2011, www.dennyburk .com/postscript-on-hell; Burk credits the illustration to a sermon he heard by his friend and mentor Joe Blankenship.

37. Thomas Aquinas, *Effects of Sin, Stain, and Guilt*, vol. 27 of *Summa Theologiae* (Cambridge: Cambridge University Press, 2006), 25.

38. D. A. Carson, *How Long, O Lord? Reflections on Suffering and Evil,* 2nd ed. (Grand Rapids: Baker Academic, 2006), 91.

39. See Lee Strobel, *The Case for Faith* (Grand Rapids: Zondervan, 2000), 169–94.

40. Craig Blomberg, *Interpreting the Parables*, 2nd ed. (Downers Grove, IL: IVP Academic, 2012), 236.

41. Augustine, *The City of God*, trans. Marcus Dods (Peabody, MA: Hendrickson, 2009), 710–11.

42. See Matthew 12:31. Theologians generally consider blasphemy against the Holy Spirit to be a lifetime of turning a deaf ear to God's initiating grace.

43. See John 19:11.

44. Genesis 18:25.

45. See Revelation 16:9–11, 21.

46. See C. S. Lewis, *The Great Divorce* (New York: Macmillan, 1946), 74–75.

47. N. T. Wright, *Following Jesus* (Grand Rapids: Eerdmans, 1995), 100.

48. See Lewis, *Problem of Pain*, 125.

49. John Calvin, *Commentary on a Harmony of the Evangelists, Matthew, Mark, and Luke*, trans. William Pringle (Grand Rapids: Baker, 1970), 1:201.

50. See Luke 16:19–31.

51. The Bible doesn't specifically call this a parable. If it falls in that genre, it's the only parable with names in it. For that reason, some think it may be more of a true account. New Testament scholar Craig Blomberg notes that the account "is paralleled by popular Jewish and Egyptian folk tales" of the era, adding that "Jesus may simply have adopted well-known imagery, but then adapted it in a new and surprising way" (*The Historical Reliability of the Gospels*, 2nd ed. [Downers Grove, IL: IVP Academic, 1987], 52–53). Steve Gregg has a helpful analysis of the various views in *All You Want to Know about Hell*, 75–84. Said Gregg, "The conclusion of many, that the imagery of the story was not necessarily intended to teach anything about the real nature of hell, nor to confirm popular lore on the subject, seems reasonably justified.

The purpose of the parable was not to reveal the nature of the afterlife, but to teach entirely unrelated lessons" (p. 83). Among the scholars who have questioned whether the parable tells us anything meaningful about the afterlife is Robert Yarbrough, who said, "It is widely accepted that this story is parabolic and not intended to furnish a detailed geography of hell" ("Jesus on Hell," in *Hell Under Fire*, ed. Christopher W. Morgan and Robert A. Peterson [Grand Rapids: Zondervan, 2004], 74).

52. Randy Alcorn, *Heaven* (Carol Stream, IL: Tyndale, 2004), 25–26.
53. Jonathan Edwards, *The Works of Jonathan Edwards*, vol. 2 (London: Ball, 1839), 11.
54. Alan W. Gomes, *40 Questions about Heaven and Hell* (Grand Rapids: Kregel Academic, 2018), 287.

Chapter 8: Escape from Hell

1. Stott's statement on annihilationism appeared in David L. Edwards and John Stott, *Evangelical Essentials: A Liberal-Evangelical Dialogue* (Downers Grove, IL: InterVarsity, 1989), 320. Stott's chapter on the topic ("Judgment and Hell") has been reproduced more recently in *Rethinking Hell: Readings in Evangelical Conditionalism*, ed. Christopher M. Date, Gregory G. Stump, and Joshua W. Anderson (Eugene, OR: Wipf & Stock, 2014), 48–55. Though there are nuances between annihilationism and conditional immortality, they are close enough that I am using the terms interchangeably, along with *annihilationist* and *conditionalist*.
2. Date, Stump, and Anderson, eds., *Rethinking Hell*, 54.
3. Robert A. Peterson, "Undying Worm, Unquenchable Fire," *Christianity Today*, October 23, 2000, www.christianitytoday.com/ct/2000/october23/undying-worm-unquenchable-fire.html.
4. John Wenham, *Facing Hell: The Story of a Nobody* (Carlisle, Cumbria, UK: Paternoster, 1991), 254, www.truthaccordingtoscripture.com/documents/death/conditional-immortality-wenham.php.
5. Wenham, *Facing Hell*, 256.
6. See Romans 6:23.
7. Peterson, "Undying Worm, Unquenchable Fire."
8. Among the endorsers of annihilationism have been Australian theologian Philip Hughes; Canadian theologian Clark Pinnock; New Testament scholar F. F. Bruce; professor of philosophy emeritus Richard Swinburne of Oxford; New Testament professor Stephen Travis (PhD, Cambridge); New Zealand philosopher Glenn Peoples (PhD, Otago); attorney and theologian Edward Fudge; British evangelist

Michael Green; Scottish New Testament scholar I. Howard Marshall; Anglican scholar Richard Bauckham (PhD, Cambridge); Baptist David Instone-Brewer (PhD, Cambridge); and John Stackhouse Jr. (PhD, University of Chicago), who says annihilationism "exonerates our good God from the appalling image of a perpetual tormenter" ("Terminal Punishment," in *Four Views on Hell*, 2nd ed., Preston Sprinkle, ed. [Grand Rapids: Zondervan, 2016], 81).

9. Quoted in Mark Strauss, "The Campaign to Eliminate Hell," *National Geographic*, May 13, 2016, www.nationalgeographic.com/news/2016/05 /160513-theology-hell-history-christianity.

10. Date, Stump, and Anderson, eds., *Rethinking Hell*, xv.

11. Date, Stump, and Anderson, eds., *Rethinking Hell*, xvi.

12. Stott, "Judgment and Hell," in Date, Stump, and Anderson, eds., *Rethinking Hell*, 51.

13. Quotes are from Stott, "Judgment and Hell," 51–55.

14. See Colossians 1:20.

15. See 1 Corinthians 15:28.

16. Stott, "Judgment and Hell," 55.

17. For example, see Matthew 3:12; 7:19; John 15:6.

18. See Hebrews 10:26–29.

19. See Genesis 19.

20. Jude 7 ESV.

21. See Jaroslav Pelikan, *The Emergence of the Catholic Tradition (100–600)*, vol. 1 of *The Christian Tradition* (Chicago: University of Chicago Press, 1971), 51.

22. See 2 Corinthians 5:3.

23. See 1 Corinthians 15:53–54.

24. See John 5:29.

25. Bart D. Ehrman, *Heaven and Hell: A History of the Afterlife* (New York: Simon & Schuster, 2020), 155.

26. See Josephus, *Jewish Wars* 2.8.14; *Antiquities* 18.1.3.

27. See Matthew 8:12; 13:42, 50; 22:13; 24:51; 25:30.

28. Robert A. Morey, *Death and the Afterlife* (Minneapolis: Bethany House, 1984), 117–18.

29. For a discussion of the meaning of *aionios*, see Steve Gregg, *All You Want to Know about Hell: Three Christian Views of God's Final Solution to the Problem of Sin* (Nashville: Nelson, 2013), 99–109.

30. Augustine, *The City of God*, trans. Marcus Dods (Peabody, MA: Hendrickson, 2009), 716.

31. G. K. Beale, *The Book of Revelation*, New International Greek Testament Commentary (Grand Rapids: Eerdmans, 1999), 762–63.

32. See Matthew 7:13.
33. See Ephesians 2:1.
34. See Matthew 5:29–30.
35. Craig L. Blomberg, *Can We Still Believe in God? Answering Ten Contemporary Challenges to Christianity* (Grand Rapids: Brazos, 2020), 29.
36. See Matthew 12:31–32.
37. 2 Thessalonians 1:9.
38. See 4 Maccabees 9:9; 10:10–11; 12:12, 18.
39. See Mark 9:48.
40. Judith 16:17 (NRSV). This same fate of fire and worms is found in the intertestamental book of Sirach 7:17. Literal "immortal" worms continually feeding on literal bodies—drawn from Isaiah 66:24 and Mark 9:48—appear in later literature such as the third-century Vision of Ezra (34) and the fourth-century Apocalypse of Paul (42).
41. Stott, "Judgment and Hell," 54.
42. Quoted in "#103: Polycarp's Martyrdom," Christian History Institute, https://christianhistoryinstitute.org/study/module/polycarp.
43. See Peterson, "Undying Worm, Unquenchable Fire." In this article, Peterson also says he does not agree that "the traditionalist-conditionalist debate on hell should be regarded as a secondary rather than a primary issue."
44. Peterson, "Undying Worm, Unquenchable Fire."
45. David Bentley Hart, *That All Shall Be Saved: Heaven, Hell, and Universal Salvation* (New Haven, CT: Yale University Press, 2019), 208.
46. See Michael McClymond, "David Bentley Hart's Lonely, Last Stand for Christian Universalism," Gospel Coalition, October 2, 2019, www.thegospelcoalition.org/reviews/shall-saved-universal-christian-universalis-david-bentley-hart. McClymond responds in this article to the three main arguments for universalism that Hart posits in his book.
47. Quoted in McClymond, "David Bentley Hart's Lonely, Last Stand."
48. Rob Bell, *Love Wins: A Book about Heaven, Hell, and the Fate of Every Person Who Ever Lived* (San Francisco: HarperOne, 2011), 107. Francis Chan and Preston Sprinkle write, "Bell never actually comes out and says this is what he believes . . . But he presents this position in such favorable terms that it would be hard to say that he is not advocating it" (Chan and Sprinkle, *Erasing Hell* [Colorado Springs: Cook, 2011], 40).
49. Hart, *That All Shall Be Saved*, 84.
50. Robin A. Parry, "A Universalist View," in *Four Views on Hell*, 2nd ed., 101.
51. Origen's views were "very complex and not always consistent." As for the church council, "a great deal of politics drove this council, as well

as other early church councils, so we shouldn't consider Origen's views heretical based solely on the decisions made at Constantinople" (Chan and Sprinkle, *Erasing Hell*, 23, 39).

52. Chan and Sprinkle, *Erasing Hell*, 23.
53. C. S. Lewis, ed., *George MacDonald: An Anthology* (San Francisco: HarperOne, 2001), xxxv.
54. See 1 John 2:2; John 1:12.
55. First Timothy 4:10 reads, "That is why we labor and strive, because we have put our hope in the living God, who is the Savior of all people, and especially of those who believe."
56. Colossians 1:22–23, italics added.
57. 2 Thessalonians 1:9.
58. Galatians 1:8–9.
59. See Mark 1:5.
60. Luke 19:10.
61. John 17:12 KJV.
62. John 19:30.
63. Isaiah 53:11.
64. William Barclay, *William Barclay: A Spiritual Autobiography* (Grand Rapids: Eerdmans, 1977), 67.
65. C. S. Lewis, *The Problem of Pain* (1940; repr., New York: Macmillan, 1962), 118–19.
66. See Zephaniah 2:11.
67. Helmut T. Lehmann and Martin O. Dietrich, eds., *Luther's Works*, vol. 43 (Minneapolis: Fortress, 1968), 53. The German reads, "Das wäre wohl eine andere Frage, ob Gott etlichen im Sterben oder nach dem Sterben den Glauben könnte geben und also durch den Glauben könnte selig machen. Wer wollte daran zweifeln, dass er das tun könnte. Aber dass er es tut, kann man nicht beweisen."
68. The term *postmortem opportunity* is taken from the title of theologian James Beilby's 2021 book *Postmortem Opportunity: A Biblical and Theological Assessment of Salvation after Death* (Downers Grove, IL: IVP Academic, 2021). Paul Copan noted that some of his reflections on this topic are drawn from Beilby's book.
69. Cited in Preserved Smith, *The Life and Letters of Martin Luther* (Boston: Houghton Mifflin, 1911), 342.
70. See Jerry L. Walls, *Heaven, Hell, and Purgatory* (Grand Rapids: Brazos, 2015), 187–211.
71. See J. Oliver Buswell, *A Systematic Theology of the Christian Religion*, vol. 2 (Grand Rapids: Zondervan, 1963), 162.
72. See John 3:16–17.

73. 1 John 2:2; notice that the only other place this phrase "whole world" is used is in 1 John 5:19, where the "whole world" lies in the hands of the evil one.

74. See Ezekiel 33:11; 1 Timothy 2:4; 2 Peter 3:9.

75. See Acts 17:30.

76. Copan's paraphrase. NIV translation of John 21:22: "If I want him to remain alive until I return, what is that to you? You must follow me."

77. See Lee Strobel, "Dreams and Visions," in *The Case for Miracles* (Grand Rapids: Zondervan, 2018), 139–160.

78. See Acts 17:30.

79. See Matthew 25:31–46.

80. See Revelation 20:15.

81. See Michael McClymond, *The Devil's Redemption* (Grand Rapids: Baker Academic, 2018).

82. Quoted in Paul Copan, "How Universalism, 'The Opiate of the Theologians,' Went Mainstream," *Christianity Today*, March 11, 2019, www.christianitytoday.com/ct/2019/march-web-only/michael -mcclymond-devils-redemption-universalism.html.

83. Chan and Sprinkle, *Erasing Hell*, 13–14.

84. Chan and Sprinkle, *Erasing Hell*, 108.

85. See John 14:6.

Chapter 9: The Reincarnation Sensation

1. Credit for the chapter's title goes to Norman L. Geisler and J. Yutaka Amano, *The Reincarnation Sensation* (Eugene, OR: Wipf & Stock, 2004).

2. Herbert Brean, "Bridey Murphy Puts Nation in a Hypnotizzy," *Life* 40, no. 12, March 19, 1956, https://oldlifemagazine.com /march-19-1956-life-magazine.html.

3. Cited in "How Many People in the World Believe in Reincarnation?" Reincarnation after Death? March 4, 2016, www.reincarnationafterdeath.com/how-many-people-believe.

4. For details of the Bridey Murphy case, I am indebted to skeptic Paul Edwards, who devotes a full chapter ("The Rise and Fall of Bridey Murphey") to the topic in his book *Reincarnation: A Critical Examination* (Amherst, NY: Prometheus, 2002), 59–79.

5. Edwards, *Reincarnation*, 60–61.

6. Edwards, *Reincarnation*, 61.

7. Noted on the back cover of the Pocket Book reprint.

8. Time-Life Books, *Psychic Voyages* (Alexandria, VA: Time-Life, 1988), 114; no author credited.

9. Edwards, *Reincarnation*, 62.

10. Shirley MacLaine, *Out on a Limb* (New York: Bantam, 1983), 362.

11. Cited in Edwards, *Reincarnation*, 86.

12. Cited in Edwards, *Reincarnation*, 86; see John Leo, "I Was Beheaded in the 1700s," *Time*, September 10, 1984, 68.

13. Cited in Edwards, *Reincarnation*, 86.

14. Quoted in Geisler and Amano, *Reincarnation Sensation*, 12.

15. William Rounseville Alger, *A Critical History of the Doctrine of a Future Life* (Philadelphia: Childs, 1964), 475.

16. Cited in Geisler and Amano, *Reincarnation Sensation*, 37.

17. See John B. Noss, *Man's Religions*, 6th ed. (New York: Macmillan, 1980), 52.

18. This translation of Plato's words in *Phaedrus* is found in Joseph Head and S. L. Cranston, eds. *Reincarnation in World Thought* (New York: Julian, 1967), 197; other translations render this as "he who employs aright these memories is ever being initiated into perfect mysteries and alone becomes truly perfect."

19. *The Bhagavad Gita*, 2nd ed., trans. Eknath Easwaran (Tomales, CA: Nilgiri, 2007), 91–92.

20. "Reincarnation," www.merriam-webster.com/dictionary/reincarnation.

21. Cited in Geisler and Amano, *Reincarnation Sensation*, 27.

22. Thomas Ryan, "25 Percent of US Christians Believe in Reincarnation. What's Wrong with This Picture?" *America: The Jesuit Review*, October 21, 2015, www.americamagazine.org/faith/2015/10/21/25-percent-us -christians-believe-reincarnation-whats-wrong-picture.

23. See Geisler and Amano, *Reincarnation Sensation*.

24. See Geisler and Amano, *Reincarnation Sensation*, 36.

25. Edwards, *Reincarnation*, 59.

26. See Ian Stevenson, *Twenty Cases Suggestive of Reincarnation* (Charlottesville: University Press of Virginia, 1978); Stevenson, *Children Who Remember Previous Lives: A Question of Reincarnation*, rev. ed. (Jefferson, NC: McFarland, 2001).

27. Cited in Stevenson, *Twenty Cases Suggestive of Reincarnation*, 48.

28. See Hans Schwarz, *Beyond the Gates of Death: A Biblical Examination of Evidence for Life after Death* (Minneapolis: Augsburg, 1981), 101.

29. See Ryan, "25 Percent of US Christians Believe in Reincarnation."

30. Herbert Bruce Puryear, *Why Jesus Taught Reincarnation: A Better News Gospel* (Scottsdale, AZ: New Paradigm, 1993), 2–3.

31. Quincy Howe Jr., *Reincarnation for the Christian* (Wheaton, IL: Theosophical, 1987), 93, 88.

32. Geddes MacGregor, *Reincarnation in Christianity: A New Vision of the Role of Rebirth in Christian Thought* (Wheaton, IL: Theosophical, 1878), 17, 24.

33. MacGregor, *Reincarnation in Christianity*, 16–17 (italics in original).

34. See Lee Strobel, *The Case for Miracles* (Grand Rapids: Zondervan, 2018), 235–53.

35. Douglas Groothuis, *Walking through Twilight: A Wife's Illness—A Philosopher's Lament* (Downers Grove, IL: InterVarsity, 2017).

36. Strobel, *Case for Miracles*, 244.

37. Douglas Groothuis, *Christian Apologetics: A Comprehensive Case for Biblical Faith* (Downers Grove, IL: IVP Academic, 2011).

38. Douglas Groothuis, *Philosophy in Seven Sentences: A Small Introduction to a Vast Topic* (Downers Grove, IL: InterVarsity, 2016).

39. Douglas Groothuis, *Truth Decay: Defending Christianity against the Challenges of Postmodernism* (Downers Grove, IL: InterVarsity, 2000).

40. Douglas Groothuis, *Unmasking the New Age* (Downers Grove, IL: InterVarsity, 1986); Groothuis, *Confronting the New Age: How to Resist a Growing Religious Movement* (Downers Grove, IL: InterVarsity, 1988); Groothuis, *Revealing the New Age Jesus: Challenges to Orthodox Views of Christ* (Downers Grove, IL: InterVarsity, 1990).

41. See Edwards, *Reincarnation*, 86.

42. Raynor C. Johnson, *The Imprisoned Splendour* (New York: Harper & Row, 1953), 381.

43. "Advaita Vedanta" is Sanskrit, with *a-* meaning "no" and *dvaita* meaning "two"—literally, "not two." In this school of Hinduism, all is one, and all is the Brahman.

44. This publication is the Indian version, not the more famous Scottish journal by the same name.

45. Quoted in Edwards, *Reincarnation*, 39.

46. Deepak Chopra, *Life after Death: The Burden of Proof* (New York: Three Rivers, 2006), 11.

47. Edwards, *Reincarnation*, 45.

48. These reviews were listed under a 2002 reprint of the book for sale at www.Amazon.com.

49. Edwards, *Reincarnation*, 79.

50. Edwards, *Reincarnation*, 66.

51. See Edwards, *Reincarnation*, 66–68.

52. Cited in Edwards, *Reincarnation*, 65.

53. Brean, "Bridey Murphy Puts Nation in a Hypnotizzy," 33; quoted in Edwards, *Reincarnation*, 68.

54. Cited in Edwards, *Reincarnation*, 69.

55. See Edwards, *Reincarnation*, 70.

56. Edwards, *Reincarnation*, 70.

57. Edwards, *Reincarnation*, 66.

58. Quoted in Edwards, *Reincarnation*, 72. Tighe died from cancer on July 12, 1995, www.nytimes.com/1995/07/21/obituaries/virginia-mae-morrow-dies-at-70-created-bridey-murphy-hoopla.html.

59. Stevenson, *Children Who Remember Previous Lives*, 43.

60. Quoted in Geisler and Amano, *Reincarnation Sensation*, 67, italics added.

61. See Geisler and Amano, *Reincarnation Sensation*, 67.

62. See Edwards, *Reincarnation*, 71.

63. Paul Edwards writes (*Reincarnation*, 71), "Bridey Murphy's knowledge of Irish history and customs was almost certainly an instance of 'cryptomnesia.'" However, Ian Stevenson writes (*Children Who Remember Previous Lives*, 274), "The case of Bridey Murphy is not a proven instance of cryptomnesia." Nevertheless, he said the case "does not provide strong evidence for reincarnation, because no person corresponding to Bridey Murphy's statements has been traced" and she "got some details about life in nineteenth-century Ireland wrong."

64. Stevenson, *Children Who Remember Previous Lives*, 3, italics added.

65. Edwards, *Reincarnation*, 256, italics added.

66. Even reincarnation researcher Ian Stevenson concedes, "Several other explanations account for many instances of this experience better than reincarnation does" (*Children Who Remember Previous Lives*, 48).

67. Stevenson, *Children Who Remember Previous Lives*, 45.

68. See Matthew 8:28–33; Luke 4:33–36; Acts 16:16–18; 19:11–16.

69. Gary R. Habermas and J. P. Moreland, *Beyond Death: Exploring the Evidence for Immortality* (1998; repr., Eugene, OR: Wipf & Stock, 2004), 242.

70. Shirley MacLaine, *It's All in the Playing* (New York: Bantam, 1987), 217–19.

71. See 2 Kings 2:9–18.

72. See Matthew 17:1–3.

73. See Matthew 17:9 KJV.

74. See Robert A. Morey, *Death and the Afterlife* (Minneapolis: Bethany House, 1984), 207.

75. For example, see Matthew 17:9 in the NIV.

76. John 1:21.

77. Luke 1:17.
78. See Howe Jr., *Reincarnation for the Christian*, 92–94.
79. Howe Jr., *Reincarnation for the Christian*, 93.
80. John 9:3.
81. See Geisler and Amano, *Reincarnation Sensation*, 145.
82. Kenneth Ring, *Heading toward Omega: In Search of the Meaning of the Near-Death Experience* (New York: Morrow, 1985), 158.
83. Origen of Alexandria (ca. 184–ca. 253) was a Christian theologian and prolific writer.
84. See Allan Menzies, ed., *The Ante-Nicene Fathers*, vol. 9 (New York: Christian Literature, 1896), 474.
85. See Mark Albrecht, *Reincarnation: A Christian Critique of a New Age Doctrine* (Downers Grove, IL: InterVarsity, 1987), 44–49; see also Joseph P. Gudel, Robert M. Bowman Jr., and Dan R. Schlesinger, "Reincarnation: Did the Church Suppress It?" *Christian Research Journal* 10, no. 1 (Summer 1987): 8–12, www.issuesetcarchive.org/articles/aissar14.htm.
86. "For it is by grace you have been saved, through faith—and this is not from yourselves, it is the gift of God—not by works, so that no one can boast" (Ephesians 2:8–9).
87. Revelation 21:1–4.

Chapter 10: On the Edge of Eternity

1. Matilde Palau's story, and other details about Luis Palau's early family life, can be found in Luis Palau, *Palau: A Life on Fire* (Grand Rapids: Zondervan, 2019).
2. Cited in "Luis Palau Association: About," www.palau.org/about.
3. Liz Robbins, "An Evangelical Revival in the Heart of New York," *New York Times*, July 10, 2015; can be viewed at https://layman.org/an-evangelical-revival-in-the-heart-of-new-york.
4. I tell Andrew Palau's prodigal story in *The Case for Grace* (Grand Rapids: Zondervan, 2015), 143–62.
5. 2 Corinthians 5:8.
6. "For to me, to live is Christ and to die is gain. If I am to go on living in the body, this will mean fruitful labor for me. Yet what shall I choose? I do not know! I am torn between the two: I desire to depart and be with Christ, which is better by far; but it is more necessary for you that I remain in the body" (Philippians 1:21–24).
7. See Jonathan Edwards, "The Pure in Heart Blessed," www.biblebb.com/files/edwards/heart.htm.

8. This phrase is from Jesus' parable of the bags of gold in Matthew 25:14–30.
9. See Matthew 7:23.
10. See John 14:30.
11. "Or do you show contempt for the riches of his kindness, forbearance and patience, not realizing that God's kindness is intended to lead you to repentance?" (Romans 2:4).
12. Rebecca Manley Pippert, *Stay Salt: The World Has Changed, Our Message Must Not* (Charlotte, NC: Good Book, 2020), 231.

Conclusion

1. Nabeel Qureshi to an unidentified audience. Tweet by @RZIMhq. September 16, 2020, 4:07 p.m. Lightly edited for clarity.
2. N. T. Wright, *Surprised by Hope* (San Francisco: HarperOne, 2008), 293.
3. See Ed Romine, "Spurgeon on the Hope of Heaven," *The Spurgeon Center*, May 3, 2018, www.spurgeon.org/resource-library/blog-entries /charles-spurgeon-on-heavens-hope.
4. Max Lucado, "Who Can Fathom Eternity?" FaithGateway, January 22, 2014, at www.faithgateway.com/who-can-fathom-eternity /#.YBMCjuhKiUk.
5. Though its origins are obscure, this quote is commonly attributed to Saint Teresa of Ávila, a sixteenth-century Carmelite nun (see, for example, www.azquotes.com/author/19882-Teresa_of_Ávila/tag/heaven).
6. Eugene Peterson, *Living the Resurrection: The Risen Christ in Everyday Life* (Colorado Springs, CO: NavPress, 2006), 67.
7. Romans 12:18.
8. See Lee Strobel, "God Can Give You Power as Power Is Needed," in *God's Outrageous Claims: Discover What They Mean for You*, 2nd ed. (Grand Rapids: Zondervan, 2005), 88–105.
9. Brother Andrew, *The Calling: A Challenge to Walk the Narrow Road* (Grand Rapids: Revell, 1996), 39.
10. Deuteronomy 29:29.
11. See Romans 2:15.
12. See Romans 1:20.
13. "You will seek me and find me when you seek me with all your heart" (Jeremiah 29:13); "God . . . rewards those who earnestly seek him" (Hebrews 11:6).
14. See Lee Strobel, *The Case for Miracles* (Grand Rapids: Zondervan, 2018), 139–60.

15. See Nabeel Qureshi, *Seeking Allah, Finding Jesus: A Devout Muslim Encounters Christianity*, 3rd ed. (Grand Rapids: Zondervan, 2018).
16. Genesis 18:25.
17. Ronald H. Nash, *Is Jesus the Only Savior?* (Grand Rapids: Zondervan, 1994), 165.
18. See 1 Corinthians 4:5.
19. See Lee Strobel, "Jesus Is the Only Path to God," in *God's Outrageous Claims*, 221–36.

What Happens After We Die?

1. Some experts speculate we might be given a temporary body in the intermediate state because, for example, martyrs are described in Revelation 6:9–11 as wearing clothes. However, this description is clearly metaphorical. "In sum, in the whole of Scripture there is nary a hint that we will receive a temporary body" in the intermediate state, said Hank Hanegraaff, known as the Bible Answer Man. For a discussion of this issue, see Hank Hanegraaff, *Afterlife* (Brentwood, TN: Worthy, 2013), 75–79.
2. See 2 Corinthians 5:2.
3. Said Timothy Phillips, "Hades has only a limited existence; Gehenna or hell is the final place of judgment for the wicked. Many English versions foster confusion by translating both terms as 'hell'" ("Hades," in *Evangelical Dictionary of Biblical Theology*, ed. Walter A. Elwell [Grand Rapids: Baker, 1996], 322).
4. Randy Frazee, *What Happens After You Die? A Biblical Guide to Paradise, Hell, and Life after Death* (Nashville: Nelson, 2017), 25.
5. Alan W. Gomes, *40 Questions about Heaven and Hell* (Grand Rapids: Kregel Academic, 2018), 139.
6. Gomes, *40 Questions about Heaven and Hell*, 141. Some may question whether Christians will be judged, since Jesus says in John 5:24 that the one who believes in him "has eternal life and will not be judged but has crossed over from death to life." However, Gomes cites such verses as Romans 14:10, showing that the final judgment is a comprehensive judgment of everyone who has ever lived, which means it would include Christians as well. Furthermore, we have passages that seem to focus on the judgment of believers specifically. These include Matthew 18:23; 25:19; Romans 2:6–7, 16; 14:10–12; and 1 Corinthians 3:11–15. Also, 2 Corinthians 5:10 reads, "For we must all appear before the judgment seat of Christ, so that each of us may receive what is due us for the things done while in the body, whether good or bad."

Notes Gomes, "From the entire context of 2 Corinthians 5, and even in the verses preceding it in chapter 4, Paul undoubtedly is addressing believers and (most likely) only them" (*40 Questions about Heaven and Hell*, 141–42).

7. Gomes, *40 Questions about Heaven and Hell*, 161.
8. Gomes, *40 Questions about Heaven and Hell*, 157, referring to Matthew 5:11–12; Luke 6:23.
9. See Matthew 6:20; 19:21; Mark 10:21; Luke 12:33; 18:22.
10. See Matthew 10:41–42.
11. Jesus uses the imagery of a lavish banquet to depict the great delights awaiting his followers (see Matthew 8:11; 22:1–10; 25:10; 26:29; Mark 14:25; Luke 13:28–29; 14:16–24; 22:16, 29–30).
12. Simon Kistemaker, *The Parables of Jesus* (Grand Rapids: Baker, 1980), 78. For a more detailed discussion about rewards in heaven for Christians, see chapter 6.
13. See Romans 6:23.
14. For a discussion on whether we can choose to follow Christ after our physical death, see chapter 8.

Discussion Guide

1. Philip Yancey, *What's So Amazing about Grace?* (Grand Rapids: Zondervan, 1997), 70.
2. Richard Purtill, "Defining Miracles," in *In Defense of Miracles: A Comprehensive Case for God's Action in History*, ed. R. Douglas Geivett and Gary R. Habermas (Downers Grove, IL: IVP Academic, 1997), 72.
3. Craig L. Blomberg, "Degrees of Reward in the Kingdom of Heaven?" *Journal of the Evangelical Theological Society* 35, no. 2 (June 1992): 159–72, www.etsjets.org/files/JETS-PDFs/35/35-2/JETS_35-2_159 -172_Blomberg.pdf.

Index

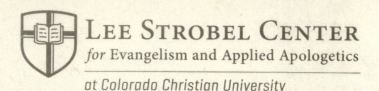